Criminology Explains School Bullying

CRIMINOLOGY EXPLAINS

Robert A. Brooks and Jeffrey W. Cohen, Editors

This pedagogically oriented series is designed to provide a concise, targeted overview of criminology theories as applied to specific criminal justice–related subjects. The goal is to bring to life for students the relationships among theory, research, and policy.

1. Criminology Explains Police Violence, by Philip Matthew Stinson, Sr.

2. Criminology Explains School Bullying, by Robert A. Brooks and Jeffrey W. Cohen

Criminology Explains School Bullying

Robert A. Brooks
Jeffrey W. Cohen

UNIVERSITY OF CALIFORNIA PRESS

University of California Press
Oakland, California

© 2020 by Robert A. Brooks and Jeffrey W. Cohen

Library of Congress Cataloging-in-Publication Data

Names: Brooks, Robert Andrew, author. | Cohen, Jeffrey W., author.
Title: Criminology explains school bullying / Robert A. Brooks and
    Jeffrey W. Cohen.
Description: Oakland, California : University of California Press, [2020] |
    Includes bibliographical references and index.
Identifiers: LCCN 2020001535 | ISBN 9780520298262 (cloth) |
    ISBN 9780520298279 (paperback) | ISBN 9780520970465 (ebook)
Subjects: LCSH: Bullying in schools. | Criminology. | Bullying in schools—
    Social aspects. | School violence—Social aspects.
Classification: LCC LB3013.3 .B766 2020 | DDC 371.5/8—dc23
LC record available at https://lccn.loc.gov/2020001535

29 28 27 26 25 24 23 22 21 20
10 9 8 7 6 5 4 3 2 1

We both thank Maura Roessner for her support in shepherding this book through to publication as well as her assistance with the book series. We also thank members of the Criminology Explains Advisory Board for their valued input.

Thank you to Alain for your enduring support of my writing, here and elsewhere.

—ROBERT A. BROOKS

Thank you to Diana for your support, love, and intellect.

—JEFF W. COHEN

CONTENTS

Introduction

We began our research on school bullying in about 2010 when we noticed the disparate coverage of two bullying-related youth suicides in Massachusetts. In the first case, an eleven-year-old African American boy named Carl Walker-Hoover died by suicide on April 6, 2009, in Springfield. In the second case, a fifteen-year-old Irish immigrant girl named Phoebe Prince died by suicide on January 14, 2010, in South Hadley. In both cases, the suicide was linked to bullying victimization. The two suicides occurred less than one year apart and in towns separated by less than twenty miles, and both youths possessed characteristics supporting an "ideal victim" construction (e.g., young, vulnerable, defenseless, and worthy of sympathy). However, only the Prince case evolved into a "signal crime," that is, involving "events that, in addition to affecting the immediate participants . . . impact in some way upon a wider audience . . . caus[ing] them to reconfigure their behaviors or beliefs in some way" (Innes 2004, 52). The Prince suicide led to the filing of charges against nine individuals, massive news coverage, and Massachusetts's enactment of a new antibullying law. The media gave the Carl Walker-Hoover suicide relatively scant attention. In conference papers and presentations, we explored issues of gender, race, and criminalization around this differing coverage.

We also rapidly expanded our research to include media reports of bullying more generally, which led to the publication of the book *Confronting School Bullying: Kids, Culture, and the Making of a Social Problem* (Cohen and Brooks 2014). In that book, we explored how the media constructed the phenomenon of school bullying from a relatively minor, localized problem through to its emergence as a major national and international public health concern. We noted that the linking of school bullying to retaliatory violence (e.g., school shootings) and to suicide had by 2013 become a dominant discourse in mainstream news media. Emphasizing such extreme outcomes—and linking them together to suggest first a trend and then an epidemic—is an important factor contributing to how school bullying came to be perceived as a serious social problem. This contrasts with the early 1990s, when the threat of bullying was usually constructed in rather mild terms. While few dismissed bullying entirely with a "kids will be kids" attitude, descriptions like the following 1993 excerpt from Lawrence Kutner's *New York Times* "Parent and Child" column were not uncommon: "A 10-year-old who is extorting milk money or threatening to chase a child home after school can loom large in the fears of an 8-year-old. Handing over a quarter a day to avoid possibly being beaten up seems a small price to pay" (October 28, 1993, C12). By 2010, bullying had been elevated to a threat of catastrophic proportions; John Quiñones opened a segment of NBC's *Prime Time Live* by asking, "Harmless bullying? A simple part of growing up? Or a tragic epidemic that leaves entire schools heartbroken, parents childless and families torn apart?" (October 29, 2010).

The confluence of exhaustive media reports, an explosion of academic research, and increased concerns from school systems led to the creation of an antibullying industry marked by consultants, experts, corporate entities, and entertainment celebrities and vehicles. The rise of the antibullying industry helped solidify bullying as a national social problem and also created a risk of cynicism and burnout (Cohen and Brooks 2014).

ACADEMIC INTEREST IN SCHOOL BULLYING

Interestingly, academic interest in school bullying is said to have begun in earnest after several suicides in Norway were linked to bullying (Beaty and Alexeyev 2008). The research was pioneered by Olweus (1993), who in addition to researching the causes and consequences of bullying also developed a leading bullying prevention program. Academic interest quickly spread to neighboring European countries and then additional ones. Research in the United States was slower to start, increasing dramatically after about 2007. Figures 1 and 2 provide representative examples of the steep increase in academic publications concerning school bullying. Each figure represents the number of academic publications returned from a search on the comprehensive academic search engine Google Scholar using the search term "school bullying" (in quotation marks). Figure 1 shows the number of academic

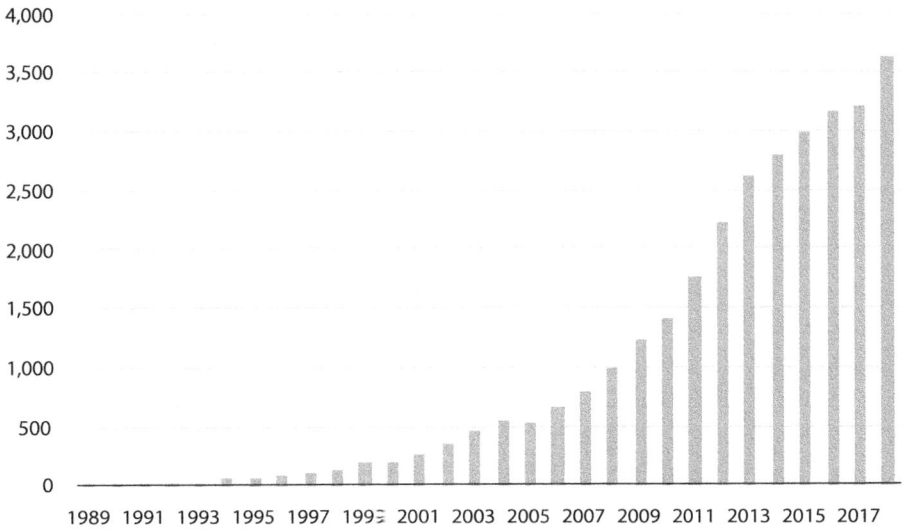

FIGURE 1. Number of new publications per year generated on the academic search engine Google Scholar using the term "school bullying," 1989–2018.

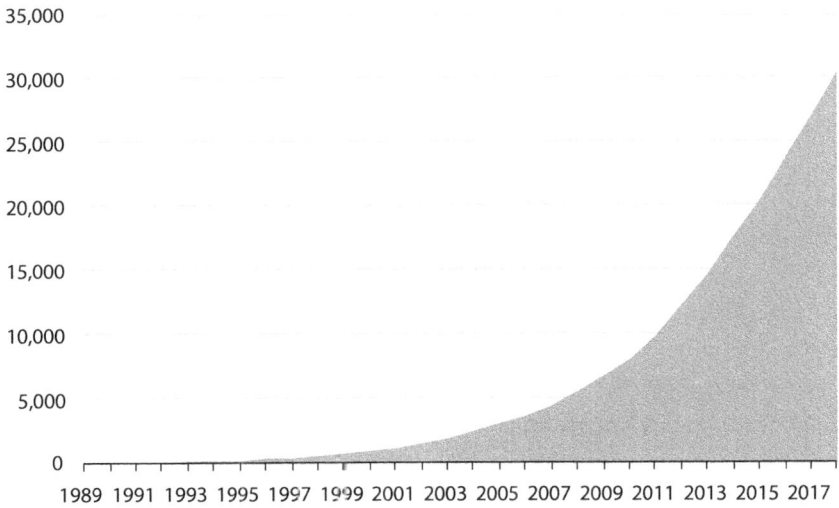

FIGURE 2. Cumulative number of publications generated on the academic search engine Google Scholar using the term "school bullying," 1989–2018.

works (e.g., articles, monographs, book chapters, and books) that were added each year, from 10 in 1989 to 3,620 in 2018. Figure 2 shows the yearly cumulative number of academic works, beginning with 10 in 1989 and increasing to 30,399 in 2018. As large as these recent numbers are, they are a vast understatement considering that many academic works on school bullying do not necessarily use the words *school bullying* in that order. A search of the term without quotation marks yielded 614 "hits" for 1989 and a cumulative 358,000 hits for the period 1989–2018. Many of these results are not on point (some results use the two terms but in an unrelated way), so it is not possible to know the precise number of publications.

Other indications of increased academic interest in school bullying include the number of papers devoted to the subject at international conferences. For instance, the 2016 meeting of the American Society of Criminology showcased fifty presentation titles addressing schools and another twenty-two addressing bullying. New journals have been introduced, including the *Journal of School Violence* in 2002 and the *International Journal of Bullying Prevention* in March 2019, the latter sponsored by the International Bullying Prevention Association. Many other journals have devoted special issues to school bullying, including *American Psychologist* (2015), *Journal of Adolescence* (2017), and the *International Journal of Environmental Research and Public Health* (2019), to name a few.

Notwithstanding this explosion of research, important questions remain about many aspects of school bullying, something we explore in detail in this volume. There are fundamental questions about how bullying and cyberbullying ought to be defined and measured, how bullying is related to and different from other forms of peer aggression, and how trajectories of bullying and victimization develop over childhood and adolescence, among many others. Because psychological approaches and quantitative measurement have dominated bullying research, there is much to learn from continuing the more recent sociological and cultural approaches as well as greater use of qualitative research methods and mixed methods research.

THE MOTIVATION BEHIND *CRIMINOLOGY EXPLAINS*

The idea for a book series arose when one of us was teaching a class that had equal numbers of criminology and psychology students and thus had to provide an overview of each field to the students. Since we were working on our book *Confronting School Bullying* at the time, we decided to introduce criminological theories by defining each and then describing how they would explain school bullying. It appeared that students more clearly saw the similarities and differences among the theories because they were being applied to the same phenomenon. We quickly applied this concept to our teaching of the course Criminology. We have found that criminology textbooks offer a detailed and comprehensive discussion of a wide variety of criminological theories and crimes, but they do not typically have a "through line" that would allow the reader to make connections across theories and chapters. Such texts frequently promise a "bio-psycho-social model" but in fact offer a section on biological influences, some on psychological theories, and some on social and cultural models. In order to overcome this, we assigned students to locate articles about bullying that used various levels of explanation, and students presented their research as we moved through the book. Again, we found that students were able to make clearer connections across theories because of the focus on the same dependent variable.

By focusing all of the theories on one problem, volumes in *Criminology Explains*, including this one, provide a through line, allowing for greater synthesis and thus deeper and longer-lasting retention of learning. Applying different (and sometimes wildly divergent and conflicting) explanatory models to the same problem serves to highlight the similarities and differences among the theories, and allows linkages across explanatory levels and across time and geography. The intent, then, is to emphasize the "social-ecological model," which views social phenomena as having multiple inputs at different levels of influence that include individuals, institutions, communities, and larger social and cultural structures and processes. We designed the volumes in part to be an adjunct to criminology textbooks, with chapters arranged in the same general order as most such textbooks.

THE DESIGN AND ORGANIZATION OF THIS VOLUME

In this volume, we have provided a broad overview of how criminological theory can enlighten our understanding of school bullying. Given the conflict between the massive amount of academic work about school bullying on the one hand, as noted above, and our space limitations on the other hand, we are not able to delve deeply into all aspects of the phenomenon. We also note that research applying criminological theory to school bullying is a relatively recent development (picking up around 2008 or 2009), and so have done our best to fill in gaps in the literature when necessary. We also included research that is not explicitly criminological but that appears to mirror or invoke criminological theories or principles. For example, much research that explains peer influences is based in psychological theories but also suggests aspects of differential association theory from criminology. We also provide an overall impression of the utility of criminological theory to explain school bullying. For example, some research suggests that school bullying is actually quite normative, and some commentators have questioned whether applying criminological theory to school bullying contributes to the criminalization of student behavior more generally. That is certainly not our intention—rather, we believe such theory can have broad application because much of it was theorized and tested in adolescent populations as to a variety of delinquency behaviors, including those based in aggression.

We have designed the chapters to be read in conjunction with corresponding chapters in criminology textbooks, but the book also stands alone. Given this focus, we have attempted to devote relatively less space to descriptions of theory and more to applications of it. Chapter 1 offers an overview of school bullying, describing its nature and extent, definitional and measurement issues and challenges, how the phenomenon has been socially constructed, and various methods of response and prevention. The chapter ends with a brief discussion of the social-ecological model. Chapters 2 through 7 apply criminological theories. Chapter 2 discusses victimization, lifestyle, and deterrence theories. Chapter 3 considers individual-level (micro) theories at the biosocial and psychological levels. Chapter 4 discusses social structure theories, including social disorganization, strain, and subcultural theories. Chapter 5 looks at social process theories, including social learning, social control, and social reaction (or labeling). Chapter 6 explores various critical theories, such as feminist theory and critical race theory. Chapter 7 addresses integrated, developmental, and life course theories as well as the social-ecological view that incorporates "nested" levels of theory (i.e., micro to macro). Each of these chapters also includes a discussion of the policy implications that emerge from the theories covered and a Policy Box that asks readers to apply theoretical constructs to school bullying response and prevention.

ONE

The Nature, Scope, and Response to School Bullying

School bullying, an age-old phenomenon, has only come to be recognized as an international public health concern in the twenty-first century (Olweus, Limber, and Breivik 2019). Research shows that bullying is correlated with serious harm to victims, bullies, and bully-victims, as well as to perpetrators, bystanders, families, and the school environment. All fifty US states and the District of Columbia have enacted antibullying statutes, and nearly all schools and school districts in the United States have adopted antibullying policies and programs. The construction of bullying as a serious social problem involved a confluence of parties (researchers and other experts, educators, and celebrities), social movements such as the demand for greater LGBTQ rights, and institutions (media, politics, and commercial interests), resulting in an "antibullying industry" (Cohen and Brooks 2014) or a "psychology-commercial complex" (Boge and Larsson 2018).

This chapter provides an overview of school bullying, including how interested parties have defined and measured it, and how prevalent it is. The chapter then details some of bullying's harms to victims, perpetrators, and others and explains how schools and other institutions have sought to prevent and respond to it. The chapter concludes with a brief explanation of the social-ecological model and its relevance to the remainder of the book.

DEFINING SCHOOL BULLYING

Many groups need to have workable definitions of school bullying, including researchers, policy makers, and legislators (Patchin and Hinduja 2015).

Educators and students also need valid bullying definitions in order to evaluate and respond to it.

Academic Definitions

Social scientists require definitions of phenomena that are clear and consistent. It is thus surprising that, despite the prominence of bullying as a social problem, the term has been inconsistently defined (Green, Furlong, and Felix 2017).

Traditional Bullying Academic research has mostly coalesced around the definition developed by Dan Olweus (Volk et al. 2012): "aggressive behavior or intentional 'harm doing,' which is carried out repeatedly and over time in an interpersonal relationship characterized by an imbalance of power" or in which the subject is unable to defend himself or herself (Olweus 1993, 8–9). The element of intentionality distinguishes bullying from harassment, which depends not on intent but on the victim's perceptions (Cascardi et al. 2014). The element of repetition emphasizes bullying's systematic nature and separates it from fighting. The power imbalance element differentiates bullying from teasing, roughhousing, and other types of aggression between equals (Green, Furlong, and Felix 2017). The power imbalance is sometimes based in physicality—that is, where the bully is bigger, stronger, or older (Langos 2012). However, the imbalance can also be rooted in social or intellectual power (Espelage 2018), including one's status in a peer network (Faris and Felmlee 2011b; Nelson et al. 2019), and in cultural norms such as notions of "proper" sexual and gendered behavior (Rosen and Nofziger 2018).

Academic researchers have further categorized bullying as direct or indirect. Direct bullying occurs in the presence of the victim and involves physical and/ or verbal aggression, while indirect bullying is aggressive communication that is not directed at the victim, such as spreading false and damaging rumors (Gladden et al. 2014, 7). Much of indirect bullying is also "covert"—that is, hidden from or not easily recognized by adults (Barnes et al. 2012). Researchers have also broken down bullying into subtypes that include physical, verbal, relational, destruction of property (Gladden et al. 2014, 7–8), and cyberbullying.

Researchers have questioned the Olweus conceptualization (e.g., Rawlings 2016; Walton 2011). Some have called for relatively minor tweaks, as in the "uniform definition" of bullying issued by US federal agencies (Gladden et al. 2014, 7). Others have argued for changes that are more significant. For example, Volk, Dane, and Marini (2014) conceptualized bullying as "aggressive, *goal-directed* behavior that harms another individual within the context of a power imbalance" (328, emphasis added). Others have gone further and suggested that bullying be seen as a multidimensional construct that includes the form of aggression (physical, verbal, social, or cyber) and its functions (offensive, defensive, or instrumental aggression; Little et al. 2003). Some researchers have also conceptualized bystander behaviors multidimensionally (e.g., Lambe and Craig 2020).

Cyberbullying A leading question is whether cyberbullying can be "plugged into" the Olweus definition (Tokunaga 2010). Because there is high correspondence between cyber and traditional perpetration, and cyber and traditional victimization (Gini, Card, and Pozzoli 2018; Modecki et al. 2014), many researchers conceptualize cyberbullying as simply bullying through electronic means (e.g., Gladden et al. 2014, 8; Kowalski et al. 2014). Other researchers have questioned whether the Olweus elements apply to cyberbullying. For instance, some have argued that "repetition" by the initial perpetrator should not be required because digital postings can be easily shared and repeatedly viewed by others (e.g., Grigg 2010; Englander et al. 2017; Langos 2012; Patchin and Hinduja 2015). Researchers have also debated the "power imbalance" element as to cyberbullying. It could be that

- power relations in the "online world" mimic those in the "real world," given that traditional bullying and cyberbullying significantly overlap, or

- power may flow from one's technical proficiency with digital communication technologies (Langos 2012; Vandebosch and Van Cleemput 2008); a claim that applied research has not clearly supported (Grigg 2010), or

- cyberspace represents an "equalizing arena for individuals of varying physical strengths to aggress" (Barlett et al. 2017, 23).

Other researchers have argued that cyberbullying relates more to other types of online aggression than it does to traditional bullying. Grigg (2010) grouped cyberbullying behaviors with electronic stalking, harassment, hacking accounts, and spreading viruses (151). Pyżalski (2012) proposed the concept "electronic aggression" after finding that a significant percentage of the Polish schoolchildren in his study had acted aggressively online against persons outside their peer group and that only 25 percent of students' online aggression qualified as cyberbullying.

Research has demonstrated differences in understandings of bullying, both within groups and between groups. An example of *intra*group differences is that teachers' perceptions "can be [differentially] shaped by time spent in the profession and confidence in managing aggressive behavior" (Chandler 2018, 37, citing Reid, Monsen, and Rivers 2004) and can vary according to the source of information being accessed (Rigby 2018). Parents' definitions also vary widely (see Harcourt, Jasperse, and Green 2014), and children define bullying differently as they develop (Smith et al. 2002). An example of *inter*-group differences is the finding that teachers and students differed as to which Olweus definitional elements to include (Naylor et al. 2006). Understandings of bullying also have cultural and linguistic influences (Maunder and Crafter 2018; Sittichai and Smith 2015; Smith and Monks 2008). Bullying manifests differently in Eastern and Western cultures (Smith, Kwak, and Toda 2016). Additionally, the word *bullying* does not always have a clear counterpart in many languages, and use of words that seem similar may result in under- or overreporting (Smith et al. 2002). Unfortunately, standardized measures may not capture these differences (Gaffney, Farrington, and Ttofi 2019).

Relatively few studies have asked participants to explain cyberbullying (Alipan et al. 2015), and studies have shown mixed results. Not all participants have supported the notion of a power differential (Vandebosch and Van Cleemput 2008), and participants' interpretation may depend on the perpetrator's intent and/or the victim's experience (Baldasare et al. 2012; Vandebosch and van Cleemput 2008). Given these differences, it is important that researchers define cyberbullying in a way that resonates with participants' understanding (Volk, Veenstra, and Espelage 2017), but this may be difficult if there is so much intragroup variability.

The News Media's Construction of School Bullying

The news media were drawn to school bullying by three "moral shocks" (see Jasper and Poulsen 1995)—the Columbine school shooting in 1999 and two deaths by suicide (termed "bullycides" by some media) in 2010, discussed further in this chapter's Policy Box. Media outlets blamed the Columbine massacre in part on the perpetrators having been bullied, although Cullen (2010) effectively debunked that long-held assumption. News media linked both suicides to clusters of supposedly similar ones (Cohen and Brooks 2014). Moreno et al. (2019) showed that much of the news coverage in the bullycides era has been fear based, more so for cyberbullying (more than 40 percent) than traditional bullying (about 20 percent). Similarly, coverage in Spanish media was sensationalist, focusing on the extreme outcome of victim suicides (see Blanco-Castilla and Cano-Galindo 2019).

While news media initially seemed to draw from the Olweus elements, they expanded the scope of the bullying "epidemic" to take in an increasing range of behavior, including less serious behaviors such as teasing or rough-housing and more serious harms such as assaults and even homicide (Cohen and Brooks 2014).

Legislative Definitions

Every US state and the District of Columbia have enacted antibullying legislation (Sacco et al. 2012), with a few states having criminalized some forms of school bullying (United States Department of Education 2011). Statutory definitions vary widely, including as to specific actions (physical, verbal, or written), the intent of the aggressor, and harm to the victim. Sacco et al. (2012) noted, "in many instances, minor language, omitted or inserted into laws, can significantly alter the way in which the behavior and circumstances are legally defined (e.g., inclusion of the terms 'physical,' 'overt,' or 'repeated')" (4).

Notably, as of 2012, few statutes followed research-based bullying definitions (Sacco et al. 2012, 5). In fact, many statutes' conceptions "go well beyond research-based definitions of bullying" because they borrow language from statutes defining harassment (United States Department of Education 2011, 17). Language in twenty-two state statutes uses the terms "bullying," "harassment," and "intimidation" interchangeably, fourteen restrict their statute to "bullying," and another eight include both "bullying" and "harassment" but define them separately (Cascardi et al. 2014, 265).

Why Definitions Matter

Researchers have also sometimes failed to differentiate bullying distinctly from harassment and other types of peer aggression, creating "the potential to obscure important differences in etiology, impact, and effective prevention" (Cascardi et al. 2014, 255). This is of particular concern because some evidence has shown that bullying has unique, and more serious, harms compared to other peer aggression (e.g., Ybarra, Espelage, and Mitchell 2014) and thus requires a different set of responses (Cornell and Limber 2015). It is difficult to develop evidence-based interventions and prevention methods if definitions vary or are uncertain (Corcoran, McGuckin, and Prentice 2015; United States Department of Education 2011).

The consistency and specificity of definitions also matter to teachers, administrators, and students. Most school districts require teachers and administrators to take action after alleged bullying incidents, such as reporting to the victim's parents and taking disciplinary action against the perpetrator. Since discipline must be consistent to be effective, teachers' and administrators' definitions should align with those of parents and students. In addition, bullying victims require different types of support than do other victims of peer harassment. Finally, a clash of definitions between those of adults and those of children can lead to poor outcomes, such as a decline in trust (e.g., Chandler 2018).

OPERATIONALIZING SCHOOL BULLYING

Operationalizing means to turn a concept into something measurable. Even after decades of research, "measurement is still the Achilles' heel of bullying research" (Volk, Veenstra, and Espelage 2017, 36) because it "is fraught with difficulty" (Vessey et al. 2014, 820).

Bullying researchers have relied mostly on quantitative measures developed in the field of psychology (Eriksen 2018). More than 80 percent of reported studies have used **self-report measures** (Vivolo-Kantor et al. 2014). As of 2011, there were at least thirty-three such measures (Hamburger, Basile, and Vivolo 2011), although there are few separate measures of cyberbullying specifically (Vivolo-Kantor et al. 2014). Self-report measures are widely used because they are low cost, quick to administer, and easy to calculate. Researchers such as Olweus (2013) have argued that students are in the best position to know their own roles and behaviors; however, there is little research as to whether self-report methods produce more accurate assessments (Vivolo-Kantor et al. 2014). Another method, **nomination**, involves asking various informants, such as teachers, parents, and (usually) peers, to identify victims and perpetrators. An emerging method is network analysis, which examines how students are connected in order to reveal social patterns of peer aggression (e.g., Faris and Felmlee 2011a, 2011b, 2014; Veenstra et al. 2013; Verlinden et al. 2014). Researchers use this method to "inform teachers about the group structure of their classroom, to give personal advice on their students' relationships, and to make a tailored plan to assist or intervene with those relationships" (Volk, Veenstra, and Espelage 2017, 38). If used longitudinally, the method can answer questions such as whether existing friend groups bully students or whether those who bully students become friends (Volk, Veenstra, and Espelage 2017).

It is important that measures be valid and reliable. **Reliability** means how free from measurement error a measure is—that is, how consistent it is. Bullying researchers have focused more on reliability than validity (accuracy). Thus, Casper, Meter, and Card (2015) suggested that researchers have sacrificed the latter for the former. Even so, rigorous analysis has provided only limited support for reliability of instruments (see Vessey et al. 2014). Peer nominations are more reliable than self-reports because they come from multiple sources. However, they are subject to "biases related to reputational effects, prejudice, or non-bullying relationship problems," and depend on peers having observed the bullying, some of which may be covert (e.g., relational or cyberbullying; Volk, Veenstra, and Espelage 2017, 38). Reliability also suffers when groups of students interpret the same behaviors differently. For instance, in one study, boys and minority students were less likely to label an incident "bullying" than were, respectively, girls and white students, even though all groups reported being subjected to similar bullying *behaviors* (Lai and Kao 2018).

Validity takes several forms; generally, it is an assessment of accuracy—how well a researcher has translated a concept into measurement (i.e., how well it measures what it is supposed to measure). Thus far, bullying research "has not strongly focused on the theoretical validity of its measures" (Volk, Veenstra, and Espelage 2017, 37). Of primary concern is variation in the assessment of bullying's elements (Cascardi et al. 2014). Assuming that the Olweus conception is the "correct" one, researchers would need to measure each of its elements in order to have **content validity** (that is, to take in all aspects of the term's meaning) However, Vivolo-Kantor et al. (2014) found fewer than half of the questionnaires in the studies they reviewed included all the elements. (This is aside from the question of whether the Olweus definition actually comports with students' own perceptions of what constitutes bullying [Harbin et al. 2019].) Even where a questionnaire defines bullying's elements, validity issues can still arise. For instance, Kaufman, Huitsing, and Veenstra (2020) administered a refined version of the Olweus Bully/Victim

Questionnaire and found that "more than half of the self-reported victims did not experience all characteristics of bullying." The "power imbalance" element was the most likely for respondents to ignore. Another challenge to validity is that bullying is dynamic and highly dependent on context and interpretation. For instance, the "power differential . . . can change depending on the circumstances of a specific aggressive episode" (Cascardi et al. 2014, 254), and children draw on context to interpret whether bullying occurred (Forsberg 2019).

There is also rather weak **concurrent validity** across measures—that is, different measures sometimes produce different prevalence rates and classify different students as bullied and nonbullied (Cascardi et al. 2014). In addition, the agreement between self-reports and nominations by teachers or peers is only modestly positive (Branson and Cornell 2009; Lee and Cornell 2009).

Many researchers have called for more qualitative research to better understand children's experiences (e.g., Tholander, Lindberg, and Svensson 2019) and to help explain the relatively low success rates of bullying interventions (see Patton et al. 2017). Qualitative research explores how participants construct their understanding of school bullying, how this understanding plays out within particular institutional and cultural settings, and how all of this fits with researchers' notions of the phenomenon (Maunder and Crafter 2018; Patton et al. 2017). It can involve methods such as in-depth interviews (e.g., Side and Johnson 2014), focus groups (e.g., Chandler 2018), content analysis (e.g., Osvaldsson 2011), ethnography (e.g., Gumpel, Zioni-Koren, and Bekerman 2014; Thornberg 2018), and other methods that involve direct observation. For instance, Craig and Pepler employed cameras and wireless microphones to record students' interactions on playgrounds (1998; Craig, Pepler, and Atlas 2000), thus capturing language and behavior that usually occur beyond adults' perceptions and "revealing new insights about [the] forms, frequency, and social structures" of school bullying (Volk, Veenstra, and Espelage 2017, 39).

Qualitative research can also explore what a student is bullying—or being bullied—*about* (e.g., physical characteristics, race/ethnicity, sexual orientation), a question absent from nearly all quantitative measures (American Educational Research Association 2013). This question is important because, for example, ethnic/cultural bullying is difficult to detect with current instruments (Rodríguez-Hidalgo et al. 2019), and it is correlated more strongly with poor health outcomes than is traditional bullying (Russell et al. 2012). However, qualitative measures have their own reliability and validity challenges. For instance, observations are better at capturing physical aggression than relational aggression, and direct observations of cyberbullying have many practical limitations. In addition, ethnographic findings may not be **generalizable** to other populations.

PREVALENCE OF SCHOOL BULLYING

Researchers have reported wide variation in the percentage of students who are involved in bullying, due to a number of factors, including the reliability and validity issues identified above (Modecki et al. 2014; Selkie, Fales, and Moreno 2016; Vivolo-Kantor et al. 2014). For instance, Selkie, Fales, and Moreno (2016) noted highly varying rates of cyberbullying perpetration (1–41 percent) and victimization (3–72 percent) in the fifty-eight studies they examined (129). Schwartz, Proctor, and Chien (2001) reported varying percentages of students who are bully-victims—from 0.4 percent to nearly 29 percent—across ten studies using self-reports. Use of peer reports results in less variation in the percentage of bully-victims (from 6 percent to 10 percent), yet this is still a large difference in relative terms (Yang and Salmivalli 2013).

Meta-analyses, which create average means across many studies, show bullying perpetration and victimization are common. For instance, a meta-analysis of eighty studies reported a mean rate of 35 percent for traditional bullying perpetration and 36 percent for traditional victimization, and 15 percent for cyberbullying and 15 percent for cybervictimization, with a great deal of overlap between cyber and traditional bullying (Modecki et al. 2014). Large-scale population studies, particularity recent ones, have shown lower but still troubling prevalence rates. One 2015 study found 20.8 percent of students in grades six through twelve had been bullied during the 2014–2015 school year (United States Department of Education 2016b), a significant decline in victimization from the rate of 27.8 percent during the 2010–2011 school year (United States Department of Education 2013). Some localized studies show decreases that are even more dramatic. For instance, self-reported bullying victimization among students in grades four through twelve in more than one hundred Maryland schools declined from 28.5 percent in 2005 to 13.4 percent in 2014 (Waasdorp et al. 2017). Changes in rates could result from actual changes in behavior or could be an artifact caused by phenomena such as **response shift** (see Shaw, Cross, and Zubrick 2015) or the **sensitization effect** (e.g., Cornell and Bandyopadhyay 2010). For instance, students in schools that have higher-quality antibullying policies sometimes report *more* victimization, with more distress (e.g., Gower, Cousin, and Borowsky 2017). One possible explanation is that high-quality policies tend to encourage more reporting, a sensitization effect.

Large studies and meta-analyses have found that girls are more likely to be victims of cyber, relational, and verbal forms, while boys are more likely to be victims of physical bullying (e.g., Waasdorp and Bradshaw 2015). However, there may be an "age × gender" effect. In their meta-analysis, Barlett and Coyne (2014) found that in high school, girls were more likely to cyberbully while younger and boys while older. As to race, studies are mixed, showing African American students reporting victimization rates that are either lower (e.g., Waasdorp and Bradshaw 2015) or higher (United States Department of Education 2016a) than those of white students, while other studies show reporting varies by race depending on the method of measurement (Lai and Kao 2018; Sawyer, Bradshaw, and O'Brennan 2008).

Cross-nationally, about one in three students reports having been bullied, but there is a great deal of geographical variation, from a low of 22.8 percent in the Caribbean to 48.2 percent in sub-Saharan Africa (UNESCO 2018). Just as in studies in the United States, cross-national studies have reported general declines in bullying perpetration and victimization (e.g., Molcho et al. 2009 [1994–2006 period]; Rigby and Smith 2011 [1990–2009 period]). However, there are indications that the rate of cyberbullying may have increased over these periods (Yang and Grinshteyn 2016). Within the United States, rates also vary widely, with one study showing a low of 14.1 percent in Alabama and a high of 26.7 percent in South Dakota, with a national mean of 19.8 percent (Hatzenbuehler et al. 2015).

HARMS ASSOCIATED WITH PERPETRATION AND VICTIMIZATION

There is a large body of research detailing negative correlates of bullying and other peer victimization. Although researchers frequently use terms like *harm* or *outcomes*, it is important to understand several complicating factors to identifying causality. (We use the term *harm* here for ease of reference.) First, researchers mostly classify bullies and victims as monolithic categories when in fact there are various "latent statuses" (subtypes) within each of these categories. In addition, while researchers classify various "types" or "subtypes," differences between bullies and nonbullies actually "are a matter of degree rather than a difference in kind" (Walters and Espelage 2019), and this is likely true for differences among bullies and among victims. Second, there are many risk and protective factors to both bullying and victimization (McDougall and Vaillancourt 2015), and thus there is no single or common outcome for either perpetrators or victims, a concept known generally as **multifinality** (Cicchetti and Rogosch 1996). Third, and relatedly, much bullying research has ignored the effects of **confounding factors** (Bouffard and Koeppel 2014; Wong and Schonlau 2013). Thus, while studies show correlations between bullying victimization and various harms, "it is difficult to identify the underlying mechanisms that explain the relation between bullying victimization and maladaptive development" (Connolly and Beaver 2016, 1236). For instance, the link between bullying involvement and suicide is likely confounded by a number of individual-level variables, as noted in this chapter's Policy Box. The same is true of causal mechanisms that link bullying *perpetration* to harm.

Harm to Victims

Victims may experience a variety of harms and can be revictimized through unsupportive responses from parents and teachers that leave the student a "rejected victim" (Tholander 2019). Victimization appears to be associated with somewhat lower academic achievement (see Delprato, Akyeampong, and Dunne 2017), including as to cyber victimization specifically (e.g., Gardella, Fisher, and Teurbe-Tolon 2017). One study found that only relational bullying (and not the cyber or physical forms) affected academic performance (Torres, D'Alessio, and Stolzenberg 2020). However, lower achievement has not been a universal finding as to traditional bullying (e.g., Georgiou 2008) or cyberbullying (e.g., Kowalski et al. 2014). Some national US studies also indicate that victimization is associated with increased absenteeism (Gardella, Fisher, and Teurbe-Tolon 2017; Grinshteyn and Yang 2017; Steiner and Rasberry 2015). Other studies have linked higher levels of teasing and bullying to poorer *school-wide* outcomes, such as standardized exam scores (Lacey and Cornell 2013; Lacey, Cornell, and Konold 2017) and high school dropout rates (Cornell et al. 2013), even after controlling for school-level variables.

Meta-analytic reviews have found correlations between bullying victimization and various internalizing symptoms (e.g., Evans, Smokowski, and Cotter

2014; Gini and Pozzoli 2009; Gini et al. 2014; Holt et al. 2015; Låftman et al. 2018; Moore et al. 2017; van Dam et al. 2012), including as to cyber victimization specifically (Kowalski et al. 2014). Some researchers have even advocated for a new disorder called "postbullying disorder" (Arnout, Alshehri, Assiri, and Al-Qadimi 2020). Other meta-analyses have found disproportionally negative outcomes among particular groups, such as sexual minority youth (e.g., Collier et al. 2013). Individual studies have linked victimization with a whole host of physiological symptoms and problems in children (Alhafez and Masri 2019; Arana et al. 2018; Chen et al. 2018; Copeland et al. 2015; Donoghue and Meltzer 2018; Du Plessis et al. 2019; Ouellet-Morin et al. 2011; Serra-Negra et al. 2017; Sutin et al. 2016). Victimization has also been correlated with externalizing behaviors, including various types of delinquent behaviors (DeCamp and Newby 2015; Park and Metcalfe 2020; Rusby et al. 2005; Valdebenito, Ttofi, and Eisner 2015; Wong and Schonlau 2013). Findings about externalizing problems in victims may seem surprising, but the relationship could be due to investigators' failure to sometimes distinguish between pure victims and bully-victims (Lester, Cross, and Shaw 2012), as well as between subtypes of victims.

Meta-analyses of longitudinal studies have found correlations between childhood victimization and internalizing symptoms as adults (Nielsen et al. 2015; Ttofi et al. 2011). Individual studies have found childhood victimization to be correlated with poorer adult outcomes in health, education, and employment (Drydakis 2014; Gorman et al. 2019; Matthews et al. 2017; Sansone, Lam, and Wiederman 2010; Sweeting et al. 2020; Wolke et al. 2013). Researchers have developed biological (e.g., Vaillancourt, Hymel, and McDougall 2013) and psychological (Swearer and Hymel 2015b) models attempting to explicate how peer victimization can cause lifelong harm.

While researchers have demonstrated correlations, they differ as to whether there is a clear *causal* link between victimization and various negative symptoms, during childhood or afterward. Much of the research is correlational—that is, researchers collected data at one time. The best evidence suggests that peer victimization is both an antecedent and a consequence of internalizing problems. In other words, there is a vicious circle where victimization causes internalizing problems while "internalizing problems . . . maintain and solidify children's standing as a victim of peer torment" (Reijntjes et al. 2010, 250; see also Averdijk et al. 2016; Forbes et al. 2019; Gini, Card, and Pozzoli 2018). Evidence supports a stronger effect for "victimization to problems" pathway than vice versa.

However, a meta-analysis (Schoeler et al. 2018) that claimed to have examined the "most stringent evidence" found that bullying victimization had only "small causal effects" (1237) on internalizing symptoms akin to those experienced after natural or human-caused disasters and that effects dissipated over time. These diverse findings may be explained by a common failure to differentiate bully-victims as well as to account for the severity or chronicity of victimization. Research has shown a **dose-response** relationship (that is, the more victimization, the more serious the symptoms), which supports the pathway where victimization causes poor outcomes. This has generally been a finding whether the "dose" is measured by the number of total types of victimization (physical, verbal, relational, or cyber; Hinduja and Patchin 2019; Hong et al. 2020; Wolke, Lee, and Guy 2017) or by its relative frequency, severity, and/or persistence (e.g., Bowes et al. 2013; Hong et al. 2020; Klomek, Sourander, and Elonheimo 2015; Randa, Reyns, and Nobles 2019; Smokowski, Evans, and Cotter 2014).

Researchers have also explored whether cyberbullying is correlated with different, or more severe, internalizing symptoms. Some individual studies have found that cyber victimization is linked to different types of internalizing and externalizing problems (e.g., Giumetti and Kowalski 2016). One meta-analysis found that victimization by bullying and cyberbullying each uniquely contributed to internalizing problems but that the difference in *severity* of symptoms was nonsignificant (Gini, Card, and Pozzoli 2018).

Harm to Perpetrators

Bullying perpetration is associated with some of the same negative symptoms during childhood as is victimization (Copeland et al. 2015; Gini and Pozzoli 2009; Kowalski and Limber 2013; Ttofi, Farrington, Lösel et al. 2016). National studies have found a higher incidence of some psychiatric disorders and negative health behaviors among men who had bullied as children (e.g., Matthews et al. 2017; Vaughn et al. 2010). However, not all perpetrators are the same; rather, there appear to be "two social worlds of aggression"; some perpetrators are popular and have high social power (even though they may not be well liked), while other perpetrators are socially rejected (Farmer et al. 2010). Perpetrators in the latter group demonstrate symptoms that are more negative than their popular peers do. This distinction may at least partly explain the dramatic differences in how researchers have portrayed bullies (see Rodkin, Espelage, and Hanish 2015) and the finding of some studies that perpetrators were not at greater risk of poor mental health (e.g., Romano et al. 2019).

Researchers have paid relatively less attention to bully-victims than to either "pure" bullies or victims. Of the three groups, bully-victims tend to have the highest rates of internalizing and externalizing symptoms as children (Kelly et al. 2015; Kowalski and Limber 2013; O'Moore and Kirkham 2001), although this finding has not been universal (e.g., Lereya et al. 2015). They also have been found to have the greatest impairment in adult functioning (Wolke et al. 2013). Thus, bully-victims tend to develop negative characteristics associated with both bullies and victims (Lereya et al. 2015). However, research has also shown that some of the attributes associated with bully-victims can mitigate the trajectories to later antisocial outcomes (Schwartz et al. 2018).

Harm to Bystanders and Others

Bystanders to bullying can suffer negative psychological consequences (Rigby and Slee 1993; Rivers et al. 2009). In addition, they may experience greater interpersonal sensitivity (i.e., witnesses worry about becoming the next victim) and heightened levels of hostility, perhaps because they need to resolve the cognitive dissonance "resulting from the discrepancy between their desire to intervene and their lack of action" (Rivers et al. 2009, 220). This is particularly true for bystanders who have also been victims (Midgett and Doumas 2019). School bullying also affects victims' families; in one study, "parents described feeling upset, disappointed, frustrated, and powerless" about their children's victimization (Harcourt, Green, and Bowden 2015, 8). In addition, school climate has been negatively correlated with school bullying, a relationship we explore in chapter 4. There are even economic costs. One California study found that the state lost an estimated $78 million in unallocated funds due to missed school days of kids who were victimized by bias-based bullying and who did not feel safe to go to school (Baams, Talmage, and Russell 2017).

PREVENTION OF, AND RESPONSES TO, SCHOOL BULLYING

There are many prevention approaches to school bullying. This section provides an overview of various methods of formal and informal social control of school bullying.

School-based programs range from one-off assemblies to "whole-school" approaches. This section focuses on whole-school interventions, which can be targeted at different "levels of influence," including students, parents, teachers, and the school climate overall (Menesini and Salmivalli 2017, 248). Programs vary a great deal in terms of content, focus, participants, and intensity. There are many programs; one meta-analysis reported sixty-five different programs among the one hundred studies it analyzed (Gaffney et al. 2019).

Most meta-analyses of prevention studies have reported a small, statistically significant reduction in bullying and/or victimization (e.g., Lee, Kim, and Kim 2015; Merrell et al. 2008; Mishna et al. 2011). Other analyses have reported somewhat larger effect sizes that suggest a theoretical reduction in bullying or cyberbullying of as much as 10–20 percent (Gaffney et al. 2019; Ttofi and Farrington 2011). The most effective approaches are whole-school programs, more intensive programs, and programs that include more components (e.g., Cantone et al. 2015; Ttofi and Farrington 2011; Vreeman and Carroll 2007), although the last was not a uniform finding in the most comprehensive meta-analysis (Gaffney et al. 2019). Besides antibullying programs, schools can also engage in other activities, such as sponsoring gay-straight alliances that are associated with a reduction in bullying against sexual minority youth (Marx and Kettrey 2016).

Some researchers suggest that schools should concentrate on tertiary prevention efforts aimed at frequent perpetrators rather than the entire student body, given (1) the relatively mild effects of school-wide interventions, (2) the percentage of interventions that have no effect, (3) methodological challenges and inconsistencies, and (4) the fact that a relatively small percentage of students engage regularly in antisocial behaviors (e.g., Pepler et al. 2008; Ryoo, Wang, and Swearer 2015). We share the "urgent questions" posed by Menesini and Salmivalli (2017, 242) as to which programs work best and what are the most effective ingredients. Thus, we welcome the use of qualitative methods to explore impediments to program effectiveness among various populations, such as teachers (e.g., Cunningham, Rimas, et al. 2016) and students (e.g., Cunningham, Mapp et al. 2016). Because cyberbullying interventions have not been shown to be widely effective (Mishna et al. 2011), there is a strong need to develop and test evidence-based programs to address cyberbullying specifically (Della Cioppa, O'Neil, and Craig 2015).

Scholars have paid less attention to policy and political aspects than they have to other aspects of school bullying (Winburn, Winburn, and Niemeyer 2014). Cohen and Brooks (2014) documented how in the United States responsibility for preventing school bullying, historically within the purview of schools and parents, shifted to the states through legislation, then to the federal level as policy makers considered laws or regulations that mandate state requirements, and then back down to the individual through the process of criminalization and civil lawsuits. Kids, of course, are easy targets, because they lack power to construct their own realities or define their own situations in ways that inform or problematize the public discourse. Thus, they are the ultimate "docile bodies" that "can be subjected, used, transferred, and improved" (Foucault 1977, 136) without the inconvenience of having to recognize their own lived experiences.

Federal Response There is no federal antibullying statute, although congressional committees have considered bills. This is not surprising because states have historically held much more control over public schools. Most federal antibullying policy has originated in executive branch agencies. For instance, the US Department of Education has issued several "Dear Colleague" letters to school authorities; one was based on Title VII (federal civil rights) and another opined that anti-LGBT bullying could be prohibited by Title IX (prohibiting discrimination based on sex; Cornell and Limber 2015). Both of these letters ignited controversy, with some praising the department's initiative and others decrying federal government overreach (see Marcus 2011; Melnick 2019). The US Department of Education issued another guideline about children with disabilities (Cornell and Limber 2015). One problem with using civil rights laws to combat bullying is that such laws are not comprehensive, protecting only students who fall into particular categories (Cornell and Limber 2015).

State Statutes By 2015, every US state and the District of Columbia had enacted antibullying laws. Most laws contain a statement of purpose/scope and a description of prohibited behavior (Cornell and Limber 2015; United States Department of Education 2011). However, the laws vary a great deal as to other areas, including the specificity (or existence) of directives to local school districts in matters such as reporting requirements, disciplinary policies, and prevention and support services (Weaver et al. 2013). About a third of the statutes prohibit bullying against members of certain enumerated groups based on, for example, race, ethnicity, or sexual minority status (United States Department of Education 2011). In some states, whether to include sexual minority students became ensnared in the "culture wars," with various conservative groups opposing granting "special status" to such students (Cohen and Brooks 2014).

Rapid diffusion of antibullying statutes occurred due to two factors. First, bullying, at least in the public's mind, is an issue of low complexity—"everyone understands the concept of bullying" (Winburn, Winburn, and Niemeyer 2014, 516). Second, the issue developed high salience through massive media coverage. States frequently enacted statutes in direct response to media reports of either school shootings or suicides said to be linked to school bullying (Cohen and Brooks 2014; Winburn, Winburn, and Niemeyer 2014). Cohen and Brooks (2014) pointed out that it was not the "bullycides" alone that whipped up media coverage, but the concomitant theme of "institutional failure," wherein schools were blamed for not doing enough to stop bullying.

Researchers and policy makers have given relatively scant attention to examining the *effectiveness* of legislation, paying more attention to outlining the content of laws (e.g., United States Department of Education 2011), their recommended components (e.g., Horn 2000), and explanations for differences in the strength or content of laws (e.g., Mallinson 2016). Studies are mixed as to their preventive effects. One national US study reported a small reduction in bullying prevalence (8.4 percent) associated with having an antibullying statute (Nikolaou 2017), while another found that implementation of particular components recommended by the US Department of Education had a moderate effect in reducing bullying rates (Hatzenbuehler et al. 2015). Other studies have found significant but small correlations between measures of strength or quality of a state statute with reduced victimization (e.g., Sabia and Bass 2017; Terry 2018). Researchers have also found that enumeration of sexual minority status in a state statute is correlated with reduced reported victimization of that class, as well as suicidal ideation and attempts (e.g., Meyer et al. 2019), but this is likely due to those states' overall commitment to equality (Waldmane 2017).

It would appear that to be effective, legal requirements must be faithfully implemented and proper resources must be allocated. Researchers have reported various contextual and resource-based impediments to implementation in several states (Bruening et al. 2018; Cron 2016; Hall and Chapman 2018; Martinez 2016). However, fidelity may not be of paramount concern. Zachry (2018) found that the degree of adherence to state requirements by 128 school divisions in Virginia was not correlated with the reported prevalence of bullying incidents in those districts.

Civil Litigation In 1999, the US Supreme Court decided *Davis v. Monroe County Board of Education*, which held schools that violate Title IX are subject to civil lawsuits if they allow sexual harassment to occur. Courts have applied the *Davis* principles to cases of bullying as well as harassment. Holben and Zirkel (2014) found 166 court decisions from 1992 to 2011; Cornell and Limber (2015) and Hinduja and Patchin (2015) discussed several specific cases where school districts have been sued for not doing enough to stop bullying. One student was awarded more than $1 million in damages when the school was found to have done little to stop years of harassment (*Zeno v. Pine Plains Central School District* [2nd Circuit, 2012]). While courts have ruled for the school districts in about two-thirds of these cases (see Holben and Zirkel 2014), this may misstate the balance, considering that districts with weaker cases are more likely to settle before trial (Cornell and Limber 2015, 336). For instance, Minnesota's Anoka-Hennepin School District settled a lawsuit for $270,000 and promised to reform its policies on sexual orientation discrimination (Bazelon 2012).

In some cases, parents have sought restraining orders against children who they claimed bullied their child at school. Sunny Hostin, CNN legal analyst, reported on a father who filed for a restraining order against his child's fourteen-year-old bully. Hostin said, "I say bravo to the father. I think it's using a tool to protect your child, and I like it" (*Newsroom,* January 27, 2012). In another instance, a restraining order was filed against a nine-year-old. When the bullying victim's father was asked why he was bringing an attorney into the situation, he said, "I ... tried to go through the school to handle these measures. Nothing was being done. My daughter was still being bullied" (CNN's *Starting Point with Soledad O'Brien,* April 24, 2012).

Criminalization As noted above, only a few states provide for potential criminal penalties for bullying per se. For instance, the Missouri legislature updated its criminal harassment law to include electronic communications, at least partly in response to concerns over cyberbullying raised by the Megan Meier case (Meredith 2010). Nevertheless, many bullying behaviors may

In this chapter, we discussed three bullycides that captured extensive attention of the media. Most of the media reports we reviewed made a direct link between the bullying and the suicides (Cohen and Brooks 2014). The claim by CNN's Tony Harris about Phoebe Prince was typical: "Hard to believe. Bullied to death, literally" (*Newsroom*, March 30, 2010). However, news media paid scant attention to other factors that may have contributed to the suicides. For instance, Phoebe Prince's prior psychiatric history, inflicting of self-harm, and loneliness about separation from her father did not emerge until after the trial (and even then, were not widely reported; Bazelon 2010). The media (along with prosecutors) also sometimes exaggerated the "abuse" that occurred, particularly in the Tyler Clementi case (see ABC's *20/20*, March 2, 2012). In each case, the criminal charges seemed to be a significant factor that created intense media interest and sustained coverage.

Prosecutors did not charge any of the defendants in these three cases with murder or causing a suicide, and it seems extremely unlikely that any of them would have been criminally charged had the suicides not occurred. The sentences in these cases make that obvious. Dharun Ravi was sentenced to twenty days in jail in the Clementi case, two students in the Prince case plead guilty to criminal harassment and were sentenced to probation, and the charges in the Rebecca Sedwick case were dismissed.

A meta-analysis by Holt et al. (2015) found that the risk of self-reported suicidal ideation and behaviors was two to four times higher in perpetrators, victims, and bully-victims compared to the noninvolved. However, most of the studies they examined did not measure other factors related to suicidality. The authors noted that bullying involvement "is likely only 1 factor among many that plays a role in youth suicidality" and that analysis by the US Centers for Disease Control and Prevention found that "relationship problems, recent crises, mental health problems, and dating partner problems are more prevalent precipitating circumstances than bullying issues" (e506). In fact, studies have shown that the bullying-suicide connection becomes much weaker or nonexistent when controlling for these other factors (Holt et al. 2015). Thus, experts believe that bullying alone would be very unlikely to drive a child to suicide. In most empirical studies, bullying accounts for a small amount of the variance in suicidal thoughts (e.g., between 4 and 7 percent in a study by Kowalski and Limber [2013] of nearly one thousand students). Thus Holt et al. (2015)

concluded, "The dearth of longitudinal studies in this area precludes sufficient examination of the long-term effects of bullying on suicidal behaviors, making statements such as 'bullying causes suicide' impossible to substantiate" (e506).

Questions

1. Emily Bazelon researched the Prince case and wrote in *Slate* (2010), "There is no question that some of the teenagers facing criminal charges treated Phoebe cruelly. But not all of them did. And it's hard to see how any of the kids going to trial this fall ever could have anticipated the consequences of their actions, for Phoebe or for themselves. Should we send teenagers to prison for being nasty to one another? Is it really fair to lay the burden of Phoebe's suicide on these kids?" How would you respond to Bazelon's questions?

2. CNN news anchor Kyra Phillips said the following on *Newsroom* (May 14, 2010): "School bullies [are] driving their victims to suicide . . . [and] in some cases, the bullies don't give their victims any outs." Do you think that reporting such as this—as well as fictional accounts of suicides that seek to lay all the blame on others—sends to those contemplating suicide the dangerous message that there is no "out" for them?

amount to criminal acts in every state (e.g., stalking, harassment, or assault). Local communities have also sometimes turned to the criminal law. As reported on CNN's *Saturday Morning News* (December 1, 2012), in response to the bullycide of Canadian teen Amanda Todd, "her hometown has launched a new antibullying campaign called 'Be Someone' that will allow police to issue fines to those caught bullying in public or online." A town in Wisconsin passed an ordinance authorizing police "to ticket parents of bullies, which could mean hefty [fines] that increase for chronic offender[s]" (CBS's *This Morning,* June 8, 2013).

It is not possible to know how many times prosecutors have filed criminal charges in bullying cases. However, three cases received a great deal of national coverage. In each case, prosecutors charged the defendants with various crimes after alleged bullycides. The students were Phoebe Prince (a fifteen-year-old from Massachusetts who hanged herself), Tyler Clementi (a nineteen-year-old first-year college student in New Jersey who jumped off the George Washington Bridge), and Rebecca Sedwick (a twelve-year-old from Florida who leapt, or fell, from a cement plant tower). Five students were charged in the bullying of Prince, which involved mostly indirect and verbal bullying. Clementi's dorm mate, Dharun Ravi, was accused of twice streaming video of Clementi kissing a man. He was eventually convicted of invasion of privacy and bias intimidation (a type of hate crime). Sedwick was said to have taken her life after being bullied for a year by what news media reported to be fifteen girls, or as many as twenty according to her mother (CNN's *Anderson Cooper 360*, October 15, 2013). The county sheriff ordered the unprecedented arrests of two of the girls (aged twelve and fourteen) for felony aggravated stalking (ABC's *World News,* October 15, 2013). In this chapter's Policy Box, we ask you to consider the ramifications of bringing criminal charges in cases of alleged bullycides.

EXPLAINING SCHOOL BULLYING

As late as 2019, researchers wrote, "our scientific knowledge about explanatory variables for bullying behavior is still limited" (Zych, Ttofi, and Farrington 2019, 3). Addressing the "why" of school bullying has typically involved investigating factors thought to be correlated with bullying or victimization, such as various traits or symptoms. Much of this research is not theory grounded. Maunder and Crafter (2018) recommended testing various sociocultural theories. Pascoe (2013) similarly called for a "sociology of bullying," noting that the differences that provoke bullying are not neutral but "reflect larger structural inequalities" (95). Similarly, Walton (2005) took note that most analysis "tends not to emphasize the ways in which markers of social difference ... inform the nature and reflect the characteristics of bullying among children" (112). In this view, bullying is just an extreme form of what is already accepted in schools (Payne and Smith 2013).

We concur with researchers calling for consideration of larger social and cultural processes (e.g., Cullingford and Morrison 1995), within which bullying's "interpersonal relationship" (Olweus 1993) takes place. This includes influence of peer social networks (Merrin et al. 2018), institutional settings of schools (Ringrose and Rawlings 2015; Søndergaard 2012), and larger social and cultural factors (Eriksen 2018), along with their development and interplay. Thus, we support the "social-ecological model" for framing school bullying in its contexts, where there are various levels of contributing causes and thus various theories at each of those levels from which to draw (see Hong and Espelage 2012).

The rest of this book is meant to shed some light on the "why" question by examining how researchers have tested (or could test) various criminological explanations of school bullying. We should note a few things before we delve into theory. First, "criminological" theories are, in truth, attempts to explain and understand deviance rather than crime (Scheider 2002). Second, there are not necessarily clear distinctions between "criminological" and "non-criminological" theories (particularly within micro theories). For example, public health models sometimes offer a similar approach to criminological ones (Ferrara et al. 2015). Third, bullying and other peer aggression may be normative behavior (i.e., nondeviant) or may be the "deviant" end point on a continuum of normative aggression (Faris and Felmlee 2011a, 2011b, 2014; Kerbs and Jolley 2007; Phillips 2003). Students may admire bullies and enable their bullying because bullies seem "cool" (Strindberg, Horton, and Thornberg 2019).

Finally, we want to be clear that while we support the emerging trend of applying criminological *theory* to school bullying—both because of the insights it can offer and because bullying has been associated with other juvenile deviance (e.g., weapons carrying; Lu et al. 2020) and adult criminality—we do not support the *criminalization* of bullying or the introduction of "zero tolerance" policies that are punitive and frequently counterproductive, something we explore in chapter 5.

TWO

Deterrence, Rational Choice, and Victimization Theories

The **Classical School**, with its focus on notions of **free will** and **rationality**, represented a radical challenge to the ruling ideologies of the time, which were based in demonology and often resulted in excruciatingly cruel and unpredictable forms of punishment meted out by the Church or other institutions of the ruling classes (Hagan 2011; Martin, Mutchnick, and Austin 1990). In particular, Cesare Bonesana, Marchese di Beccaria (Cesare Beccaria; 1738–1794) and Jeremy Bentham (1748–1832) argued for the reform of systems of punishment (Hagan 2011). Drawing on a utilitarian framework, Bentham based his understanding of human behavior (including deviance and crime) on the notion of a **hedonistic calculus**, or a rational consideration of the balance between pleasure and pain. Both Beccaria and Bentham believed the goal of punishment should be to tip the scales so that the pain associated with engaging in crime was greater than the pleasure one derives. Beccaria, Bentham, and other classical theorists started from the notion that all people are driven by the pursuit of pleasure; therefore, they did not concern themselves with explaining *why* someone might engage in deviant or illegal behavior. Instead, they focused on the creation of systems of law and punishment that would deter individuals from engaging in those behaviors.

While **neoclassical theories** draw on the Classical School's emphasis on free will and rationality, they also reflect and incorporate aspects of **positivism**. As Walsh and Hemmens (2011) point out, neoclassical theorists rely on **soft determinism** "because although they believe that criminal behavior is ultimately a choice, the choice is made in the context of personal and situational constraints and the availability of opportunities" (77), or what Williams and McShane refer to as "**soft free-will**" (2010, 183). Unlike the pure rationality of classical theories, where behavioral choices are assumed to be made in a cultural and social vacuum, neoclassical theories attempt to explore more deeply the processes through which rational decisions are made and how those decisions are shaped by individual (e.g., emotional), cultural (e.g., familial belief systems), societal (e.g., socioeconomic forces), and other factors.

The resurgence of classical thought through the development of neoclassical theories was influenced by the rise in political conservatism of the late 1970s and 1980s and the concomitant attention paid to the systematic study of victimization trends. These factors resulted in the development of a variety of theories that focused not only on rational decision-making, but also on the influence of victim characteristics and physical spaces. This chapter explores the application of classical and neoclassical theories of crime to school bullying. It begins with a discussion of individual **unit theories** that have emerged from these broader theoretical perspectives. For each unit theory, we include a brief description of its basic tenets and a more detailed discussion of how that theory has been applied to school bullying.

DETERRENCE THEORY

In his essay *On Crimes and Punishments* (originally published in Italian in 1764), Beccaria articulated his formulation of appropriate punishment:

> In order for punishment not to be ... an act of violence of one or of many against a private citizen, it must be essentially public, prompt, necessary, the least possible in the given circumstances, proportionate to the crimes, [and] dictated by the laws. (99, as cited in Hagan, 2011)

Here we can see the foundations of **deterrence theory**, as well as the articulation of the importance of individual rights and due process of law. We can also see an emphasis on proportionate punishment, a concept that Bentham also supported. Bentham considered punishment to be a form of evil that should only be used to deter other, more serious forms of evil (Williams and McShane 2010).

Deterrence theory has three primary components: celerity (swiftness), certainty, and severity. According to deterrence theory, a punishment that is swift, certain, and severe will be more likely to have a deterrent effect. In many ways, deterrence theory underlies current US criminal justice systems' organization and operation. As we discuss shortly, US schools have also predominantly operated under similar frameworks in formulating responses to school bullying and other forms of misbehavior. Both Bentham and Beccaria believed swiftness and certainty were more important components than severity. Ironically, contemporary applications of deterrence theory focus almost exclusively on the severity of punishment, an issue we discuss more fully in relation to the criminalization of school bullying.

Deterrence takes two primary forms: (1) **specific deterrence**, which is aimed at the individual who engaged in the behavior, and (2) **general deterrence**, which is aimed at sending a message to other individuals who might engage in similar behaviors. Deterrence theory is a theory of law making that assumes people operate with free will and make rational decisions regarding their behavior based on a calculation of whether the pleasure associated with a particular behavior will outweigh the pain associated with it. This requires that the consequences (i.e., punishment) of a behavior be made clear through the articulation of the law (or, in our case, school policies) and that the state (or school) implement punishments with due process and attention to the rights of individuals to be free from the arbitrary application of power.

Deterring School Bullying

Direct empirical tests of specific deterrence in relation to school bullying are rare and offer mixed results. Ayers et al. (2012) analyzed a subset of data from 1,221 students collected as part of the School-Wide Information System (SWIS) surveys to measure the impact of discipline practices on the likelihood of a disciplinary referral for the reoccurrence of bullying or aggressive behavior (542). The original SWIS data, from which this study drew a subset, came from 166 schools in sixty-five school districts across seven states (542). Their findings suggested a specific deterrent effect for interventions that involve "loss of privileges . . . that inhibit interaction with peers outside the classroom" and those that involve "parent-teacher conferences" and other "disciplinary strategies that involve the parents, teachers, and/or administrators" (546). Exclusionary discipline strategies such as detention and suspension had no deterrent effect for youth in their study. These findings suggest that forms of punishment that are seemingly less severe but focus on the relational aspects of a student's life are more likely to deter future bullying behavior than harsher, more severe punishments. Similarly, in their study of one thousand middle school students, Patchin and Hinduja (2018) found that "students are deterred more by the threat of punishment from their parents and the school, and least deterred by the threat of punishment from the police" (190). They further reported that students perceived school punishment as most likely to occur in response to in-school bullying, while parental punishment was most likely to occur in response to cyberbullying. The youth perceived punishment by the police to be least likely, compared to school-based or parental punishment, suggesting a lack of *certainty of punishment*, which would reduce the deterrent effect of the punishment, as suggested by deterrence theory.

As further support for the importance of certainty of punishment, Hall (2017) conducted a systematic review of empirical studies that tested the effectiveness of policy interventions for school bullying. Hall found only a small proportion of studies (21 of 489) actually collected and analyzed data on the effectiveness of policy interventions, but noted the importance of "fidelity of implementation" as a mediating factor "between policy adoption or presence and the targeted policy outcome of student bullying" (58). It is not enough to have a policy on the books; schools must ensure consistent implementation of their policies so that students perceive punishment to be certain. We were unable to identify research that directly or indirectly tested the notion of celerity (swiftness) of punishment, although Hall's notion of fidelity of implementation may imply the need for swift punishment. What Hall did not discuss, however, was the severity of punishment, which, like in the criminological literature, tends to be the focus of contemporary applications of deterrence theory. We turn now to how punishment severity manifests in the bullying literature.

Severity of Punishment As we discussed in chapter 1, there has been a trend toward the criminalization of school and cyberbullying over the past several decades, especially in regard to the creation of state statutes and the exercise of prosecutorial discretion (see Cohen and Brooks 2014). Initial support for these types of approaches was common. For instance, in response to growing concerns regarding cyberbullying, Manuel (2011) articulated the need for a clear definition of cyberbullying as a criminal offense:

> The elements of a criminal cyber-bullying ... would be similar to that of criminal harassment: (1) willfully and knowingly engage in (2) malicious conduct, (3) directed at a specific person, (4) which seriously alarms and would cause a reasonable person of a similar disposition to suffer conditions of substantial emotional, psychological, or physical harm, including but not limited to psychiatric admission or suicide (5) through the arena of virtual

space: including but not limited to blogs, social networking websites, electronic mail, telecommunication devices, and Internet communications. (248)

Notice than Manuel's suggested elements of cyberbullying as a criminal offense do not actually address important aspects of the common definition of bullying (i.e., repetition or power imbalance), meaning that a wide range of behaviors not necessarily defined as bullying would be included in this criminal statute. This is consistent with state antibullying statutes that are based on harassment, as discussed in chapter 1. Manuel (2011) went on to suggest punishment that could include "imprisonment for no more than two years" (248). Manuel grounded this argument in the discourse of deterrence theory, suggesting that by "imposing this legislation, there would be a hope that criminalization would dissuade future cyber-bullies from victimizing one of their peers" (249). Albertson (2014) made a similar argument for the imposition of criminal sanctions for bullying in the state of Indiana, but with a more direct call to deterrence theory: "if criminal liability were imposed on children who committed acts of bullying, there would *almost certainly be a general deterrent* effect on other would-be bullies" (266; emphasis added).

Despite the fact that the originators of the Classical School placed least emphasis on severity of punishment, contemporary applications of deterrence theory are based in increasing severity, including "get tough" frameworks such as criminalization and zero tolerance school discipline policies. However, that focus may do little to actually deter bullying, and often, as we discuss in later chapters, may exacerbate inequities for students. Moreover, Borgwald and Theixos (2013) found that zero tolerance policies are ineffective and may have a kind of displacement effect, causing bullying to become more covert or hidden, and, therefore, more difficult to identify and address. Borgwald and Theixos (2013) also pointed to prior research suggesting that punitive policies such as zero tolerance are "statistically counterproductive in reducing bullying in school" (151).

Others have similarly recognized the lack of evidence supporting a deterrent effect for punitive responses to bullying that focus on severity alone. In their analysis of antibullying legislation, Edmondson and Zeman (2011) noted, "most states relied exclusively on coercive laws, such as those authorizing expulsion or criminal indictments for bully conduct, that have induced schools to adopt policies proven ineffective in reducing bullying" (37). Swearer et al. (2017) seemed to agree with this assessment, noting that the push for zero tolerance policies "persists despite the overwhelming evidence that this approach does not reduce bullying behavior and may even have significant costs in terms of greater school disengagement and involvement in the juvenile justice system" (26). Some of those who would be responsible for implementing responses grounded in the criminalization of school bullying, namely police, also agree. Through in-depth interviews with Canadian street patrol officers and school resource officers, Broll and Huey (2015) found that these officers did not "endorse attempts to criminalize everyday cyberbullying activities" (170), preferring, instead, approaches grounded in prevention through education. Dayton and Dupre (2009) similarly argued for legislative responses that focus on proactive, preventative approaches as opposed to punitive, reactive measures.

Despite the fact that classical theorists specifically downplayed the importance of punishment severity in comparison to swiftness and certainty, and the consistent evidence that harsh punishment and the criminalization of bullying are ineffective or counterproductive, support for such policies remains among the public, policy makers, and school administrators. In an analysis of perceptions of zero tolerance policies for school violence in South Korea, for instance, Kim and Oh (2017) found that some stakeholders (including students, parents, and school personnel) perceived such policies as creating a secure atmosphere and demanding full responsibility from students, and thus found them desirable despite their negative side effects. Other stakeholders in this study perceived zero tolerance policies to emphasize punishment over education. Regardless of which of these perceptions the stakeholders held, they all believed that zero tolerance policies "require consistency and detailed criteria to minimize potential side effects" (74).

The "Lost" Element of Deterrence Deterrence theory not only argues for swift, certain, and proportionately severe punishments, it calls for due process and fairness in the application of those punishments. While the school bullying research does not support the severity aspect of deterrence theory, it does provide relatively strong support for due process and fairness in the application of punishments. For instance, a major review of school crime control and prevention literature noted, "schools in which rules are clearly stated, are fair, and are consistently enforced, and in which students have participated in establishing mechanisms for reducing misbehavior, experience less disorder" (Cook, Gottfredson, and Na 2010, 317). Looking at school bullying specifically, Kupchik and Farina (2016) analyzed data from 4,288 students surveyed for the School Crime Supplement of the National Crime Victimization Survey (SCS-NCVS). They found strong support for their hypothesis that "students in schools with rules and punishments perceived to be fair are less likely than others to be victims of bullying" (157). Importantly, they also noted, "the growing body of literature on school punishment demonstrates how rigid policing in schools, high suspension rates, and other hallmarks of contemporary school punishment and security erodes students' perceptions of fairness" (157). In other words, a focus on increasing severity of punishment is ineffective in and of itself and also serves to decrease perceptions of fairness and due process, which in turn decreases the deterrent effect of those very policies.

In the school bullying literature, the notion of fairness in punishment is found within the concept of **authoritative school discipline/climate**, which consists of the imposition of strict but consistent rules, fairness, and respect (due process; Gerlinger and Wo 2016). Authoritative school discipline/climate combines these disciplinary structures with student support efforts, such as encouraging positive and supportive teacher-student relationships (Cornell and Huang 2016). Multiple studies have identified an association between authoritative school discipline/climate and lower rates of bullying (Cornell and Huang 2016; see also Cornell, Shulka, and Konold 2016; Gregory et al. 2010). Gerlinger and Wo (2016) found similar support for authoritative school discipline in their analysis of data from a sample of 23,974 twelve- to eighteen-year-olds in schools across the United States. Gerlinger and Wo measured authoritative school discipline through student self-reports of their perception that (1) school rules were fair and strictly enforced, (2) punishment for breaking school rules was the same for all students, and (3) teachers treated students with respect. Where students perceived all of these characteristics to be true, the school was considered to have an authoritative discipline strategy. Gerlinger and Wo measured the association between authoritative discipline strategy and three types of bullying victimization—verbal, physical, and relational—and found "the dual presence of school structure and support mechanisms was related to significantly lower levels of bullying" (147) for all three types.

In summary, deterrence theory's focus on swift, certain, and (proportionately) severe punishment finds mixed support in the literature on school bullying. However, this mixed support may be due to inaccurate interpretations of deterrence theory. A focus on only increasing severity (i.e., criminalization and zero tolerance) will likely continue to be ineffective and, in many ways, counterproductive. However, if authoritative punishment regimens are developed, then the deterrent effect of punishment will likely increase.

In an early articulation of rational choice theory, Clarke and Cornish (1985) explained criminal behavior "as the outcome of the offender's broadly rational choices and decisions" (147). As a neoclassical theory, rational choice attempts to explain the process through which people make decisions, including factors that influence or constrain an individual's range of choices. According to rational choice theory, these choices are oriented around the fulfillment of commonplace needs (Williams and McShane 2010). As Walsh (2012) noted, rational choice theorists focus less on the creation of motivated offenders and more on "the process of their choices to offend," which is referred to as **choice structuring** (47). Choice structuring takes into consideration not only the costs and benefits of engaging in a particular behavior, but also the relative opportunities to do so. Similar to other classical and neoclassical theorists, Clarke and Cornish (1985) were particularly concerned with crime control policy.

According to Clarke and Cornish (1985), rational choice theory makes the important distinction between decisions related to being involved in crime (**involvement decisions**), including initial involvement, continued involvement, and desistance, versus decisions regarding how to engage in particular types of crime (**event decisions**). Further, Clarke and Cornish (1985) asserted that the ways in which individuals go about making both types of decisions are crime specific. In other words, involvement and event choices related to engaging in school bullying are significantly different from the choices related to engaging in shoplifting or murder. We were unable to find direct tests of rational choice theory's applicability to school bullying, but many of the concepts articulated by Clarke and Cornish (1985) have similarities with constructs articulated in the victimization theories considered in more detail here.

Victimization Theories

It is perhaps not surprising that much criminological theory attempts to explain why individuals or groups engage in criminal behavior. There have been, however, attempts to understand crime through the behaviors of crime victims. Some of these victimization theories problematically evoke notions of **victim blaming**. For instance, **victim precipitation theory** suggests that in some instances the behavior of the victim contributes to their experience of victimization. As originally developed by Marvin Wolfgang (1957), the notion of victim precipitation was limited to instances of homicide. This seems reasonable enough; however, the concept of victim precipitation was later expanded to include other forms of violence, such as aggravated assault (see Curtis 1974; Miethe 1985) and, in significantly problematic ways, rape (see Amir 1967). It is not hard to see why attempts to explain rape or other forms of sexual violence through victim precipitation theory would generate critique as a form of victim blaming. However, other victimization theories provide a less problematic analysis of victim behavior and its role in victimization.

Cohen and Felson (1979) developed **routine activity theory** (or what they themselves refer to as the routine activity approach) with a focus on how everyday patterns of social interaction can be used to explain differences in crime rates (see also Williams and McShane 2010). Routine activity theory employs neoclassical and rational choice perspectives at the macro level as a way to explain broader crime trends, not as an explanation of individual criminal behavior. The basic tenet of routine activity theory is that crime results from a convergence of likely offenders, suitable targets, and the absence or lack of capable guardians (Cohen and Felson 1979). Similarly, **lifestyle theory** (see Hindelang, Gottfredson, and Garofalo 1978) posits that "variations in lifestyle (the characteristic way individuals allocate their time to vocational and leisure activities) cause differential probabilities of being in particular places at particular times and coming into contact with persons who have particular characteristics" (Gottfredson and Hindelang 1981, 124). While routine activity theory and lifestyle theory employ similar theoretical constructs, the former does so to explain variations in crime rates at the macro level, while the latter uses these constructs to explain differences in victimization patterns across social groups. However, researchers have applied both of these theories at the individual level to explain school bullying victimization.

Building on the work of Hindelang, Gottfredson, and Garofalo (1978) and others, Lauritsen, Sampson, and Laub (1991) presented the **proximity hypothesis** as an explanation for higher levels of victimization among individuals who engage in deviant, delinquent, or criminal behavior. Their proximity hypothesis "suggests that independently of individual characteristics, neighborhood levels of crime represent an important structural determinant of risk" (269). In other words, the mere fact of being in spaces wherein crime is likely to occur puts individuals at greater risk for victimization.

In an expansion of the proximity hypothesis, Papachristos and colleagues have researched the influence of **social proximity** on risk of victimization through social networks analysis. For instance, Papachristos and Wildeman (2014) analyzed co-offending networks among eighty-two thousand residents living within a six-square-mile area that they regarded as at high risk for homicide victimization based on established socioeconomic indicators. Their measure of co-offending networks was based on "instances in which 2 or more people were arrested together for the same crime" (144). In line with the proximity hypothesis, they hypothesized that "greater exposure to homicide victims in one's social network increases one's own probability of victimization" (146). The results of Papachristos and Wildeman's analysis supported their hypothesis, leading them to conclude that "an individual who associates with or is in close social proximity to other homicide victims exists (and acts) in a social world where risky people, situations, and behaviors are present" (148). They also noted that the influence of social proximity is not limited to an individual's own friends, but also by their friends' friends, indicating a larger indirect effect. In another social network analysis focused on proximity to gang members, Papachristos et al. (2015) found similar results, noting "those who are closer to gang members in their co-offending network are at an elevated risk for victimization" and that "being directly connected to a gang member increases a nongang associate's probability of being shot by 94 percent" (643).

Meier and Miethe (1993; see also Miethe and Meier 1990) integrated previous victimization theories into their **structural-choice theory** of victimization (also referred to as **opportunity theory**). Integrating foundational constructs from routine activity theory, lifestyle theory, and the proximity hypothesis, Miethe and Meier (1990) theorized that "routine activities may predispose some persons and their property to greater risks, but the selection of a particular crime victim within a sociospatial context is determined by the expected utility of one target over another" (245; as cited in Meier and Miethe 1993, 475). Structural-choice theory combines macro-level factors as articulated by routine activity theory (i.e., criminal opportunity structure) and micro-level factors as articulated by lifestyle theory (i.e., target selection). Meier and Miethe hypothesized the importance of four explanatory constructs: exposure, proximity, target attractiveness/suitability, and guardianship. This is very similar to lifestyle routine activities theory (LRAT) developed by Cohen, Kluegel, and Land (1981).

Empirical tests of the applicability of victimization theories have found mixed support for LRAT as an explanation for bullying victimization in schools and online. As we will see below, most of these studies incorporate measures of two or more of the constructs articulated by LRAT. In addition, different researchers use the same measures as indicators of different theoretical constructs. We will revisit these potential measurement issues at the end of this section.

Exposure and Proximity LRAT theorizes that individuals who engage in routine activities that **expose** and place them in close **proximity** to risky and vulnerable situations where motivated offenders are present are more likely to experience victimization than those who do not. As theoretical constructs, exposure and proximity were first applied to explain the relationship between social identity group membership (e.g., young, male, unmarried, low income, person of color), lifestyle routines (e.g., in public more often, living in high crime areas), and differential victimization patterns. In the school bullying literature, exposure and proximity are often measured using the same or similar indicators, including (1) participation in curricular and extracurricular activities in and out of school, (2) presence and rates of other types of misbehavior/crime at the school, and (3) engagement in school misbehavior or involvement with peers who engage in misbehavior.

Researchers tend to combine several of these measures in their studies. Analyzing data from the SCS-NCVS, Popp (2012b) measured exposure and proximity using participation-type indicators (i.e., students' participation in classroom-related activities, school clubs, and school sports), engagement in misbehavior (i.e., fighting and skipping classes), and presence of school problems (i.e., drugs, guns, and gangs in school). Popp (2012b) found that "the greater the student's exposure and closer his or her proximity to motivated offenders and crime-prone environments, the greater the student's chances of being bullied" (327).

Cho and Wooldredge (2018) conducted a cross-cultural analysis of youth victimization in South Korea and the United States using nationally representative samples of adolescents in both countries. These researchers employed participation in school and nonschool clubs, athletics, and employment as measures of exposure to motivated offenders and found a correlation between several of their exposure measures and bullying victimization, including participation in nonschool clubs and having a part-time job. Analyzing data from the SCS-NCVS, Cho et al. (2017) found that exposure to motivated offenders and exposure to illegal substances and firearms increased an individual's risk of being bullied, concluding that "unsafe and crime-prone environments are positively associated with bullying and victimization" (310). Choi et al. (2019) drew a similar conclusion from their analysis of data from the SCS-NCVS, noting that "it is clear that the school environment as a way of exposing targets to motivated offenders is significant in correlation with cyber and non-physical bullying victimization" (17). Cho et al. (2017) also measured proximity based on how close students lived to school and the mode of transportation they utilized when going to/from school, concluding that "adolescents who walk to school or use a school or public bus are likely to experience both nonphysical and physical peer victimization" (310).

These findings may also relate to the theory of deviant places. Rodney Stark (1987) formed a theory of **deviant places** as an ecological theory of crime in an attempt to explore how physical spaces within neighborhoods influenced crime rates. Stark's articulation of deviant place theory included thirty integrated propositions. In summary, Stark combined five well-established urban neighborhood–level factors related to crime and deviance (density, poverty, mixed use, transience, and dilapidation) with "some specific *impacts* of the five on moral order as *people respond to them*" and how those responses "further *amplify* the volume of deviance through [various] consequences" (895; emphasis in original), including the attraction of deviant others and activities, the driving out of those less deviant, and reductions in social control. These same processes may be at play in various schools, leading to increased exposure and proximity to motivated offenders.

Researchers have also used measures of participants' own offending as indicators of exposure and proximity to motivated offenders. In their analysis of the influence of school context on victimization, Peguero et al. (2013) found "engagement in school-based misbehavior is found to increase the odds of victimization at school across each of the distinct school demographic contexts [urban, rural, suburban]" (12). They concluded, "the relationship between exposure and adolescent victimization may not be moderated by distinct school contexts" (12). In an analysis of data from 2,844 fourth-grade students in Korea, Cho (2017b) found that "youth involved in risky lifestyles (affiliating with delinquent peers and/or engaging in offending behavior) are more likely to place themselves in a risky situation by exposing themselves to motivated offenders" (76).

When looking at LRAT in relation to cyberbullying, researchers have tended to measure exposure and proximity in ways similar to the studies described above, with the addition of measures specifically oriented to amount of time spent online and the types of activities engaged in. For instance, using data from surveys of 434 students in a Kentucky middle and high school, Bossler, Holt, and May (2012) tested the applicability of routine activity theory to online harassment victimization. They employed five measures of proximity, including (1) total number of hours spent online, (2) whether the student had a social networking site page, (3) whether the student had friends who engaged in peer online harassment, (4) whether the responding student engaged in computer deviance, and (5) online harassment offending themselves. Bossler, Holt, and May (2012) found that the odds of experiencing online harassment victimization were greater among those who maintained a social network page and those who associated with peers who harassed others. They found that in addition to the amount of time spent online, the specific types of activities engaged in also mattered, noting "individuals who participate in specific activities that focus on information sharing, such as communicating in chatrooms, instant messaging, e-mailing, using social network sites, and downloading images via file-sharing programs . . . increase their exposure to motivated harassers" (503). They found a similar relationship between involvement in online deviance and likelihood of online victimization, arguing that individuals who engage in online deviance experience greater exposure to other motivated offenders.

Park, Na, and Kim (2014) collected data via face-to-face interviews with twelve hundred adolescents in South Korea, using a multistage stratified random sampling method to analyze the relationship between online activities, netiquette, and cyberbullying. These researchers found that "victims were more likely to be active information and social users of the Internet" (78), meaning that they use the internet for socializing as opposed to one-to-one communication. Those who perpetrated cyberbullying also spent more time online and were particularly active in social networking sites. This supports the notion that participation in these activities exposes victims and puts them in proximity to motivated offenders.

There is also some evidence to suggest that school-based factors may influence exposure to cyber victimization. In their analysis of data from the 2013 SCS-NCVS, Choi et al. (2019) found that the school environment served as a mechanism through which targets were exposed to motivated cyberbullying offenders (17). Their measures of school environment included indicators similar to those used by Cho et al. (2017) and described above, such as availability of illicit substances, students using drugs and/or alcohol at school, and the presence of guns and gang activity at school.

Target Suitability Simply engaging in routines that increase one's exposure and proximity to motivated offenders may not result in increased victimization experiences at the individual level. **Target suitability** is one additional factor that, when combined with exposure and proximity, can increase likelihood of bullying or other forms of victimization. Researchers have employed a variety of operational definitions of target suitability. These include demographic characteristics such as gender, race, and ethnicity; age; socioeconomic status; ability status; and various psychological characteristics. We discuss many of these factors in later chapters but focus on other measures of target suitability here for several reasons. First, a consideration of victim characteristics aligns with original formulations of LRAT because these characteristics signify membership in social identity groups that differentially shape our daily routines and, therefore, our relative suitability as a target; however, they do not represent direct measures of such routines. Second, focusing on victim characteristics without a concomitant discussion of the structural location of individuals who hold those characteristics fails to fully capture their impact. Therefore, we consider the influence of these characteristics in our discussion of psychological theories in chapter 3 and our discussion of feminist, critical race, and other conflict theories in chapter 6. Finally, in the school bullying context, these characteristics are often treated as control variables, not as direct measures of target suitability, which suggests that empirical tests of the applicability of LRAT to school bullying focus on other measures of target suitability.

For example, Popp (2012a) intentionally set out to problematize the common use of demographic characteristics as proxy measures for target suitability. Analyzing data from multiple waves of the SCS-NCVS, Popp (2012a) found that individuals who possess characteristics that have been shown to make them vulnerable to victimization *and* who experience bullying victimization are perceived as more suitable targets than those who possess those same characteristics but have not experienced bullying. This finding suggests that more direct measures of target suitability than demographic characteristics may be more valuable in understanding the applicability of LRAT to bullying. This research also suggests that bullying victimization should not only be analyzed as a dependent variable in tests of victimization theories but can also serve as an independent variable measuring target suitability. In other words, motivated bullies may perceive those who have already been victimized as more vulnerable, and, therefore, more suitable targets for continued bullying.

Another measure of target suitability is participation in particular types of extracurricular activities. In explaining their finding that individuals who participated in non-sports-related activities were more likely to be victims of direct and indirect bullying, Cecen-Celik and Keith (2016) argued that "those who attend non-sports-related activities may be perceived as a weaker [more vulnerable] target for motivated offenders" (3826). Cho et al. (2017) found that "in terms of target attractiveness . . . adolescents who engage in activities related to arts are likely to be victims of both physical and nonphysical peer victimization, whereas involvement in student government minimizes the likelihood of physical peer victimization" (310). They surmised that particular types of activities may mark students as more vulnerable compared to other types of activities. It is also possible, of course, that different types of activities draw students with different vulnerabilities or protective factors, once again emphasizing the need for longitudinal research that can address temporal ordering. Researchers have reported similar findings regarding cyberbullying and other forms of online victimization (see Choi et al. 2019; Kalia and Aleem 2017).

Guardianship Individuals who experience greater exposure and proximity and who are perceived as suitable targets by motivated offenders still may not experience elevated levels of victimization. A fourth and final component of LRAT must also be present, or in this case, missing, in order for individuals to experience a greater likelihood of victimization. Specifically, the combination of exposure, proximity, and target suitability must emerge in spaces where there is a lack of capable guardianship, both formal and informal. Formal guardianship includes factors such as physical security and the presence of police/school resource officers. Informal guardianship includes more relational dynamics, such as social/peer networks, the school's rule environment, and involvement of teachers and parents. Similar to the findings related to the other components of LRAT, support for the influence of capable guardianship is mixed. For instance, Cho et al. (2017) found that some measures of both formal and informal guardianship were associated with reductions in peer victimization, but school security measures had little impact.

Informal Guardianship In their comparative analysis of youth victimization across the United States and South Korea, Cho and Wooldredge (2018b) found a higher risk of bullying victimization for youth who participated in nonschool clubs in both countries, linking this higher risk with the extent and quality of adult supervision in these settings. We mentioned the influence of participation in school and nonschool activities in our discussion of exposure and proximity as well, suggesting that different types of activities may result in differing degrees of vulnerability. As Cho and Wooldredge (2018b) pointed out, these mixed results may be partially explained by the extent to which the activities involve the presence of capable guardians.

Researchers have found correlations between other forms of informal guardianship and school bullying. Popp (2012b) found students who had a strong social support system had significantly lower odds of being bullied. Popp also found lower bullying rates in schools whose rules were fair and strictly enforced, suggesting that the deterrent effect of authoritative discipline in schools discussed earlier in this chapter is a form of capable guardianship. Similarly, Choi et al. (2019) found that "teacher relationships might be relevant from the standpoint of capable guardians" (18). In their analysis of data from the SCS-NCVS, Cecen-Celik and Keith (2016) incorporated measures of interactionist security, including students' reports of having an adult or friend who cares about them, having a friend they can talk to, and belief that school rules are known, fair, and strictly enforced. Their findings support the conclusion that these forms of informal guardianship were significantly related to lower likelihood of bullying victimization.

Formal Guardianship Generally speaking, it appears that formal guardianship tends to be less effective in reducing the likelihood of victimization than informal guardianship. While there seems to be at least some support for the influence of informal guardianship in the literature, formal guardianship does not fare as well. Cho et al. (2017) found that school security measures, which included the presence of school safety security guards, safety staff or adults in hallways, metal detectors, locked doors, sign-in of visitors, locker checks, required ID badges, security cameras, and a safety code of conduct, had little impact on victimization. Popp (2012b) drew a similar conclusion from an analysis of SCS-NCVS data, noting that this is consistent with prior research on the relationship between school security measures and victimization. This is also consistent with findings from numerous studies that have been conducted since Popp's analysis (see Choi et al. 2019; Peguero et al. 2013). In one of a few longitudinal studies of the impact of school security on victimization, Fisher, Mowen, and Boman (2018) analyzed data from 7,659 students from two waves of the Educational Longitudinal Study 2002. They measured school security with twelve different indicators and found that these measures were unrelated to two forms of victimization and actually "predictive of an increase of approximately 12% in the odds of being threatened with harm in 2004 while controlling for the 2002 levels of victimization and a series of potentially confounding variables" (1233).

Similar to the ineffective and sometimes counterproductive influence of harsh punishments in the name of deterrence theory, the imposition of more restrictive forms of physical security also appears to be counterproductive in terms of guardianship, or, at the least, ineffective. Or, as Perkins, Perkins, and Craig (2014) put it, "all types of harassment and bullying victimization occur across both unstructured and structured spaces within the school context regardless of whether these locations are supervised" (815). One explanation for the lack of effectiveness of school security in reducing school bullying victimization may be that school resource officers do not see school bullying as an issue that rises to the point that they should intervene. For instance, Choi, Cronin, and Correia (2016) conducted semistructured qualitative interviews with school resource officers and other personnel and found that officers "were consistently hesitant about using their law enforcement authority to deal with school misconduct problems," even though "they understood that their unique authority presented a kind of 'backstop' against ongoing or particularly serious forms of bullying behaviors" (156). In order for resource officers or other figures of authority to serve as capable guardians, motivated offenders must perceive a likelihood that they will intervene in situations. The hesitancy of the officers that Choi, Cronin, and Correia (2016) interviewed also seems to stem from a lack of a clear definition of what constitutes school misconduct and what constitutes particularly serious forms of bullying behavior, an issue we addressed in our discussion of the challenges of defining bullying in chapter 1.

The lack of evidence supporting the implementation of school security measures to decrease likelihood of bullying victimization is particularly relevant given that one of the major policy implications of LRAT is the development of **crime prevention through environmental design** (CPTED). Proponents of CPTED argue that by altering the physical space, we can

In this chapter, we discussed the relative lack of evidence supporting the use of physical security in reducing bullying victimization. We also mentioned that while CPTED has found utility in some contexts (e.g., stores), there is little evidence to support its implementation in schools. However, this does not mean that the physical layout of schools is irrelevant when thinking about how to increase guardianship and decrease victimization. In their qualitative study at a Mississippi elementary school, Fram and Dickmann (2012) set out to explore how the built environment of the school exacerbates bullying and peer harassment.

Fram and Dickmann (2012) collected multiple forms of data related to the school. This included policy documents, survey data (from teachers, interventionists, service providers, and administrators), and photos of the school's physical spaces (232). After analyzing this data and engaging in a multilayered coding process, Fram and Dickmann concluded that aspects of the school environment exacerbate bullying and peer harassment. They went on to discuss how the built environment interacts with policies and practices to create conditions conducive to bullying victimization and harassment. First, survey respondents identified the playground and hallways as locations prone to bullying. The researchers noted that the school's hallways were closed off and created small, isolated areas where bullying is more likely to occur. Second, physical aspects of the playground (e.g., large, isolated, poorly lit, and some distance from the school itself) made surveillance of misbehavior difficult. Based on their analysis, Fram and Dickmann (2012) concluded "spaces that exhibit specific elements can exacerbate tendencies for bullying that may exist at a school" (241). They went on to suggest that "the findings showed a disconnect between school policies and actual practices as they relate to school safety and crisis situations" and that "spaces inside and outside the school were reported to be places of negative social and peer interactions" (241). Fram and Dickmann's research points to the influence of the built design of a school on bullying behaviors and victimization. While policies and practices aimed at bullying prevention are important, so too is the built environment within which those policies and practices are implemented.

Questions

1. Think of a time when you experienced or witnessed peer victimization at school. Where did it take place? How might the built

environment of that location have influenced the likelihood that you or another were victimized in that place?

2. Which aspects of the built design of a school you are familiar with would you change to reduce the likelihood of bullying victimization based on Fram and Dickmann's study? How are these changes informed by the theories and research discussed throughout this chapter?

increase guardianship as a protective factor in particular locations. Various institutions have incorporated CPTED into their security practices, including retail stores that employ security cameras, locked display cabinets, scanning devices, and (non)uniformed loss prevention personnel and police officers. Similarly, schools have increased their use of such practices, especially those in high crime areas such as inner-city communities of color. However—and perhaps unsurprisingly given the lack of support as a deterrent or form of capable guardianship—these practices more often serve as a mechanism of criminalization that expands and deepens the **school-to-prison pipeline** and disproportionately impacts economically disadvantaged youth and youth of color, an issue we explore in more detail in chapter 6.

Why the Mixed Results? As the review of relevant literature above suggests, the components of LRAT have received mixed support in empirical tests of their applicability to school victimization broadly, and school bullying in particular. There may be several reasons for this. First, different researchers have used the same measures as indicators of different theoretical constructs. This is due partially to lack of clarity in the operationalization of these constructs and likely also the heavy reliance on secondary analysis of large, nationally representative data sets not originally designed to test these constructs. Second, and relatedly, the overlap in operational definitions of the major constructs makes it difficult to identify why they function as they do.

For instance, Cho, Wooldredge, and Park (2016) conducted a combined cross-sectional and longitudinal test of the applicability of lifestyles/routine activity theories to school bullying victimization, using a nationally representative sample of junior high school students in South Korea. Their measures of capable guardianship included direct and indirect parental and teacher supervision. They measured target suitability using measures of students' routines, including two types of group-based leisure activities. The first, participation in school clubs, was hypothesized to be inversely related to bullying victimization because participation would increase guardianship through the presence of teachers and administrators. The second, participation in "cyberclubs," was hypothesized to be positively correlated with bullying victimization as "these activities occur off school premises and are not carefully monitored by adults" (297). The other measures of target suitability included hours per week spent studying and working, both of which they hypothesized to be negatively correlated with bullying victimization. They measured proximity to motivated offenders by indicating if the student attended school in Seoul (the largest city in South Korea with the highest crime rate) or elsewhere.

Their cross-sectional findings were mixed. For instance, they found a positive correlation between capable guardianship (in the form of parental relationships) and bullying, meaning increased guardianship was related to increased bullying victimization. However, a student's relationship with their teacher (as a measure of guardianship) was negatively correlated with bullying victimization, suggesting that teachers may play a more significant guardianship role than parents. In terms of routines/lifestyles and susceptibility to bullying, Cho, Wooldredge, and Park (2016) found that participation in off-site activities like cyberclubs correlated with higher likelihood of bullying victimization; however, there was no significant relationship between school club participation and bullying victimization in their cross-sectional models. Similarly, neither hours per week studying nor working were significantly related to bullying victimization in their sample.

In their longitudinal model, only participation in school club meetings showed a significant relationship to likelihood of bullying victimization, but in the opposite direction than hypothesized. That is to say, "greater participation over time in school club meetings coincided with increased odds of being bullied" (Cho, Wooldredge, and Park 2016, 303). They offered several explanations for this unexpected outcome, including that adult supervision during these after-school activities may not be as robust as when school is in session, as well as the idea that involvement in these activities provides greater opportunity for motivated "offenders" to develop familiarity with and assess the relative vulnerability of potential targets.

As we have discussed throughout this section, support for the applicability of victimization theories to school bullying is mixed. There is research that supports the notion that victims' lifestyles and routine activities may place them at differential risk for victimization both at school and online. This suggests that programs and policies aimed at changing victim behaviors may offer some degree of protection, with the caveat that such programs and policies not blame victims for their own victimization. Moreover, policies and practices aimed at increasing capable guardianship also show promise, especially those that attempt to increase informal guardianship, such as the fair and consistent enforcement of school rules and enhancement of teacher-student relationships (see, for instance, Choi et al. 2019), as well as supporting bullying victims in the development of social skills and peer relationships (see Hong et al. 2014). For instance, Evans and Smokowski (2016), offering advice to school social workers, suggested that "victims and potential victims should be brought into welcoming social groups, linked to higher functioning children or adult mentors to nurture friendships, and given the opportunity to play some type of role in the school community to develop pride in their social contribution" (372). Improving victims' relationships with their peers can also increase the likelihood of bystander interventions, a potentially effective prevention practice in schools we discuss in more detail in chapter 5.

THREE

Micro-Level Theories

Micro-level theories operate at the individual level and fall into two categories: biosocial and psychological. Biosocial theories attempt to explain behavior through the interaction of biological factors with psychological and social ones. Psychological theories fall into two general orientations, the *intra*personal and the *inter*personal. The former examines people's internal processes, while the latter focuses on how people interpret their world and relate to and are influenced by others. There is overlap among and within biosocial and psychological theories, but due to space constraints, the chapter mostly discusses theories individually.

BIOSOCIAL THEORIES

Researchers have increasingly explored how genes and other biological influences interact with the environment in the development of criminal behaviors (Rudo-Hutt et al. 2016). Such studies show that the risk of antisocial behavior (ASB) increases when biological risk factors combine with social risk factors, including maternal rejection and family instability (van Hazebroek et al. 2019), and contact with the criminal justice system (Motz et al. 2019). There also appear to be genetic/environmental differences in violent *victimization* (Eastman et al. 2018).

Children whose parents exhibit ASB have an increased risk of developing ASB (Besemer et al. 2017). Similarly, prospective longitudinal studies have found that children who have a parent who has been convicted of a crime are at high risk of being convicted (e.g., Farrington, Coid, and West 2009). There are several, probably interrelated, pathways that may explain this. Social learning theory (discussed below and in Chapter 5) posits that children learn antisocial behaviors from parents and other caregivers, either directly or indirectly. There also may be other genetic and home environmental influences (Besemer et al. 2017).

Genetic/Environmental Factors

Researchers have examined the influence of genetic factors on ASB and its subtypes through exploring (1) commonalities and variations in behavior and symptomology between twins or other siblings raised together (twin studies) and raised apart (adoption studies), (2) variations in specific genes between people (**polymorphisms**), and (3) variations across the entire genome (**polygenic variation**) between people.

General Heritability: Family, Sibling, and Twin Studies Meta-analyses of twin studies show genes have a large influence on ASB, from 41 to 50 percent, (Mason and Frick 1994; Malouff, Rooke, and Schutte 2008; Rhee and Waldman 2002) as well as on traits associated with it, such as impulsivity (Bezdjian, Baker, and Tuvblad 2011) and psychopathy (Brook et al. 2010). Most studies show higher heritability for tendencies toward violent ASB as opposed to nonviolent ASB and for more serious violence than less serious violence (Raine 2019). Studies of childhood aggression have shown similar heritability likelihood of ASB (e.g., DiLalla 2017; Lubke et al. 2018).

Bullying perpetration and victimization tend to run in families (Allison et al. 2014; Farrington 1993). However, twin and adoption studies are relatively rare in bullying research and have tended to focus on victimization rather than perpetration. Studies have reported heritability rates of victimization from 32 to 77 percent (see Veldkamp et al. 2019). It appears that only two studies to date have examined perpetration. Ball et al. (2008) found 61 percent heritability for perpetration at age ten. The authors also found that heritability fully accounted for bully-victim behaviors. The study by Veldkamp et al. (2019) disaggregated types of bullying and found 70 percent heritability for all forms, with a somewhat lower likelihood for each specific form. More indirectly, studies also show large genetic influences on personality traits linked to bullying behaviors, such as callous-unemotional traits (e.g., Henry et al. 2016, finding 58 percent heritability).

Contributions of Specific Genes Researchers have found mild associations between ASB and polymorphisms on genes associated with some neurotransmitters and with brain structures associated with mood and reward (Ficks and Waldman 2014; Tielbeek et al. 2016). A prospective longitudinal study looking at polymorphisms in genes associated with the neurotransmitter serotonin showed a modest relationship with delinquency, explaining 9.6 percent of the variance (Langevin et al. 2019). Some studies have shown that low levels of the enzyme monoamine oxidase-A (MAO-A), which affects the neurotransmitters dopamine, norepinephrine, and serotonin, are associated with more serious violence (Vassos, Collier, and Fazel 2014). However, a meta-analysis of 185 studies did not find a significant relationship between aggression/violence and any specific gene (Vassos, Collier, and Fazel 2014).

There have been few studies attempting to link specific genes with childhood externalizing problems or peer aggression/bullying. One study found that polymorphisms in genes related to the hormones oxytocin and vasopressin correlated with externalizing problems (Wade et al. 2016). Another study found a small association between peer aggression and polymorphisms on a single gene (Lundwall, Sgro, and Wade 2017).

Polygenic Variation Complex behaviors are likely "not primarily driven by single genes or even a set of polymorphisms [multiple differences] in related genes" (Musci et al. 2018, 194, citing Duncan, Pollastri, and Smoller 2014). Bullying is likely one of those complex behaviors. Thus, researchers have looked at **polygenic** influences by taking DNA samples from persons exhibiting certain conditions, traits, or behaviors and then determining if there are common variants of genes across the entire genome. Comparing a person's genome to the combination of gene variants results in a **polygenic score.** The largest study to date on the genetic basis of ASB among adults found multiple genetic correlates, but the effect size was small, explaining just 10 percent of the heritability (Tielbeek et al. 2017). Wertz et al. (2018) found a modest correlation between ASB and polygenic factors related to low educational attainment and criminal offending, and further found the greatest correlation with a life-course persistent pattern of offending. The authors hypothesized that the pathway could operate indirectly through factors that are associated with criminal offending: (1) subjects completed less school, (2) subjects experienced poor school performance and academic frustration, or (3) other related traits were present, such as lower cognitive ability and self-control (Wertz et al. 2018, 792).

The largest study to date concerning aggressive behavior in children found 10–54 percent of childhood aggression was tied to genome-wide variation

(Pappa et al. 2016). (The authors explained that the wide variability in results among studies might be due to the method of sample collection, environmental differences, and different age cohorts.) However, there has been limited research as to polygenic influences on bullying specifically. Musci et al. (2018) tested the relationship between polygenic scores related to risk for conduct disorder (see Dick et al. 2011) with peer-reported bullying behavior in a sample of 561 children and found no statistically significant associations. As of this writing, there appears to be only one study that examined polygenic variation with regard to bullying victimization (Schoeler et al. 2019). That study found that genes related to intelligence, body mass index, and risk taking were correlated with victimization, while genes related to specified personality traits (e.g., neuroticism) and to some mental disorders, such as bipolar disorder, were not. Limited research has examined whether childhood adversity (including school bullying) affects DNA methylation, when examining either specific sites (Efstathopoulos et al. 2018) or across the entire genome (Mulder et al. 2020). Methylation is a process whereby methyl groups are added to the DNA molecule. This addition can change genetic expression without changing genetic form. Prior research has found certain patterns of methylation to be associated with childhood adversity. Research as to bullying is early as of this writing. Findings are mixed and the research faces technological limitations.

Other Physiological Indicators

Neurological Arousal and Reactivity One of the most-studied suspected correlates of aggression involves the operation of the sympathetic nervous system (SNS), which coordinates the body's "fight or flight" response to threat. The SNS is one of the two branches of the autonomic nervous system (ANS). The other branch, the parasympathetic nervous system (PNS), controls the body's "rest and digest" responses.

There are two leading theories as to why low SNS arousal is a risk factor for ASB. The **fearlessness hypothesis** posits that low arousal is due to temperamental fearlessness; fearless individuals are unlikely to be concerned about the repercussions of their aggressive conduct and are resistant to socialization efforts (Raine 2002). The **stimulation-seeking theory** suggests that low arousal is a negative state, and thus individuals with low arousal pursue activities, such as aggression, that will bring their arousal up to a more comfortable level (Zuckerman 1990). Woods and White (2005) studied 242 secondary school students and found that direct bullies had the lowest level of arousal (measured by a standardized self-report questionnaire), while direct bully-victims had the highest. Sesar, Simic, and Sesar (2013) also found that bully-victims had the highest arousal levels. However, they also found, contrary to most studies, that *high* arousal was associated with various externalizing behaviors.

Researchers have reported similar findings when they measured arousal through physiological methods rather than self-reports. Low arousal has a variety of physiological indicators, including low resting heart rate (LRHR) and low skin conductivity. LRHR is strongly associated with ASB (see Ortiz and Raine 2004) and violent criminal behavior among men (e.g., Latvala et al. 2015) and adolescent boys (e.g., Murray et al. 2016). Bullying studies have reported mixed results (see Farrington and Baldry 2010). Researchers using a different measure—skin temperature—found that children who were victims had higher reactivity than did students overall and that bullies had lower reactivity (Mazzone et al. 2017).

Endocrinology Many hormones play a role in regulation of aggression and reactions to it, including cortisol, alpha-amylase, and testosterone.

Cortisol and Alpha-amylase The body releases cortisol in response to stress; with chronic stress, the body can become desensitized to its effects. Cortisol dysregulation has been implicated in various mental health problems. Salivary alpha-amylase (sAA) is another hormone implicated in the stress response. Studies have looked at two aspects of these hormones: basal levels (that is, those found in a resting, "neutral" state) and reactivity (that is, whether the hypothalamic-pituitary-adrenal [HPA] axis is underactivated or overactivated in response to a stressor). Studies are mixed both as to whether aggression is correlated with low versus high basal levels of these hormones and from under- versus overactivation of the HPA (Rudolph, Troop-Gordon, and Granger 2010).

A few studies have tested relationships among cortisol/alpha-amylase, stress, and peer aggression or victimization. One study found no significant relationship between bullying and cortisol levels in a small sample of ninth-grade students (Williams et al. 2017). González-Cabrera et al. (2017) found that cybervictims and cyberbully-victims had greater cortisol secretion compared to cyberbullies and cyberbystanders. Kliewer et al. (2012) found that victims of both relational and direct bullying had higher sAA reactivity when describing a stressful situation compared to nonvictims but found no differential relationship with stress and cortisol.

Researchers have also tested two hypotheses as to why some victims become aggressive. The **diathesis-stress hypothesis** suggests that a dysregulated HPA (as measured by either low or high cortisol levels) makes one vulnerable to being triggered into aggression by negative peer behavior. The **differential susceptibility hypothesis** posits that HPA dysregulation depends on context; peer aggression can trigger aggression, but a more supportive environment may result in low aggression (Vaillancourt et al. 2018). Rudolph, Troop-Gordon, and Granger (2010) conducted a laboratory-based test and found among other things that heightened levels of cortisol and sAA predicted aggression after peer victimization but only at a high level. Ungvary et al. (2018) studied adolescents who were told they were to play a game with peers. Participants who had higher levels of anticipatory cortisol (that is, levels rose more after being informed of pending contact with peers) were more likely to engage in both proactive and reactive aggression during the game. The authors theorized that higher anticipatory cortisol levels indicated difficulties in regulating emotions. Other researchers have found complex relationships involving a variety of mediators (see, e.g., Lafko, Murray-Close, and Shoulberg 2015; Vaillancourt et al. 2018).

Testosterone Much research has noted a positive correlation between testosterone (T) and aggression, and more clearly, dominance. There are two hypotheses relevant here as to why higher T levels might be associated with aggression or domination. The **biosocial status model** posits a bidirectional relationship where men with higher T are prone to dominate (Mazur and Booth 1998). The **challenge hypothesis** suggests that T and aggression correlate only in times of instability or challenge; this may predict dominance more than aggression (Archer 2005).

There are fewer studies involving T in youth compared to studies of adults. Van Bokhoven et al. (2006) found that higher T levels at age sixteen were positively associated with self-reported criminal offending but that different forms of delinquent and aggressive behavior were related to T, thus suggesting contextual influences. There are even fewer studies in very young children. One found a positive correlation between T and peer aggression in preschool boys but not girls (Sánchez-Martin et al. 2000). Another study of preschool children did not find T correlated with aggression but did find a positive relationship between androstenedione (a weak androgen and T precursor) and provocative aggression in boys (Azurmendi et al. 2006). A different study also found no relationship between T and aggression in children aged four to ten; however, the sample was small and consisted of children who had been hospitalized for their behavior (Constantino et al. 1993). Another study involving boys five to eleven years of age found that T levels positively correlated with aggression in older but not younger boys (Chance et al. 2000). However, that study, too, involved a small sample of boys diagnosed with disruptive behavior disorders. The reason for mixed findings may be explained by the biosocial environment. For example, one study found in a sample of youth aged six to eighteen that higher T was associated with risk taking (for boys) and lower T was associated with depression (for girls), but only when the quality of the parent-child relationship was poor (Booth et al. 2003).

Only a few studies have tested androgen levels among bullying *victims*. One study found a negative relationship between androstenedione and victimization (Azurmendi et al. 2006). Another study involving a community sample of youth aged twelve and thirteen reported that victimized girls had lower T levels and victimized boys had higher T levels than their nonbullied counterparts (Vaillancourt et al. 2009). The latter finding was contrary to the authors' hypothesis that victimized boys would have lower T than their nonbullied peers, consistent with findings from other studies of lowered T in men who lost social status.

Brain Structures Raine (2019), summarizing the findings of neuroimaging studies, wrote, "There is little doubt that violent offenders have brain impairments, as documented by structural and functional brain imaging" (89). Raine noted a meta-analysis of twenty-nine studies found reduced structure/function in the prefrontal cortex; however, studies have shown differences between offenders whose violent behavior is reactive and impulsive versus proactive and planned. Imaging studies dovetail with genetic studies such as the one by Van Donkelaar et al. (2018), which found a correlation between aggression and two genes relating to particular brain structures (the nucleus accumbens, which is involved in the "reward circuit" in the brain, and the amygdala, which is involved in processing emotion). Amygdala volume has been correlated negatively with aggression and psychopathic traits, particularly where the behavior is more serious and/or begins in childhood (Pardini et al. 2014).

Brain imaging studies in children with conduct disorder and callous-emotional traits also show brain structural or functional differences (Choy, Focquaert, and Raine 2020). However, not all studies have shown reduced brain functioning. Raine (2019) pointed out that *increased* functioning in some brain areas, such as those governing the reward system, have also been associated with violence. There is at least one neuroimaging study involving peer victimization (McIver et al. 2018). That study involved college students and found when subjects were exposed to peer isolation, activity in several brain areas was higher in peer-victimized participants than in other groups. The authors suggested this might offer insight into why peer victimization is associated with poor mental health outcomes. We know of no neuroimaging studies involving peer aggression perpetration specifically; however, some studies have found **minor physical anomalies** (MPAs; an external manifestation of abnormal neural development) to be predictive of peer aggression as early as age three as well as of violent delinquency and violent adult offending (Raine 2019).

Early Health and Environmental Risk Factors for Violence

Research has shown aggression is correlated with a number of early health factors (Liu 2011; Raine 2019) and with exposure to environmental toxins, such as lead (Carpenter and Nevin 2010). There likely are interactions among these factors, as well as with social factors, that increase risk. There are two hypotheses as to why lead exposure is correlated with offending and aggression. First, exposure reduces IQ, and reduced IQ is associated with both property and violent offending. Second, research has found "small but consistent correlations between . . . lead exposure and symptoms of conduct problems, inattentiveness and hyperactivity . . . [which] increase the risk of ASB in adolescence and young adulthood" (Hall 2013, 156).

Studies have also shown that poor fetal nutrition, as well as signs of malnutrition in young children, is associated with increased risk of juvenile and adult ASB. Because low IQ mediated this relationship, Raine (2019) suggested that poor nutrition results in brain maldevelopment. However, it seems that the link between ASB and poor nutrition can be due to impaired neural *functioning* as well as abnormal neural *structures.* One twin study showed that children with poor diets at ages four to five were more likely to develop ASB in kindergarten (Jackson 2016).

Another study found that bullying perpetration increased twofold among youth aged ten to sixteen in a forty-one-nation sample who scored high on all three study measures of poor nutrition (Jackson and Vaughn 2018). However, victimization was not related to poor nutrition. Perception of food insecurity (measured by the frequency of going to bed hungry) has also been associated with both bullying perpetration and victimization (Edwards and Taub 2017). Edwards and Taub (2017) suggested that bullying involvement is related to both direct and indirect effects of food insecurity.

PSYCHOLOGICAL THEORIES

Psychological theories draw from knowledge about human cognition, attitudes, emotions, and behaviors. They can be intrapersonal (involve the inner working of the mind) or interpersonal (involve how people's understanding of, and relationships with, others influences their psychological functioning). Most psychological theories were not developed specifically to explain criminal, deviant, or antisocial behavior but rather have broad application. In fact, criminal offending can be understood as a relatively minor part of a "syndrome of antisociality" that includes early parental neglect, substance abuse, unemployment, and social rejection (see Zara and Farrington 2016).

Psychoanalytic and Psychodynamic Theories

Psychodynamic and psychoanalytic theories have their origin in the work of Sigmund Freud ([1923] 1989) and his disciples. One important aspect of psychoanalytic and psychodynamic theories is the concept of attachment, developed by John Bowlby and Mary Ainsworth (Ainsworth and Bowlby 1991). Bowlby (1988) saw healthy mother-child attachment as a "secure base." Today we view the attachment as between the child and any primary caregiver. How the caregiver responds to the child's needs influences how the child interprets "the reliability of their caregiver, consequently affecting how they view other people" (Ward et al. 2018, 195). Nonsecure attachment has been correlated with externalizing behaviors, delinquency, and low social skills (Nikiforou, Georgiou, and Stavrinides 2013). A meta-analysis of sixteen studies by Ward et al. (2018) found a small, significant negative relationship between attachment security and peer victimization/bullying. The authors hypothesized that the relationship is likely indirect, where lower attachment decreases trust in others and reduces one's sense of self-worth. Low-attached children may see relationships through a "biased lens that makes them more likely to view themselves as victims of bullying" (Ward et al. 2018, 204). (We return to this idea when we discuss social information processing, below.) It is also likely that those with healthier attachments have more empathy and engage in more benevolent actions toward others. Some studies have also shown that higher quality of attachment is positively related to bystander intervention (Nickerson, Mele, and Princiotta 2008).

In addition to explaining causes of bullying, psychodynamic theories have been applied in various prevention and response methods. For instance, one method is a "psychodynamic social systems approach addressing the co-created relationship between bully, victim, and bystanders" that was found effective in reducing bullying and aggressive bystanding (Fonagy et al. 2009).

Mental Disorders

In the United States, mental disorders are defined in the *Diagnostic and Statistical Manual of Mental Disorders* (DSM-5; American Psychiatric Association 2013). Conduct Disorder (in children) and Antisocial Personality Disorder (APD; in adults) are disorders most linked to offending because both list a variety of antisocial behavior as symptoms. However, the relationship between mental disorder and violence is attenuated and involves underlying individual-level mediators, including substance abuse, paranoid symptoms, age, sex, and severity of symptoms, as well as meso-level mediators such as neighborhood disorganization.

A population-based study of more than sixty thousand children aged six to seventeen years found children with depression, anxiety, and attention-deficit/hyperactivity disorder (ADHD) had about a threefold chance of being identified as a bully by a parent or guardian (Turcotte, Vivier, and Gjelsvik 2015). Limited studies have also shown that bullies, bully-victims, and victims are all at risk for various eating disorders (e.g., Copeland et al. 2015). These findings are consistent with reports from population studies that link adult psychiatric involvement with a self-reported history of childhood bullying (e.g., Vaughn et al. 2010). It is possible that the relationship between mental disorder and bullying behaviors is direct (in either or both directions); however, it is "most likely multifactorial in nature whereby family structure and socioenvironmental factors such as exposure to other forms of violence play a role in the development of [both] mental health disorders and bullying behavior" (Turcotte Benedict, Vivier, and Gjelsvik 2015, 791).

Twin studies have shown that bullying victims are also at risk for mental disorders and symptomatology, including anxiety, depression, and substance use, and that negative psychiatric states such as anxiety and depression are both a cause and a consequence of victimization (Silberg et al. 2016), findings discussed in chapter 1. A study of more than five thousand children in Sweden found that victimization at eight years of age was associated with psychiatric disorder at age twenty-eight, even after controlling for childhood psychiatric problems (Sourander et al. 2016). A meta-analysis found that bullying victimization both at school and at work was strongly associated with symptoms of post-traumatic stress disorder (PTSD), although all studies were cross-sectional and few involved an actual diagnosis (Nielsen et al. 2015). Another meta-analysis of a small number of studies found that victimization was associated with later development of psychosis and that this was more likely when victimization was severe, but other intervening factors needed to be explored (Cunningham, Hoy, and Shannon 2016). A subsequent correlational study found an association between childhood bullying victimization and psychosis, likely moderated by depressive and paranoid symptoms (Moffa et al. 2017). Children with other disorders, such as ADHD (Efron et al. 2018) and autism spectrum disorder (Maiano et al. 2016), are at elevated risk of victimization, but individual and contextual factors have strong influences.

Personality Trait Theories

Basic personality traits are patterns of thought, behavior, and emotion that are established in early childhood and remain relatively stable over time. Researchers study the influence of individual traits as well as combined traits thought to be the basic "building blocks" of personality (see Zuckerman and Cloninger 1996). Others have examined the correlates of multiple negative related traits, including the "Dark Triad" of Machiavellianism, narcissism, and psychopathy (Paulhus and Williams 2002).

Psychopathy Psychopathy is treated here as a trait rather than a mental disorder because it is not included in the DSM-5. One conception of psychopathy combines callous-unemotional (C-U) traits, narcissism, and impulsivity (van Geel, Toprak et al. 2017). A person who has C-U traits lacks remorse and empathy and has a general uncaring attitude. Individuals high in narcissism have a sense of entitlement, believe they are more important than others, and have a grandiose yet fragile self-image. Impulsivity means the tendency to act without thinking about consequences. Psychopathy is strongly linked to ASB (Hart and Hare 1997) and criminal offending (Beaver et al. 2017), as are each of its elements individually.

Research has shown correlations between C-U traits and school bullying (Orue and Calvete 2019; van Geel, Toprak et al. 2017). Callous children may bully because they are less sensitve to the suffering of others, impulsive children may bully because they do not consider consequences, such as discipline by teachers or others, and narcissistic children may bully to boost their sense of self-importance or to gain entrance into a social group. Research by Fanti and Kimonis (2013) suggests that each trait contributes independently, "suggesting an additive effect in which their combination confers the greatest level of risk" (403). Individuals exhibiting psychopathy are less likely to respond to typical interventions and thus "strong links between psychopathic traits and bullying may help to explain why so many typical anti-bullying interventions are ineffective" (van Geel, Toprak et al. 2017, 769).

Empathy A meta-analysis by Jolliffe and Farrington (2004) found low empathy correlated with various offending behaviors; however, the relationship disappeared after controlling for intelligence and socioeconomic status. Although educators have long targeted increasing empathy in perpetrators to reduce bullying (e.g., Farrington 1993), studies are mixed as to whether bullies (as well as victims, bully-victims, and interveners) have lower or higher empathy than the noninvolved individuals (Zych, Ttofi, and Farrington 2019). Part of the reason for the mixed findings may be that empathy has two dimensions—cognitive and affective—and research sometimes measures one or the other, and frequently both (Zych, Ttofi, and Farrington 2019). Affective empathy is the ability to *feel* the emotions of others, while cognitive empathy is the ability to *understand* the emotions of others. Several meta-analytic and systematic reviews have found that bullying perpetrators scored low on empathy measures (typically lower on affective than cognitive measures; Mitsopoulou and Giovazolias 2015; Van Noorden et al. 2015; Zych, Ttofi, and Farrington 2019; Zych, Baldry et al. 2018). However, Zych, Ttofi, and Farrington (2019) noted that these findings are based on cross-sectional studies, and thus we do not know if low empathy caused bullying or if it is related to other factors that are the cause. It may also be that bullying leads to low empathy through processes of moral disengagement (discussed below) or neutralization (discussed in chapter 5).

Personality Taxonomies The Big Five, also known as the Five Factor Model (FFM), is a well-known taxonomy for classifying personality. The five factors are Openness to Experience, Conscientiousness, Extraversion-Introversion,

Agreeableness, and Neuroticism. Each of these traits is measured as a continuous variable. For example, the factor Openness to Experience has two poles—inventive/curious versus consistent/cautious—with most people scoring at various points in between. The HEXACO model includes six traits: Honesty-Humility, Emotionality, eXtraversion, Agreeableness, Conscientiousness, and Openness to Experience (see Volk et al. 2019). There are other similar models, including the Big Three and the Alternate Five (see Zuckerman and Cloninger 1996).

Researchers have tested the relationship between personality taxonomy traits on the one hand and bullying perpetration or victimization on the other. As to the FFM, one meta-analysis found that both bullies and victims demonstrated lower levels of Agreeableness and Conscientiousness and higher levels of Neuroticism and Extraversion (Mitsopoulou and Giovazolias 2015). However, there was a great deal of variation in the studies they analyzed, and the effect sizes for each of these factors was small. One study of the FFM and cyberbullying found perpetrators had higher scores on Extraversion and lower scores on Agreeableness and Conscientiousness (Festl and Quandt 2013), while another found that perpetrators scored low only on Agreeableness (van Geel, Goemans et al. 2017). As to HEXACO, a study found several traits were related to social dominance and, indirectly, to bullying behaviors (Volk et al. 2019).

Cognitive Functioning

Intelligence Low intelligence is a very robust predictor of a number of life outcomes, including juvenile delinquency and adult offending. Researchers have replicated this association at higher levels of aggregation, including neighborhoods, states, and countries (Schwartz et al. 2015). Not surprisingly then, high intelligence is a protective factor against criminal offending, with greater protection for the high-risk versus low-risk group (Ttofi, Farrington, Piquero et al. 2016). This association is quite strong. Schwartz et al. (2015) found the risk of acquiring a felony conviction by age twenty-one to be 3.6 times higher for those in the three lowest intelligence categories (out of nine) than in the three highest categories (115).

Although the intelligence/offending association is robust, there is considerable debate about the relationship. First, researchers have questioned whether general intelligence, verbal intelligence only, or some other aspect of intelligence is the driver. It is also not clear if low verbal ability is a direct cause of delinquency because it reflects a diminished capacity to monitor and control one's own behavior or whether it is an indirect cause through its negative effect on school success (Bellair, McNulty, and Piquero 2016). More broadly, the way intelligence is typically assessed (through standardized testing) may simply be a proxy for school performance ability rather than a "true" test of intelligence. Cognitive psychologists tend to define intelligence as the relative ability to (1) learn from experience, (2) adapt to one's environment, and (3) understand one's own thought processes (Sternberg 2018). These are not the prime foci of standardized intelligence measures.

A meta-analysis of studies of ASB found that the difference between Performance IQ and Verbal IQ was negligible in children, increased to six points in adolescents, and declined to three points in adults (Isen 2010). Thus, Isen (2010) suggested that delinquency is intertwined with school failure as verbal-educational deficits accumulate through childhood. This supports the prominent social control model suggested by Hirschi and Hindelang (1977). Another indirect effect may result from the correlation between intelligence and other personality characteristics. For instance, those with higher levels of intelligence tend to be more dependable and conscientious, "suggesting that they are likely to consider the moral consequences of their actions," while persons with lower intelligence tend to be more impulsive (Schwartz et al. 2015, 114).

Low IQ has been associated with conduct problems and aggression in children (Verlinden et al. 2014). Given the strong negative association between intelligence and aggression, it is surprising that researchers have rarely evaluated the link to bullying specifically. Farrington and Baldry (2010) suggested that intelligence is probably related to bullying behaviors, but this has not been clearly established. They found in their own study that low nonverbal intelligence was a predictor of later bullying behaviors and that bullies at age fourteen had lower verbal and nonverbal IQ and were more likely to leave school at the earliest possible age (15). However, it is likely that findings will vary depending on the type of bullying behavior, with reactive bullying tied to lower intelligence and proactive bullying to average or above-average intelligence.

Executive Function Executive function has to do with the ability to control impulses, plan, and solve problems. It has been posited to have four sequential phases: problem representation, planning, execution, and evaluation. Problems at each stage could lead a child to act aggressively (Séguin and

Zelazo 2005). This is akin to the concept of social information processing, discussed below. Lower executive function has been linked to aggression, but few studies have examined executive function and bullying involvement. Verlinden et al. (2014) found that lower preschool executive functioning predicted involvement as a bully, bully-victim, and victim, with the strongest predictor for bully-victim and the weakest for victim.

Moral Disengagement and Neutralization

The leading theory of moral development in children was first proposed by Jean Piaget and then refined by Lawrence Kohlberg. Kohlberg's theory holds that moral development occurs over several stages that are consistent across cultures and time (Kohlberg and Hersh 1977). Children begin by differentiating right and wrong in terms of their own self-interest and increasingly incorporate consideration for others as they develop. Kohlberg believed that most people will become "stuck" at a particular stage. However, he also believed that schools can, and should, help children in their moral development (Kohlberg and Hersh 1977).

The link between moral reasoning and moral behavior can be tenuous. Reaching a particular moral stage of development does not mean that one will always act in accordance with it. Bandura (1990) proposed a social cognitive theory wherein moral behavioral control can be disengaged. Moral disengagement (MD) involves several mechanisms through which a person might, among other things, portray immoral conduct as warranted, minimize one's role, disregard or distort the consequences of one's actions, or blame others. In this way, a person can resolve the **cognitive dissonance** between their moral belief system and their bad behavior. Bandura's theory is similar to neutralization theory, developed by Sykes and Matza (1957; see chapter 5).

Research has demonstrated that endorsement of MD beliefs is associated with aggressive behavior (Gini, Pozzoli, and Hymel 2014). A meta-analysis of twenty-seven studies found a "statistically significant and practically meaningful" link between MD and bullying behaviors that was larger than the effects of other notable contributors to aggression, including hostile attributions (discussed below) and social competence (Gini, Pozzoli, and Hymel 2014). Gini, Pozzoli, and Hymel (2014) found no difference in the effect size between boys and girls (although they were not confident about this unexpected finding) and found that the link between MD and bullying was stronger for older children. The latter finding is consistent with Bandura's

(1990) suggestion that children need time to develop MD techniques. At least one study found that the link between MD and bullying was rendered nonsignificant for those students who had positive perceptions of school climate (Teng et al. 2020). Some research has found that cyberbullying is associated with lower levels of MD than traditional bullying, perhaps because it takes less effort to morally disengage when the relationship is virtual (Gini, Pozzoli, and Hymel 2014; Pornari and Wood 2010).

Because most studies about MD and bullying behaviors have been cross-sectional, they do not answer the question of which came first or whether the two are reciprocal. Limited longitudinal studies are mixed, with at least three finding MD came first (Sticca and Perren 2015; Walters 2019; Wang et al. 2017) and at least one finding that bullying preceded MD (Obermann 2013). Researchers have also found other factors mediate or moderate the relationship between MD and bullying, including certain psychopathic traits (Orue and Calvete 2019), moral emotions (empathy, sympathy, and guilt; Thornberg et al. 2015), and institutional factors, such as differences among classroom environments (Kollerová, Janošová, and Říčan 2014).

Problem Behavior Theory

Problem behavior theory (PBT) holds that children and adolescents who engage in any problem behavior are more likely to engage in other problem behaviors and are less likely to engage in prosocial behaviors (Jessor and Jessor 1977). The largest psychiatric epidemiological study to date found that adults who retrospectively identified themselves as having bullied others also reported "a broad array of antisocial behaviors such as getting into numerous physical altercations, school attendance problems, lying, cruelty to animals, stealing, and harassment" (Vaughn et al. 2010, 190). Cross-sectional studies have associated bullying perpetration with various problem behaviors (see the discussion in chapter 1). However, the relationship depends on the form of bullying, with physical aggression rather than relational aggression having a stronger relationship to other problem behaviors (Farrell et al. 2016). This is perhaps unsurprising given that relational aggression is seen as being more normative than physical aggression.

A longitudinal study of fifteen hundred students in grade eight and then grade nine found that both bullying perpetration and victimization predicted problem behaviors (Lester, Cross, and Shaw 2012). In that study, involvement in problem behaviors increased with bullying frequency; however, problem behaviors declined as victimization of perpetrators (bully-victims) increased. Victims' involvement in problem behaviors was initially low and increased as their level of victimization increased.

Social Cognition Theories

Social cognition theories involve a person's assessment and internalization of the social environment. Within these theories, the social information processing (SIP) model posits that "children's behavioral responses in a social situation are a function of the . . . encoding [and interpretation] of internal and external cues" and then the selection of response and enacting it (Harris 2009, 7, citing to Crick and Dodge 1994). Problems with encoding of internal and external cues has been associated with aggression (Guy, Lee, and Wolke 2017). However, researchers have contested the relationship between encoding and bullying behaviors. Some claim that bullies have superior abilities to appraise and control situations, while others contend they have deficits. Studies have shown that bullying victimization is associated with poor social cognition, but it is not clear that this is related to encoding or other factors. The salience of the second stage—interpreting cues—in relation to bullying and victimization is also contested. Misappraisal is associated with aggression, but its application to bullying specifically is uncertain. Guy, Lee, and Wolke (2017) did not find perpetrators in their study had early stage SIP deficits.

However, the relationship of misappraisal to bullying victimization is much clearer. A meta-analysis found that victims tend to misappraise cues by overestimating threat and engaging in characterological self-blame attributions—that is, they blame themselves for their victimization (van Reemst, Fischer, and Zwirs 2016). Victims tend to overappraise threat even in the face of neutral stimuli (Guy, Lee, and Wolke 2017; Pornari and Wood 2010). Overappraisal is a form of paranoid thinking, which itself is associated with victimization (Jack and Egan 2018). Research has shown a cyclical relationship where victims' maladaptive schemas—that is, broad pervasive themes regarding their victimization—contribute to continued bullying (Calvete et al. 2018; see also Schacter et al. 2015).

Social Learning

Social learning theories posit that behavior is learned from significant others. Here, we discuss the role of parents and siblings, while in chapter 5 we address peer and larger social influences. There is a significant amount of intergenerational transfer of violent behavior, as the discussion above made clear. This could be due to the influence of genetics, general home environment, direct modeling of parental behavior, or psychological stress caused by mistreatment or witnessing violence. A meta-analysis demonstrated that negative parenting (abuse, neglect, and maladaptive parenting) is associated with both being a bully-victim and a victim (Lereya, Samara, and Wolke 2013). Many individual studies have also found that harsh parenting practices increase children's risk of involvement as both bullying perpetrators and victims (Davis et al. 2020). Parents' overprotective behaviors also have been associated with victimization (Plexousakis et al. 2019). However, there remains the question of causality. It is clear that parent-child relationships are bidirectional (Kuczynski and De Mol 2015). Thus, a fragile child who is victimized could induce overprotective parental behaviors, while having a child who is better adjusted could encourage a more even approach.

Witnessing intimate partner violence is also associated with bullying perpetration and victimization. Voisin and Hong (2012) in a review of studies suggested that the relationship is indirect—that is, it is not based on modeling parental behavior but rather is mediated by children's problem behaviors, lower school success, and problematic peer interactions. Conversely, children who rate their parents higher on encouraging their autonomy, having a sense of humor, communicating well, and being affectionate are less likely to be involved in bullying behaviors (Gómez-Ortiz, Romera, and Ortega-Ruiz 2016). Only a few studies have examined the role of victimization by siblings. One longitudinal study found that victimization by siblings predicted peer victimization, "possibly due to personality characteristics and generalization of relationship skills" (Tucker, Finkelhor, and Turner 2019, 753). One longitudinal study found that witnessing violence was associated with later bullying behaviors; witnessing violence resulted in self-serving cognitive distortions (that is, the rationalizing of violence), which then resulted in bullying behaviors (Dragone et al. 2020).

Psychological Evolutionary Theory

Psychological evolutionary theory explains how human psychological traits and behaviors are shaped by adaptation—that is, as the functional product of natural selection. Evolutionary theory has been used to explain very diverse phenomena, from people's interactions with digital games (Lange et al. 2018) to police use of excessive force (James, Todak, and Savage 2018). It can be useful in understanding human tendencies toward aggression and dominance, which have been functional over human development. Evolutionary theory is supported by findings of correlations between genes associated with higher reproduction and those associated with antisocial behavior (see Tielbeek et al. 2018) and by findings that bullies tend to have more sexual partners (Provenzano et al. 2018). Thus, evolutionary theory can explain how adolescent bullying particularly can be seen as an adaptive behavior (Volk et al. 2012; Volk et al. 2015). Koh and Wong (2017) crystallized this view in the title of their article "Survival of the Fittest and the Sexiest."

Many argue that the "dominance hierarchy" in societies and groups—the stratification of people according to relative power—has "kept the peace" and is thus a survival mechanism (see Kolbert and Crothers 2003). So while many seek to stigmatize bullying and other peer aggression, studies show that children are accustomed to a level of "normal violence" (Phillips 2003; discussed in chapter 7) and that adolescents particularly use bullying and other aggressive behaviors as a method of achieving dominance in peer groups (Faris and Felmlee 2011a, 2011b, 2014). Thus, bullying can be advantageous and is not necessarily maladaptive. This does not mean that behaviors that are "normative" or "functional" are also "good" or "desirable." Accepting that some bullying is functional has the danger of normalizing it (Rodkin, Espelage, and Hanish 2015).

POLICY IMPLICATIONS OF BIOSOCIAL AND PSYCHOLOGICAL THEORIES

Biosocial theories propose genetic and other physiological risk factors are not destiny but rather that they interact with the environment in the formation of ASB (van Hazebroek et al. 2019). To date, criminologists and policy makers have supported and tested a large number of primary and secondary prevention programs designed to alter environments. For instance, early life intervention with children exposed to lead largely reverses adverse exposure effects (Billings and Schnepel 2018). Remediation efforts also address the effects of social inequalities, because the economically disadvantaged and persons of color are disproportionately exposed to environmental risk factors (Ard 2015). Interventions that address family contributions to ASB have also been shown to be effective (e.g., Piquero et al. 2016). A few studies have found that nutritional supplementation resulted in less ASB and aggression in both children and adult inmates, at least in the medium term (see Raine et al. 2016).

To date, most prevention efforts are either directed at populations (primary prevention) or identify at-risk persons or populations through psychological and social factors (secondary prevention). Even though a growing body of evidence demonstrates the contribution of biological factors, including genetic predisposition, "very few researchers are considering [such] ideas . . . and an even smaller number are using empirical data to test such research questions" (Vaske 2017, 991). The reasons for this scant attention likely include the costs of both biological screening and individualized treatment; uncertainties that tailored interventions will be effective; the nascent state of research; ethical questions concerning collection and use of biodata, including stigmatization, labeling, unnecessary treatment, informed consent, and privacy breaches; as well as negative unintended legal and social consequences. These concerns are especially salient in early interventions involving children (Focquaert 2018). More broadly, using biosocial markers in treatment runs the risk of "medicalizing deviance" and thus individualizing social problems (Conrad 2017).

Notwithstanding these challenges, some researchers have called for more use of noninvasive biological methods to study peer aggression/bullying in children, such as taking saliva samples or using medical imaging (e.g., Hazler, Carney, and Granger 2006; Mazzone et al. 2017). However, the practice remains uncommon, even though saliva collection methods have been shown to be feasible in various settings, including high schools (Williams et al. 2017). In addition, of course, it is a long leap from research to practice. This chapter's Policy Box asks you to think about the conditions under which you believe "benign" biological interventions are appropriate.

Applying psychological theories to crime prevention and control is more widely accepted and practiced. The same can be said of bullying response and prevention programs, many of which are based implicitly or explicitly on psychological concepts, such as building empathy (see Gaffney et al. 2019). Psychologically based programs are subject to some of the same risks identified above for biosocial theories. In addition, uncritical acceptance of any theory is unwise. For instance, the fact that bullying may have evolutionary functions suggests to some that prevention efforts ought to work within a dominance framework and not against it. Many antibullying programs

Glenn and Raine (2014) analyzed the emerging field of neurocriminology and its application to better understand, predict, and prevent
crime. They wrote, "If biological factors could predict future violence
over and above predictions based on social variables, even opponents
of a neuroscientific perspective on crime would have to agree that
neurobiology has added value" (59). They pointed out that as they
wrote, such capacity was low, but advances would likely enhance the
predictive power of biological markers. As to prevention, researchers
have advocated for "benign" biological interventions, such as tran-
scranial direct current stimulation; the latter has been shown in some
studies to reduce proactive aggressive tendencies (Choy, Focquaert,
and Raine 2018).

One important question is whether future biological interventions
should be mandatory or voluntary. Douglas (2014) noted that consent
currently is not required for the imposition of fines, community service, and other correctives and asked why then should consent be
required for biomedical interventions, which he termed "medical correctives." As to the role of biological factors in punishment, researchers have reported interesting findings. In responses to questionnaires
using vignettes, participants have viewed individual biological contributors to crime as reducing moral responsibility, yet this sentiment
may be at least counterbalanced by a concern that a biological contributor to crime may also increase the perception of the offender's
future dangerousness or risk of recidivism (Appelbaum and Scurich
2014; Berryessa 2017).

Questions

1. If you were satisfied that a particular biological risk factor was
   correlated with peer aggression or school bullying, would you
   favor testing students for that risk factor (e.g., through cheek
   swabs to detect for the presence of stress hormones or particular
   genes)? Would your response be affected by whether there was
   an effective and safe "medical corrective"?

2. If you could determine which children were at elevated risk of
   bullying or victimization, would you support biological interventions designed to reduce the risk? Would your answer be affected

by (a) how strong the correlation was, (b) how safe and effective the treatment was, (c) the age of students, (d) students' ability to meaningfully consent, or other factors?

3. If you were a school administrator and determined a bullying perpetrator had significant biosocial risk factors for aggression, would that affect your choice of response? For instance, would this knowledge make you more or less sympathetic, and would it make you more or less likely to mete out punishment rather than some other response?

encourage victims to be assertive in response to bullying, but Kolbert and Crothers (2003) suggest it might be better to help students understand the dominance hierarchy "and learn to assess the context in which it is effective to be assertive" (86). In fact, an entire intervention program, Meaningful Roles, is built around the premise that bullying is a goal-directed, functional behavior (see Ellis et al. 2016).

While we agree that pathologizing bullying perpetrators or victims is not helpful, it also seems that requiring individual victims to understand the complex school politics of domination and then to ascertain the right context in which to defend themselves seems woefully short of a solution, especially considering the research findings discussed above that victims tend to overappraise threat. Moreover, it is not clear what victims should do in those situations where the "context" is not right to defend themselves. Flee? Cower? It seems necessary to take a "bigger picture" look at bullying contexts. It may be that the "moral order" that the bully is defending could be utterly objectionable, and it thus rests on teachers and other interveners to help the bully "see the limitations on themselves and others of the normative moral order they are intent on maintaining" (Davies 2011, 284). This kind of inquiry requires an examination of influences to bullying at various social levels, and over time. We explore these "bigger picture" contributors in the succeeding chapters.

FOUR

Social Structure Theories

This chapter introduces sociological criminology, which is where the modern study of crime began. A sociological view suggests that there are social structures that contribute to crime, beyond individuals' tendencies, character traits, or behaviors. Social structure theories have three branches: social disorganization, strain, and subcultural. Social disorganization theories suggest that crime occurs when there is a breakdown in social controls over behavior. This can be due to rapid changes in society, deep divisions among various classes of persons, large-scale deprivation, or lack of social capital. Strain theories claim that crime is caused by the anger, frustration, and other negative emotions that people experience when their abilities and opportunities are not sufficient to achieve their goals or when they are confronted with other negative stimuli. Subcultural (or culture conflict) theories posit that crime arises because the values of particular groups of people support crime and other antisocial behavior.

While not one of the three branches described above, we begin with a discussion of the influence of socioeconomic status (SES) because large variation in SES can be a source of disorganization, and many theories in this chapter include some measure of SES as a component.

SOCIOECONOMIC STATUS

Socioeconomic status is "an aggregate concept comprising resource-based (i.e., material and social resources) and prestige-based (individual rank or status) indicators . . . which can be measured across societal levels (individual, household, and neighborhood) and at different periods in time" (Tippett and

Wolke 2014, e48). There is no standard measure of SES; it can be assessed using individual measures such as wealth, income, occupation, or some combination of these, or it can be aggregated at various geographic levels. Much research on crime and SES has focused on explaining the correlation between low SES and "street crime." For instance, research has shown that childhood poverty is a predictor of both juvenile delinquency and life-course offending. However, the relationship is complex and largely indirect (Heberle and Carter 2015; Odgers and Adler 2018). A large multiyear study in the Netherlands found that the pathway from poverty to offending was mediated by several intervening factors, including family adversity, childhood adjustment problems, school problems, and affiliations with delinquent and substance-using peers (Fergusson, Swain-Campbell, and Horwood 2004, 963). When the authors controlled for these intervening factors, the relationship between SES and offending became nonsignificant. These factors act cumulatively rather than separately, and thus multiple hardships greatly increase the likelihood of crime or deviance.

SES and School Bullying

Researchers have found SES to be correlated with bullying involvement by comparing results across students (Alikasifoglu et al. 2007), schools (Winnaar, Arends, and Beku 2018), and geographic areas, including nations (Due et al. 2009). Tippett and Wolke (2014) conducted a meta-analysis of twenty-eight studies. They noted that (1) most studies measured risk of victimization rather than perpetration; (2) most studies found significant associations between low SES and victimization, bullying, and bullying/victimization; (3) of the studies that found an association, its strength ranged widely; and (4) measures of SES varied greatly across studies, with some using a single SES indicator, such as parental education, wealth, income, or occupation, while other studies used composite measures that combined two or more such indicators.

Tippett and Wolke (2014) found that victimization was positively associated with low SES. The authors discussed possible explanations for the association. A direct explanation might be that children of lower SES backgrounds are bullied due to their reduced ability "to afford lifestyle goods or resources available to the rest of the peer group," while higher SES might protect children from victimization due to "greater access to intellectual resources" (Tippett and Wolke 2014, e5). However, given the weak correlation, the authors believed that an indirect relationship was more likely. Children from lower SES families have more adverse home environments that may include harsher parenting, abuse, and exposure to violence, each of which has been associated with victimization. The authors found that bullying perpetration was not related to low SES but was (weakly) negatively correlated with high SES. The authors noted that this might seem surprising because aggression and antisocial behavior (ASB) have been strongly linked with low SES. However, the authors pointed to findings that many bullies do not exhibit behavioral difficulties but use aggression strategically "as a means of raising their social profile and attaining dominance over their peers" (Tippet and Wolke 2014, e56). In addition, the costs of bullying behaviors are relatively low. Thus, "bullying perpetration would be expected in any socioeconomic strata in which there are potential gains to be made" (Tippet and Wolke 2014, e56).

While the relationship between SES and bullying roles is relatively weak and may be mostly indirect, many studies after 2014 have continued to find a negative correlation between SES and victimization in a variety of places, including Finland (Knaappila et al. 2018) and Jordan (Shaheen et al. 2018). Some studies have also found a negative correlation between SES and bullying perpetration (e.g., Knaappila et al. 2018), while others have found bullying perpetrators to have higher SES, such as a finding in Columbia (Chaux and Castellanos 2015). Research has yet to parse out the mechanism that links SES and bullying/victimization. Qualitative research may be particularly useful in testing hypothetical explanations such as those offered by Tippett and Wolke (2014), discussed above. However, it appears that the amount of *inequality* (both within schools and at a macro level) is a stronger predictor of bullying/victimization than is *absolute* SES, as we explore next.

SES Inequality and Relative Deprivation

Many studies have confirmed that SES inequality is positively associated with bullying behaviors. A systematic review of thirty-one studies on bullying and victimization found that individual factors were the largest contributors but that inequalities were associated with bullying/victimization at the school, city, and country levels (Azeredo et al. 2015). The rate of poverty was not associated with bullying. Similarly, Due et al. (2009) reported results from the study Health Behavior in School-Aged Children (HBSAC) that collected data in 2001–2002 from children and adolescents across thirty-five countries. The authors found that the level of victimization was not related to a country's overall gross domestic product (GDP) but *was* positively correlated with inequality, at the level of individual schools as well as across countries. Another study using HBSAC data for multiple years, with 117 different country-level samples, found that both victimization and bullying perpetration were positively correlated with income inequality (Elgar et al. 2013). Studies within countries have reported similar results. Chaux, Molano, and Podlesky (2009) found that inequality (measured in terms of land ownership) was positively correlated with bullying behaviors in Columbian schools but absolute poverty was not.

Inequality's correlation with ASB is complex. It may be that inequality fosters "a societal norm of accepting socioeconomic inequality [that] may lead to more widespread approval of behaviors associated with status differences, such as bullying" (Due et al. 2009, 913). It is also possible that "individuals in societies with greater inequality are more likely to draw comparisons of relative position, which can elicit status anxiety or stress and erode social resources that inhibit violence" (Napoletano et al. 2016, 3445). This relates to Runciman's (1966) development of relative deprivation (RD) theory, which posits that people are influenced more by their relative position than their absolute position; that is, people feel most deprived when comparing themselves to others as opposed to a theoretical state. RD has intuitive appeal because it helps explain contradictions in other theories, such as why crime does not rise with deep recessions or depressions but does rise as economies are improving. RD would suggest that in bad economic times most people feel that everyone is doing poorly, but when conditions are improving some people feel left behind and thus relatively deprived. RD can also explain offending across all class levels instead of just lower-class offending, to which some strain theories and subcultural theories (discussed below) limit themselves. Because people construct their own sense of class and class relations, "relative deprivation can be found in those with money as well as those without" (Webber 2007, 104).

RD has been tested at micro and macro levels. In experiments with individuals, Greitemeyer and Sagioglou (2017) found that RD increased participants' aggressive affect and behavior. At the macro level, researchers such as Blau and Blau (1982) have found RD to be positively related to violent crime. More recently, Burraston, McCutcheon, and Watts (2018), in a study of US counties, found that both absolute and relative deprivation predicted rates of violent crime, with income inequality interacting with the relationship.

A study by Napoletano et al. (2016) is one of the few to have directly measured RD at the individual student level. That study found that RD was associated with both bullying perpetration and victimization, with the strongest relationship involving the bully-victim group. The authors noted that comparing oneself unfavorably to others can create negative feelings "and [a sense of] overall lack of control over one's life" (3457), and this exacerbates other problems. Thus, "it is understandable why individuals with higher levels of RD are more likely to become engaged in both perpetrating bullying and being victimized" (3457). Results from these and other studies remind us "bullying is not a 'natural' adolescent behavior, but is conditioned by the surrounding social environment" (Due et al. 2009, 912).

A counterintuitive correlate of RD is a finding that victims of bullying in countries where bullying is less frequent report lower life satisfaction. Arnarsson and Bjarnason (2018) suggested that where bullying is infrequent, victimization can "exacerbate the victim's negative feelings.... Being the only one bullied in your class is therefore likely to cause much more harm to your life satisfaction than, for example, if it also happens to a third of your classmates" (1535). Garandeau and Salmivalli (2019) also hypothesized about RD and offered additional hypotheses about negative outcomes flowing from this "healthy context paradox," including that victims may be more likely to engage in self-blaming attributions (see chapter 3) in a low-bullying environment. All of this has potential implications for prevention efforts as well as providing victim assistance. If antibullying programs reduce bullying overall, they might also cause an increase in perceived harm to those who remain victimized. There appear to be no extant studies that have explored this potentiality (see Garandeau and Salmivalli 2019).

SOCIAL DISORGANIZATION THEORIES

Social disorganization refers to the inability of a community to realize the common values of its residents and to maintain effective social controls (Kornhauser 1978, 120). The measure of a community's organization (and its "social capital" or "collective efficacy") is the extent of informal (e.g., friendships) and formal (e.g., schools) networks, and their ability to exert social control. In turn, the amount of organization in a community dictates the extent to which the community can supervise and control youth behaviors, including the formation of gangs.

The Chicago School and Its Progeny

Shaw and McKay (1942) developed the first social disorganization theory. The two worked at the University of Chicago, and thus their work and that of their colleagues is referred to as coming from the "Chicago School." Shaw and MacKay, along with their colleagues, developed an "ecological" theory that suggests that the confluence of several structural factors—low economic attainment, high ethnic heterogeneity, and high residential mobility—disrupt community organization and invite crime. Research continues to support Shaw and McKay's model (e.g., Sampson and Groves 1989). In the United States, social disadvantages are concentrated in high-poverty urban communities (Sampson and Wilson 1995). For children, adverse social conditions interact with individual and family hardships and strain to accumulate over the life span and entrench disadvantage (Sampson and Laub 1997).

Social disorganization theories fell out of favor in the 1960s and 1970s as social process theories (see chapter 5) and critical theories (see chapter 6) became more prominent, but they have seen a resurgence in recent years (Sampson 2018), including in combination with other criminological theories, such as routine activity theory (e.g., Piscitelli and Doherty 2018).

Neighborhood, School Climate, and Antisocial Behavior

Researchers have found that both community and school-level variables are correlated with juvenile delinquency and with peer aggression, including school bullying/victimization. Results vary as to the strength of the association due partly to how researchers conceptualize and measure disorganization. One multinational study found neighborhood social capital was negatively correlated with both juvenile crime and victimization (Binik et al. 2019). A study of Boston adolescents found that neighborhood income inequality was positively associated with some boys' level of aggression and violence (Pabayo, Molnar, and Kawachi 2014). Studies have also shown small-to-moderate correlations between youth antisocial behavior and factors such as schools' structural characteristics (e.g., Pauwels and Svensson 2015) and perceived strength of the school community (e.g., Battistich and Hom 1997). Other studies that have looked specifically at peer aggression and victimization have shown a small-to-moderate relationship with neighborhood conditions. In a study of middle and high school students in North Carolina (United States), researchers found neighborhood disorder was positively associated with physical, verbal, and cyber bullying (Holt, Turner, and Exum 2014).

Many studies have also found small-to-moderate relationships between school climate and problem behaviors, including peer aggression. School climate is defined as the "pattern of students', parents', and school personnel's experience of school life [that] reflects norms, goals, values, interpersonal relationships, teaching and learning practices, and organizational structures" (Cohen et al. 2009, 182). The construct has been conceptualized as, among others, "school attachment," "school commitment," "school connectedness," "teacher attachment," "school satisfaction," "school bonding," and "school environment" (see Reaves et al. 2018). Cohen et al. (2009) identified four measurable dimensions of school climate: safety, relationships, teaching, and learning. Others have included more or different elements (see discussion in Reaves et al. 2018). School climate has been operationalized mostly through participants' self-reported perceptions, using standardized measures as well as those designed for particular studies (see Reaves et al. 2018), and has been measured at the level of the classroom or the entire school (Williford and Zinn 2018). A meta-analysis of thirty-six studies showed a moderate relationship between perceptions of school climate and violence at school (Steffgen, Recchia, and Viechtbauer 2013). A later meta-analysis of thirteen studies showed a small but significant relationship between school climate and problem behavior, including violence, general misconduct, and delinquency (Reaves et al. 2018). Both articles noted the high degree of heterogeneity among the studies, and neither was able to identify any specific moderators of the climate-behavior relationship. This might be because only some aspects of negative climate predict bullying behaviors (Dorio et al. 2019).

Most studies that have examined the relationship between various school-level climate factors and bullying/victimization specifically reported a small but significant effect. Azeredo et al. (2015) found that the thirty-one studies they reviewed used a wide variety of measures of school climate, with some assessing general climate indicators and others specifically measuring the antibullying climate. Two of the general measures—school size and class size—showed inconsistent results, with some studies reporting positive associations with bullying, some negative, and some no significant association. (We suggest that school and class size are rather weak and indirect measures of school climate.) Higher scores on two of the antibullying climate measures (whether schools had clear rules and regulations around bullying, and whether they encouraged antibullying and provictim attitudes) were correlated with less bullying (Azeredo et al. 2015). Individual studies have found correlations between most aspects of school climate and rates of most bullying behaviors and victimization types in many countries, whether the indicator was called "school climate" (Fink et al. 2018; Han, Zhang, and Zhang 2017; Holfeld and Leadbeater 2017) or other terms such as "social capital" (Carney, Liu, and Hazler 2018), "school social climate" (Mazur, Tabak, and Zawadzka 2017), "collective efficacy" (Olsson, Låftman, and Modin 2017), or "school ethos" (Modin, Låftman, and Östberg 2017), or by its negative counterparts, "normlessness" (Mann et al. 2015) and "negative school perceptions" (Harel-Fisch et al. 2011). There have been very few studies that have investigated the relationship between school *physical* disorder and bullying. One such study reported conflicting findings: the number of broken lights was positively associated with bullying, while the amount of graffiti was negatively associated (Bradshaw, Waasdorp, and Johnson 2015).

Researchers have raised the question of causality in these studies, that is, whether perceptions of school climate lead to antisocial behavior or if committing antisocial behavior (or being victimized or witnessing it) results in negative perceptions of school climate. Longitudinal studies have shed light on that question. For instance, Holfeld and Leadbeater (2017) found that perceptions of better school climate predicted lower rates of cyberbullying victimization one year later among more than six hundred Canadian elementary school students. Dorio et al. (2019) found that bullying participation (as perpetrators and supporters) was predicted by "students' observations of delinquency and illegal behaviors on school grounds" but (unexpectedly) not by "students' observations of incivility and disruptive behaviors among peers" (12).

Another question involves interactions between different levels of analysis. Winnaar, Arends, and Beku (2018) noted, "schools are miniature versions of the surrounding community, and hence . . . the risk factors experienced in the community increases [sic] the schools' predisposition to violence" (S1, citing to Burton and Leoschut 2013). Similarly, Mazur, Tabak, and Zawadzka (2017) reported that school climate was highly correlated with neighborhood-level social capital in their study of more than four thousand students in Polish lower secondary schools. Just as schools are "nested" in neighborhoods, classrooms are "nested" in schools, and thus classroom-level climate can be strongly influenced by school-level climate (Williford and Zinn 2018). While it appears that school-level variables also have the potential to reduce or magnify the effects of community factors (Mann et al. 2015), it is not always clear as to whether between-school differences are due to individual, classroom, or school-level factors. Jansen et al. (2012) found that school-level SES differences became nonsignificant after controlling for family SES. Thus, between-school differences in their study were completely explained by the aggregation of family-level disadvantage. It is also important to note that while many individual-level variables cannot directly change institutional ones, it is quite possible that institutional-level factors (e.g., widespread bullying) can shape individual perceptions (e.g., feeling safe at school; see Azeredo et al. 2015). Climate has been shown to interact with individual-level factors, such as student self-control (Holt, Turner, and Exum 2014); positive school climate can offer compensating effects to individual risk factors for delinquency (Kirk 2009). We explore these mutual influences more deeply in chapter 7.

STRUCTURAL STRAIN THEORIES

The origins of structural strain theory can be found in the work of Émile Durkheim (1858–1917). Durkheim was a **functionalist**—that is, he was concerned with the ordering of social institutions and relations, and their positive effects. He saw industrial societies as having moved from simple "mechanistic" forms to complex "organic" ones made up of many interdependent parts. Durkheim saw that society was becoming more organized around occupational roles that were increasingly diversified. He did not necessarily see this as a problem because individuals needed to cooperate in order to provide for themselves (Marks 1974). However, this division of labor could take on various "abnormal forms" where solidarity does not occur. Durkheim referred to this state as **anomie**, wherein there are deficiencies in social interaction that result in moral dysregulation—that is, a mismatch between individual and societal expectations. Durkheim believed that rates of crime and deviance would increase under anomic conditions, particularly in times of rapid social change.

Merton's Anomie Theory

Robert K. Merton (1938) further developed Durkheim's concept of anomie and its relationship to deviance and crime. Merton developed a typology that combined two variables: cultural goals and institutionalized (socially accepted) means. In the United States, a main cultural goal is to achieve material success, and the accepted means are to use one's own initiative and talent to "get ahead." However, many people—due to either personal characteristics or blocked opportunities—are not able to achieve desired goals. Under Merton's typology, individuals can either accept or reject the cultural goals and institutionalized means, creating four potential responses:

- "conformity," in which a person accepts the goals and means;
- "innovation," where a person accepts the goals but rejects the means (individuals could innovate using alternative legal means, or they could engage in deviance or crime to get what they want);
- "ritualism," where a person rejects the goals but accepts the means; and
- "retreatism," involving rejection of both the goals and means.

Merton also suggested a fifth option ("rebellion"), wherein a person fights to overturn the system in order to inject new goals and means. Merton claimed that anomie occurs in a society where there is widespread disjunction between goals and means.

Merton's emphasis on economic goals makes his strain theory not obviously directly applicable to school bullying. However, there may be indirect connections. For instance, experiencing bullying could lead a victim to engage in less aggressive forms of delinquency like substance use, a form of "retreatism" identified by Merton (Cullen et al. 2008). In addition, students who are not able to achieve popularity may "innovate" by using bullying to attempt to achieve that status.

General Strain Theory

Early strain theories such as Merton's drew many criticisms. Among them was a perceived overemphasis on economic goals as opposed to those from other life realms. Robert Agnew (1992) attempted to correct some of the perceived deficiencies in Mertonian strain theories and proposed a general strain theory (GST). Agnew (1992) drew from research in the medical literature about the effects of stress, from the social-psychological literature on equity/justice, and from psychological insights into frustration-aggression and social learning. As first proposed, GST was a social-psychological model and thus focused on individuals and their relationships with their immediate social environments, with a particular focus on adolescents. Agnew (1992) proposed three sources of strain that arise from negative relationships. He wrote, "other individuals may (1) prevent one from achieving positively valued goals, (2) remove or threaten to remove positively valued stimuli that one possesses, or (3) present or threaten to present one with noxious or negatively valued stimuli" (50). Strain leads to negative emotions, including disappointment, depression, and fear, but most relevantly, anger.

Experiencing strain creates "a predisposition for delinquency . . . in those cases in which it is chronic or repetitive" (60). GST is one of the most tested criminological theories and has been applied to diverse phenomena, including terrorism (Agnew 2010). Studies have generally supported the core ideas of GST (Moon and Jang 2014, 2149). We note that because GST considers self-control, peer and parental influence, and social bonds, studies testing GST also have found support for other criminological theories that incorporate those variables (Cullen et al. 2008; Jang, Song, and Kim 2014; Lianos and McGrath 2018; Moon and Jang 2014). Agnew (1999) also proposed how GST can operate at the macro level, such as across communities, a theory that has come to be known as macro strain theory (MST). MST has not been widely tested, but authors of one study involving delinquency found partial support for it and suggested it be further developed (Brezina, Piquero, and Mazerolle 2001).

Many researchers have applied GST to bullying, with most reported results confirming the theory, whether explaining the roles of perpetrators, bully-victims, or victims. We discussed in chapter 1 how many studies have associated bullying victimization with delinquency. It is relatively easy to see how GST can provide such a link. In his further development of GST, Agnew (2001, 2006) identified several types of strain that he suggested are more likely to influence deviant or criminal activity. First, there are strains that are high in magnitude, are chronic, or threaten a person's identity. Bullying is by definition a chronic phenomenon because it involves repeated negative behavior. In addition, the content of the bullying behavior is frequently related to the victim's identity, such as attempting to enforce "appropriate" heteromasculine and feminine behavior (Cohen and Brooks 2014). Second, there are strains that a person sees as unjust or as violating a justice norm. Victimization "should be a potent type of strain to individuals because it is an intentional behavior where the victimized are purposely singled out" (Keith 2018, 69). Third are "strains that are associated with reducing social control (e.g., strains that reduce what an individual has to lose by engaging in deviance)" (Keith 2018, 69). This type of strain appears salient here because studies have shown that victimization leads to decreased school attachment and perhaps lower academic achievement. Last are strains that create an incentive to engage in deviant or criminal activity. In the case of victimization, this could occur because the perpetrator provides a deviant model or because retaliation gives the victim an immediate—albeit temporary—release of strain. In fact, Agnew (2006) specifically identified "abusive peer relations, especially among youth" (70) as one of the "strains more likely to cause crime" (72). Agnew (2001) also noted that it "has been neglected as a type of strain" (346).

Research has also generally supported GST as an explanation for the bullying victimization-delinquency relationship. A cross-sectional study involving a sample of 2,437 middle school students in Virginia reported a significant but weak relationship between victimization and delinquency in both girls and boys, and with substance use in boys (Cullen et al. 2008). Hay, Meldrum, and Mann (2010), in a study involving four hundred adolescents from a southeastern US state, also found a significant and "relatively large" relationship between victimization and delinquency (137), and an even larger relationship between victimization and internalizing behaviors (self-harm and suicidal ideation).

Other cross-sectional studies have suggested that the strain of victimization can lead to perpetration. A study analyzing nationally representative US schoolchildren found peer victimization to be the strongest correlate of perpetration (parental rejection and negative school experience were nonsignificant; Yang, Nelson-Gardell, and Guo 2018). Yang, Nelson-Gardell, and Guo (2018) also found that anger mediated the relationship, consistent with GST. Similarly, a cross-sectional Australian study of a small sample of young adults (aged eighteen to thirty) found that victimization (here, by cyberbullying) was the strain that was most associated with cyberbullying perpetration (beyond academic and financial strain; Lianos and McGrath 2018). Longitudinal studies of Korean youth also found support for GST (Jang, Song, and Kim 2014; Park and Metcalfe, 2020). For instance, Park and Metcalfe (2020) found that victimization increased the likelihood of delinquent behaviors. Jang, Song, and Kim (2014) found that youth who were victimized by traditional bullying were later more likely to engage in cyberbullying perpetration, even as the level of cyberbullying among all youth declined. The authors hypothesized that victimized youth were "externalizing their strain in cyberspace" (92), but it is also possible that social learning was a factor. Given data limitations, it is unknown whether victimized youth in the Jang, Song, and Kim study were "taking it out on" their bullies or on neutral targets. An important finding is that prior victimization was a stronger predictor of later cyberbullying than was strain associated with parents, homework, and finances. Researchers have also applied strain theory to explain the relationship between victimization and lower academic achievement (e.g., Torres, D'Alessio, and Stolzenberg 2020).

Studies that have examined sources of strain besides victimization have also found general support for GST. A cross-sectional study of approximately two thousand middle school students found a relationship between both a multidimensional measure of strain and a measure of anger-frustration on the one hand, with traditional bullying and cyberbullying on the other hand (Patchin and Hinduja 2011). However, the authors found—contrary to GST predictions—that anger-frustration was an independent contributor to bullying and did not mediate the strain-perpetration relationship. Moon and Jang (2014) also found strain to be correlated with bullying behaviors (here measured only in their physical and psychological forms). The four sources of strain in their study of 296 middle school students from a southwestern US state were family conflict, racial discrimination, criminal victimization, and teachers' emotional punishment. Anger mediated the first three sources of strain, as GST would predict. However, the last source—teachers' emotional punishment—was a direct contributor to bullying behaviors. This might be because poor treatment by teachers operates through a social learning process rather than a strain-anger one.

Institutional Anomie Theory

Messner and Rosenfeld (1994) developed institutional anomie theory (IAT), a macro-level strain theory that starts with two related propositions. First, US cultural norms highly value material success, to the detriment of other areas of family, social, and civic life. Second, the United States has disproportionately more serious crime, particularly violent crime, than other developed nations. Messner and Rosenfeld (1994) posited that the desire to obtain monetary rewards produces strong pressure to attain those rewards by the most efficacious means (84–85). This is similar to Merton's strain theory; however, Messner and Rosenfeld departed from Merton by arguing, among other things, that expansion of economic opportunities increases rather than decreases societal anomie due to constant striving. They also suggested that in advanced capitalist societies—and particularly in the United States—all societal institutions become monetized and subservient to economic interests and thus cannot operate as a check against anomic conditions. For instance, they wrote, "education is regarded largely as a means to occupational attainment, which in turn is valued primarily insofar as it promises economic rewards" (Messner and Rosenfeld 1994, 78).

Researchers have also applied IAT at the meso or micro level, hypothesizing that the same forces that create a society that overemphasizes material success encourage concomitant individual and institutional attitudes and behaviors (Messner, Thome, and Rosenfeld 2008). In this vein, Hövermann et al. (2015) introduced the concept of a "marketized mentality" (MM). They saw MM as an individual-level counterpart to the collective anomie of advanced industrialized nations MM consists of orientation to achievement, excessive individualism, universalism (standards of success apply to everyone regardless of ability or opportunity), and a fetishistic attitude toward money (that is, getting more money is *the* key to success). Groß, Hövermann, and Messner (2018) are some of the few researchers that have attempted to explain juvenile delinquency using IAT at the individual level. The authors worked with data from 4,150 students in sixty-nine German schools. They found violent delinquency was higher where there was a more anomic school climate and where individual students reported higher levels of MM (361–62).

We are unaware of any studies that have applied IAT to bullying specifically. It would seem that if theories are correct that peer aggression is largely a goal-directed behavior (Volk, Dane, and Marini 2014), with a primary goal of achieving greater social status (Faris and Felmlee 2011a, 2011b, 2014), then IAT might be a fruitful avenue of exploration. Interestingly, one experimental study showed that peer rejection decreased implicit self-esteem and boosted materialism (Jiang et al. 2015). If this finding applies more broadly, there could be a feedback loop between materialism and at least some forms of school bullying.

SUBCULTURAL/CULTURE CONFLICT THEORIES

Culture conflict theories arose in about the middle of the twentieth century. They are based in the idea of cultural deviance, which refers to "conduct which reflects socialization to subcultural values and derivative norms that conflict with the law" (Kornhauser 1978, 21).

These theories suggest that subcultures are not entirely distinct or separate but share many of the values of the larger culture. The three most prominent culture conflict theories suggest that class (SES) is a major determinant of culture and thus a major contributor to crime. Cloward and Ohlin (1960) studied the formation of youth gangs and developed their theory of **differential opportunity**, which posits that low SES juveniles choose to become part of subcultures due to the discrepancy between cultural aspirations and the ability of those in the lower SES strata to achieve them through legitimate means, echoing Merton. Cohen (1955) argued that delinquency arises when low SES youth fail to live up to middle-class standards, particularly when it comes to schooling. If working-class juveniles fail to succeed in school, they join a delinquent subculture that provides them an opportunity for status attainment through different means, also invoking Merton's conception. Miller (1958) developed **focal concerns theory** to explain adolescent gang formation. Miller felt that those in the lower SES strata have a different set of values and "focal concerns" that differ from mainstream culture and that contribute not just to crime but also to their own impoverishment. He identified these focal concerns as trouble, toughness, smartness, excitement, fate, and autonomy. Miller thought that youth learned to adhere to these concerns through exposure to the subculture as opposed to being a reaction to blocked opportunity.

Subcultural theories are not prominent as we write, for several reasons. First, there is little empirical support for the existence of large-scale, distinct subcultures that approve of crime and delinquency (Kornhauser 1978, 214–18). Second, the theories' emphasis on "lower-class values" as criminogenic is problematic at best. Research shows that juveniles and adults in all segments of society engage in significant delinquent or criminal behavior (Braithwaite 1981), yet there is little discussion of "subcultures" that approve of, say, insider trading. Third, the theories do not go far in explaining why most youth in low SES strata do not choose to join gangs or engage in significant violence. Last, the theories—and particularly that of Miller—appear to blame those living in poverty for their own condition, a position that should feel unpalatable to many.

While there has been extensive criminological research on subcultures, these theories have not been applied much to peer aggression, including school bullying. Braithwaite (2006) suggested that bullying perpetrators are alienated from the school, and they solve the negative feelings (mostly shame) that arise "by constituting a delinquent subculture with values that invert those of the school—for example toughness instead of control of aggression, contempt for property instead of respect for property. By inverting the school's values, rejected children collectively create a subculture that interprets them as a success rather than a failure" (Braithwaite 2006, 406).

However, this is likely not the case for most children who engage in bullying. Empirical research has demonstrated that bullies tend to be popular (if not always well liked), bullies do not share common characteristics, and children frequently change roles over time.

A specific avenue that seems more promising involves the subculture of organized sports. Few studies have examined whether sports aggression among children "spills over" into nonsport peer relationships (Vveinhardt, Komskiene, and Romero 2017). Most studies have been limited to examining bullying or harassment within the sport (i.e., player on player) and within community-based as opposed to school-based leagues (e.g., Gendron and Frenette 2016; Vveinhardt, Komskiene, and Romero 2017). We first describe research on the relationship between sports participation and delinquency and other antisocial behavior before turning to a discussion about sports and peer aggression more specifically.

Research with children and youth concerning the association between sports participation and antisocial behavior or delinquency is complex, and findings are mixed. Most studies show that engagement with sports is associated with less overall delinquency and a greater likelihood to graduate from high school and to attend college (see Kreager 2007). At least one study showed that participation in high school sports diminished the association between childhood conduct disorder and adult antisocial behavior (Samek et al. 2015). Sports participation is said to promote development of positive character traits such as self-esteem, self-regulation, cooperation, and perseverance, all prosocial traits that are associated with less juvenile delinquency (Spruit et al. 2016). These findings are consistent with control theories discussed in chapter 5 as well as routine activity theory discussed in chapter 2. However, some studies show that participation in team sports is positively associated with delinquent behaviors, perhaps due to decreased moral judgment. This is consistent with subcultural theories as well as social learning (chapters 2 and 5), differential association theory (chapter 5), and cultural criminology and masculinity theories (chapter 6). For instance, behaviors such as using banned performance-enhancing drugs "stem directly from the normative definitions learned in sports, a concept [Hughes and Coakley (1991)] call 'positive deviance'" (Kreager 2007, 708).

Large-scale analyses have also shown mixed results. A meta-analysis of fifty-one studies found that sports participation was not associated with overall juvenile delinquency or any of several delinquency submeasures (Spruit et al. 2016). Spruit et al. (2016) also found that participation in individual sports was related to less delinquency but that participation in team sports was not related to delinquency. The authors considered several hypotheses for the null effect, including that the positive and negative characteristics of sports are countervailing. This is supported by two studies of boys and young men (aged nine to nineteen) from soccer clubs in the Netherlands that found that prosocial *and* antisocial behavior could be traced to elements of the playing environment (Rutten et al. 2008, 2011). However, a smaller systematic analysis of eleven studies found a positive correlation between sports participation, alcohol use, and aggression and violence (Sønderlund et al. 2014). That analysis included three studies of middle or high school students, each of which showed correlations among the variables.

Kreager (2007) noted, "By applying lessons learned in sports, athletes may perceive violence and intimidation as acceptable means of achieving off-the-field goals and solving problems unrelated to sports" (708). The opposing "cathartic effect" hypothesis—that competitive sports provide an opportunity for discharge of aggression—has received little empirical support (Endresen and Olweus 2005). Many youth sports—whether community- or school-based—involve a substantial amount of unnecessary aggression that is approved by coaches, players, or parents and thus seen as normal. "These behaviors may take place covertly, but the fact that they occur appears to be an open secret in the sporting world" (Vveinhardt Komskiene, and Romero 2017, 235). Gendron and Frenette (2016) noted that aggression in sports "is merely a reflection of its prevalence in society as a whole" (51). However, different sports appear to encourage more violence than do others (Gendron and Frenette 2016; Vveinhardt. Komskiene, and Romero 2017). In addition to how violence-prone the sport is, the sports/aggression link would appear to be highly contingent on the contexts of local subcultures whether at the community, school, or individual team level (Gendron and Frenette 2016). Individual effects (the character and predisposition of athletes) may also contribute.

In addition, sports participation may affect only particular subtype(s) of aggression. Sherrill and Bradel (2017) conducted a quasi-experimental study with a sample of men college students. The authors found that subjects who had regularly participated in team contact sports in high school were significantly more likely to exhibit a greater disposition to instrumental aggression (that is, nonprovoked aggression directed at an opponent during a competition) but not to hostile aggression (aggression in response to a provoking situation). The authors hypothesized that athletes quickly learn that aggression is rewarded if it is in service of the team's goals, but that retaliatory/hostile aggression is discouraged. This outcome is worrying if we agree with researchers such as Volk, Dane, and Marini (2014) and others that bullying is a goal oriented, adaptive behavior.

Kreager (2007) analyzed data from the US National Longitudinal Study of Adolescent Health involving students in grades seven through twelve and found that boys who participated in the closest contact sports had highly elevated involvement in serious fighting (40 percent higher for football players and 45 percent higher for wrestlers, each compared to nonathletes). This was true even when controlling for selection effects—that is, that violence-prone youth may choose to play aggressive contact sports. Playing baseball and basketball were not associated with fighting, and playing tennis was associated with a reduced likelihood (35 percent) of fighting. In addition, boys whose friends mostly played football also had increased risk of involvement in fighting, as compared to boys whose friends mostly played other sports. In another study, Endresen and Olweus (2005) collected data from 1,592 boys in Bergen, Norway, three times over the course of two years. They measured boys' participation in "power sports" (wrestling, weightlifting, martial arts, and boxing) and administered two questionnaires that measured antisocial behavior and violence outside of the sporting activity. The authors found "the correlations [between involvement in power sports and both measures] were positive, of substantial magnitude, and highly significant" (472). They also found that there were no selection effects—that is, it did not appear that the increase in antisocial and violent behavior was due to the boys' having chosen the sport because they were aggressive to begin with. The relationship with violence was strongest for boxing and weakest for martial arts. The authors found this unsurprising because of the former sport's explicit encouragement of interpersonal violence while the latter emphasizes defensive capacity. The authors hypothesized that violence and ASB result "from the practice of the sport itself, and very likely, from repeated contact with 'macho' attitudes, norms, and ideals with a focus on muscles and physical strength and a belief in the value of toughness, and maybe violation of societal norms" (477).

The sports-bullying relationship appears underexplored, particularly as to girls' sports participation. One small study of sixty-nine adolescent girls who played in community-based athletic programs found that bullying prevalence rates were twice that of the national average for low-level bullying and three times the national average for more serious bullying (Volk and Lagzdins 2009). However, there are few similar studies, so this finding needs further testing and replication. Another area of exploration is the mechanisms behind the positive associations between sports participation and bullying, including determining whether bullying outside of the sport flows from the nature of the sport, from cultural practices associated with the sport, such as hazing, or from other factors. It is also of interest that, while various studies have implicated "cultures" or "subcultures" (Gendron and Frenette 2016, 53, 56, 60, 61; Vveinhardt, Komskiene, and Romero 2017, 236, 240), including "macho subcultures" (Endresen and Olweus 2005, 469–70), few have applied established subcultural *theories*.

Some studies have examined the relationship between bullying roles and participation in school-based physical education (PE) classes. Jiménez-Barbero et al. (2020) conducted a systematic review of quantitative and qualitative studies regarding PE and bullying and drew the following conclusions:

- Victims are less likely to participate in, and enjoy, PE classes than are other students. Because victims' participation is non-self-determined, they may be less likely to engage in physical activity outside of PE classes. This is concerning, because regular exercise has been shown to be a protective factor for negative outcomes of at least some forms of bullying (see also Sibold et al. 2020).

- Risk factors for victimization in PE classes include being overweight and having nontraditional gender expression, social and motor skills deficits, and low academic achievement.

- There is evidence that PE can provide an opportunity for victims to develop self-esteem and to foster a class climate favoring empathy and reducing bullying behaviors, but PE classes can also be a subject where bullying is highly prevalent.

- PE teachers can reduce the likelihood of bullying by supporting students' "basic psychological needs for autonomy, competence, and relatedness" (88; see also Montero-Carretero, Barbado, and Cervelló 2020). However, they can also encourage further bullying "by ignoring school violence, using curricular options that may favor bullying, or by reproducing social discourses that can promote negative experiences in PE classes" (93).

- Few studies have empirically explored or evaluated the use of antibullying methods in PE classes.

WOULD MANDATING PUBLIC SCHOOL UNIFORMS
REDUCE SCHOOL BULLYING?

A uniform dress code in public schools is common in many countries, including England and some of its former colonies, such as Australia, and in those nations that emphasize collectivist values, such as Japan. However, mandating school uniforms for US public school students has been controversial—as have dress codes in many schools—because it invokes issues involving class, race, gender, politics, and law. A school in Baltimore is believed to be the first in the United States to have introduced them (in 1987), as part of an effort to reduce both parental costs and social pressures on children (Brunsma 2005). The Long Beach Unified School District was the first large school district in the United States to mandate school uniforms, in 1994 (Lopez 2003). Later, other schools in the United States introduced them as part of an effort to reduce gang violence (King 1998). Reportedly, school uniforms are on the rise—21 percent of public schools in the United States in 2016 required them compared to about 12 percent in 2000 (Bain 2018). Proponents believe that they reduce tardiness, absenteeism, peer aggression, and costs to parents while eliminating dress-based competition and improving school climate, unity, and discipline. Opponents claim that they reduce children's experience with diversity, stifle individuality, and interfere with First Amendment rights of expression (see Brunsma 2005). High uniform costs sometimes pose a barrier to education (see Mazzoli Smith and Todd 2016; Sabic-El-Rayess et al. 2019). Mandatory uniform policies can reduce differences between kids and thus result in less stigmatization of students from low SES families. However, school uniforms can also have the unintended consequence of more broadly serving as markers of social inequality in the United States because they are disproportionately required in urban schools (see Grob-Plante 2017).

There has been little empirical research on the effects of school uniforms on school climate, peer relationships, school bonds, or other factors, and the results have been mixed. In a doctoral dissertation, Brookshire (2016) reported that a Georgia school that enacted a uniform policy had a more positive school climate and less bullying than did a comparison school. A similar study found no difference in school climate (Wade and Stafford 2003). Wade and Stafford (2003) also found that in schools that required uniforms teachers reported less gang presence, but students reported somewhat lower levels of self-worth. Another study found no correlation between mandatory uniforms and school-wide academic performance (Yeung 2009). Some research has shown that the introduction of school uniforms is associated with a decline in assaults, weapons carrying, and other crimes (e.g., Granberg-Rademacker, Bumgarner, and Johnson 2007). However, there is very little extant empirical research on the relationship between mandated school uniforms and bullying rates. One study found that students tended to perceive that school uniforms helped reduce bullying, but that study did not measure actual rates of bullying before and after the introduction of uniforms (see Sanchez, Yoxsimer, and Hill 2012).

Questions

1. Considering all of the pros and cons—setting aside questions of peer aggression for now—are you in favor of requiring uniforms for public school students in the United States? Do you have a different answer for elementary schools versus high schools?

2. Do you believe that requiring school uniforms would reduce bullying or other peer aggression? Would your answer be different based on the type of bullying (physical, relational, verbal, and cyber)?

Studies examining the relationship between sports participation/PE and violence/bullying tell us that sports participation as a youth violence prevention measure will be effective only if coaches and parents emphasize prosocial values of the sports process rather than a deterministic focus on competition and winning.

POLICY IMPLICATIONS OF SOCIAL STRUCTURE THEORIES

There is a wide variety of school-based programs meant to address structural inequalities. Many early intervention programs have been shown to have immediate positive effects as well as ongoing ones. For instance, results from a preschool-to-third-grade program resulted in a 25 percent increase in average annual income for the participants at age thirty-four (Reynolds et al. 2019). There is also evidence that reducing racial inequalities in school discipline could reduce race-based inequality in adult arrests, thus altering the school-to-prison pipeline (Barnes and Motz 2018).

Reducing social inequalities has been shown to reduce ASB, including peer aggression. A study that used data from the 2011–2012 National Survey of Children's Health reported neighborhood disadvantage was significantly associated with bullying perpetration, with the effect stronger for African American and Hispanic youth (Sykes, Piquero, and Gioviano 2017). However, the authors also found that participation in need-based programs designed to attenuate poverty reduced the disadvantage-race-bullying relationship to nonsignificance, underscoring the importance of large-scale interventions to reduce disadvantage. Schools can also reduce sources of strain in their environments by improving school climate by increasing social cohesion and reducing excessive competitiveness. Many of the "whole school" prevention programs are intended to alter the school climate as well as provide information and incentives to individual students. However, many antibullying programs remain overly individual focused. Temko (2019) argued for a "sociostructural model of bullying" that takes into account how social institutions act as socialization agents that can implicitly normalize and reproduce societal inequalities. Temko concluded that one of the leading prevention programs, developed by Dan Clweus, fails to account for institutional and cultural influences on the bullying environment.

Temko's argument illustrates that public policy itself can be viewed "as one aspect of the larger social structure. Policy is a set of rules, often supported by resources, that attempts to constrain or channel behavior in particular directions through regulative, normative, or cognitive means" (Coburn 2016, 466). Thus, "individual choices are constrained by the individual's location in the social structure; policy shapes individual choice by influencing this social structure" (467). Thus, it is important that policies affecting schools involve the participants in their design and implementation, increasing understanding and buy-in, and that institutions assess their own role in encouraging or perpetuating social inequalities.

Social structure theories are highly compatible with each other. The negative elements in social disorganization theory can be conceptualized as community-level strains. Anomic conditions at the level of the school could be seen as creating subcultures that encourage violence or economic striving.

In the next chapter, we introduce and apply theories of social process. The reader will notice some complementarity between theories of social structure and social process. For instance, both the social climate theories and strain theories discussed above dovetail with social process theories involving social bonds.

FIVE

Social Process Theories

While the social process theories we cover in this chapter each offer a different perspective on the form, function, and influence of social interactions and socialization processes, they all take as their starting point the notion that individual behavior is influenced by external forces, such as the family, peer networks, and other formal and informal institutions. We focus the chapter on the three main categories of social process theories in criminology: learning, control, and labeling. For each category, we discuss its development, specific unit theories, and each theory's applicability to school bullying.

LEARNING THEORIES

Learning theories focus on the process of learning through interaction with others, emphasizing processes of socialization. We focus here on the two main versions of learning theories in the criminological literature: Edwin Sutherland's theory of differential association and Ronald Akers's social learning theory. Sutherland's (1947) theory of **differential association** is the foundational learning theory in criminology. Sutherland theorized that (1) criminal and delinquent behavior is learned just like any other type of behavior, (2) one's likelihood of engaging in criminal or delinquent behavior is based on the ratio of definitions favorable or unfavorable to law violation, and (3) those definitions are learned through interaction with intimate others, such as family and friends.

It is important to note that Sutherland's theory of differential association is focused on the learning of definitions favorable to law abiding or law violating, not necessarily the association with individuals who do or do not violate the law. In other words, it is quite possible that someone would learn law-abiding definitions from individuals who engage in criminal behavior just as it is quite possible to learn law-violating definitions from individuals who rarely engage in criminal behavior. We note this because many tests of differential association theory focus on association with delinquent peers, which is not a direct measure of Sutherland's theory.

Two important early critiques of Sutherland's theoretical work were that it does not offer a clear conceptualization or operationalization of *definitions* and that it lacks an explanation of the process through which definitions are learned (see Akers 2000; Cressey 1960). Donald Cressey attempted to address these limitations of the theory in his research on financial crimes and compulsive crimes (see Akers 2000). Building on this work, Sykes and Matza (1957) introduced the notion of **techniques of neutralization** as an example of definitions favorable to law violation. They argued that individuals use various techniques as a means to sever their ties to prosocial values and therefore gain the freedom to justify their committing deviant or delinquent acts. These techniques include denial of responsibility, denial of injury, denial of victim, condemnation of condemners, and appeals to higher loyalties. Ronald Akers's (1973) **social learning theory**, developed in collaboration with Robert Burgess, includes aspects of **differential association-reinforcement theory** and is the most influential modification of Sutherland's theory. Burgess and Akers revised Sutherland's theory to more explicitly incorporate Skinnerian principles of operant conditioning. Akers has continued to refine and test this theory, most recently as a general theory of crime (Akers 2000). Akers's social learning theory has been widely tested within the criminological literature, with a particular focus on youthful delinquent and deviant behavior.

We focus here on the four primary components of Akers's social learning theory: differential association, definitions, differential reinforcement, and imitation. Each of these has received varying degrees of attention in the school bullying literature. However, that literature to date does not appear to have addressed Akers's addition of social structural factors, outside of employing demographic characteristics as control variables.

Differential Association

Of the four components of social learning theory, differential association has garnered the most attention in the school bullying literature. Differential association has two aspects: (1) "direct association and interaction with others who engage in certain kinds of behavior" and "indirect association and identification with more distant reference groups" (Akers 2000, 76), and (2) "different patterns of norms and values to which an individual is exposed through this association" (76). Hong, Kim, and Piquero (2017) found that deviant peer affiliation increased the likelihood of bullying perpetration among their sample of South Korean adolescents. Similarly, in a longitudinal study of 1,194 students from four middle schools in a Midwest county in the United States, Grant et al. (2019) found higher average levels of bullying among those who also reported higher levels of peer deviance. However, not all studies support these findings. In an oft-cited study, Moon, Hwang, and McCluskey (2011) tested differential association in relation to other theoretical explanations for school bullying. In their longitudinal analysis of data from 655 youths in three schools in South Korea, Moon, Hwang, and McCluskey (2011) found that "differential association theory offers little power to explain the extent of school bullying" once variables from competing theoretical perspectives are included (868).

The link between deviant peer associations and bullying behaviors is supported more consistently in studies of cyberbullying. Hinduja and Patchin (2013) analyzed data from a random sample of approximately 4,400 sixth- through twelfth-grade students from thirty-three schools in a large school district in the southern US. They found students who reported having many friends who bullied (at school, while using a computer, and/or with their cell phone) were significantly more likely to report that they also cyberbullied others. Gofin and Avitzour (2012) found similar results among a sample of 2,610 junior high school students in Jerusalem. Studies in South Korea found that youth having deviant peers was correlated with online harassment (Lee 2018) and sexual harassment activities (Choi, Lee, and Lee 2017). A study of middle and high school students in Kentucky (United States) similarly found that higher levels of deviant peer associations increased the likelihood of cyber deviance (Holt, Bossler, and May 2012). The study also found association with deviant peers mediated (or explained away) the relationship between low self-control and cyber deviance.

Definitions

As a component of social learning theory, **definitions** represent "one's own attitudes or meanings that one attaches to given behavior" (Akers 2000, 76).

Akers (2000) stated that definitions can be both general (e.g., larger cultural beliefs) and specific (e.g., beliefs about specific acts). Further, definitions favorable to law violation or deviance can be positive (meaning they support the behavior) or neutralizing (meaning they justify or excuse the behavior). In their analysis of the relationship between witnessing intimate partner violence and bullying behaviors, Voisin and Hong (2012) noted, "by observing violence within the home, youth learn to accept aggression as a legitimate way to resolve peer conflicts and to interact with others" (487). Few studies have incorporated explicit measures of definitions even though researchers recognize definitions both as an important component of social learning theories and an explanation for bullying. This is particularly true for general and positive forms of definitions. However, we did find one study that examined general definitions. Georgiou et al. (2013) studied 231 randomly selected students from eleven different schools in urban and rural areas of Cyprus and analyzed the relationship between cultural value orientation (a form of general definitions), authoritarian parenting, and bullying perpetration and victimization. They found a statistically significant positive correlation between bullying perpetration and vertical individualism (an orientation toward wanting to become distinguished and acquire status, especially through direct competition with others). Conversely, they found a negative correlation between bullying and horizontal collectivism (a tendency to see oneself as similar to others and to emphasize common goals and interdependence).

Studies that look at specific forms of definitions related to bullying or analogous behaviors are more common. Williams and Guerra (2007) found that probullying definitions were positively correlated with all types of bullying (as cited in Cesaroni, Downing, and Alvi 2012, 208). Choi, Lee, and Lee (2017) incorporated a specific measure of definitions, which included asking respondents how they perceived the relative seriousness of a series of online sexual harassment behaviors. This measure represents a neutralizing definition because it assessed the degree to which individuals downplay the seriousness of a behavior. They found that "definitions provided more substantial contributions to engaging in online sexual harassment activities when compared to differential association" (121). This suggests, in support of social learning theory, association with deviant peers must be accompanied by the internalization of definitions favorable to law violation in order to have the predicted effect.

Similarly, Moon, Hwang, and McCluskey (2011) included a measure of definitions in their longitudinal study of South Korean schoolchildren, employing a "legitimacy of violence" index that measures whether the use of violence can be justified to defend one's rights (a neutralizing definition) or through positive definitions, such as achieving respect, obtaining fair treatment, resisting exploitation, or avoiding appearing weak (859). They found that "students' attitudes toward the use of violence were a significant predictor of bullying . . . but the effect on bullying disappears with the inclusion of variables from competing theoretical perspectives" (868).

Differential Reinforcement

According to Akers (2000), "differential reinforcement refers to the balance of anticipated or actual rewards and punishments that follow or are consequences of behavior" (78). The notion of differential reinforcement draws on the work of Bandura (1973) and other learning theorists and aligns well with early conceptions of the motives for bullying. Powell and Ladd (2010) pointed out that Olweus's (1993) three suggested motives for bullying—a strong need for dominance and power, family environment, and the reaping of rewards—align with Bandura's three forms of reinforcement, including *external reinforcement* such as tangible or social rewards, *vicarious reinforcement* such as witnessing parents or other role model aggression, and *self-reinforcement*, which includes the child knowing and understanding they can reap benefits from their behavior" (199; emphasis in original).

In terms of empirical studies, differential reinforcement is often tested in terms of actual or expected peer responses to bullying behavior. Simon and Nail (2013) noted, "children who underestimate peers' pro-social attitudes were more likely to join the bully" (84). Hymel et al. (2015) made a similar point, noting that "when peer bystanders were more passive in their responses to bullying, children were more likely to blame the victim and to like them less" (17; see also Gini, Albiero et al. 2008; Gini, Pozzoli et al. 2008). Similarly, Williams and Guerra (2007) found that perceived peer support for bullying, a form of positive reinforcement, was positively correlated with all types of bullying.

In a more direct analysis of differential reinforcement, Tapper and Boulton (2005) analyzed victim and peer group responses to peer aggression among seventy-seven children in years three and six in two British primary schools. They found that "direct aggression most often resulted in retaliation or withdrawal from victims" (247), a form of negative reinforcement. They also found that aggression resulted in support for the aggressor from peers, a form of positive reinforcement. In a further deconstruction of the process of differential reinforcement, Ziv, Leibovich, and Shechtman (2013) applied a social information processing model (see chapter 3) to understand bullying and victimization among a sample of 105 adolescents in one middle school in Israel. They found "bullies show more consistent patterns of negative processing, expecting others to be hostile and aggressive (like victims), selecting aggressive goals, and choosing aggressive responses" (489). This suggests that those who bully are expecting forms of negative reinforcement (victim responses) that support their choosing to engage in bullying behaviors. Ziv, Leibovich, and Shechtman (2013) also found that bully-victims showed similar social information processing patterns as those categorized as bullies.

Finally, Nocentini, Menesini, and Salmivalli (2013) conducted a longitudinal analysis of three years of data from a sample of 515 adolescents from forty-one high school classrooms in the United States. They found that "aggressive adolescents had a high risk for bullying others especially in classrooms where bystanders tended to provide reinforcement and social rewards for bullying" (502). This finding was supportive of prior research that found that "the more bystanders reinforce the bully's behavior by verbal or nonverbal socially rewarding cues . . . the more frequently bullying occurs in a classroom" (497). Conversely, they also noted that "the more classmates tend to defend the victimized peers . . . the less frequently bullying takes place in a school classroom" (497). This speaks to a major policy implication of social learning theory, namely, the promotion of bystander intervention programs, which we explore in this chapter's Policy Box.

Imitation

Akers's (2000) conception of **imitation** is that individuals are more likely to engage in a particular behavior subsequent to having observed that or similar behaviors in others. Observation may take place in close or intimate relationships (e.g., among peers or family) or through more vicarious means (e.g., media influences). Imitation is also contingent upon observed consequences of behavior, including relative reinforcement or punishment. While there has been some attention paid to the relationship between consumption of violent media and delinquent and/or criminal behavior in general, the results of that research are mixed at best (see Bender, Plante, and Gentile 2018; Ferguson 2015). We were able to identify only one study that looked at consumption of violent media and bullying. Ferguson and Olson (2014) studied the

Bystander intervention programs aim to train students who witness bullying to intervene with specific strategies. Polanin, Espelage, and Pigott (2012) conducted a meta-analysis of eleven studies of bullying prevention programs and found that they had a statistically significant impact on bystander intervention behavior. These researchers concluded that bullying prevention efforts should "provide opportunities to role-play and practice bystander intervention in vivo" (61). Johnston et al. (2018) conducted a mixed-methods evaluation of a brief bullying bystander intervention program that included role-plays. Their analysis showed that program participants increased their knowledge and confidence to intervene, and awareness of bullying in school. Moreover, 100 percent of the participants who reported having witnessed bullying in the thirty days following participation in the program employed one or more of the intervention strategies taught to them during the training. In another evaluation of the same brief intervention program, Midgett, Doumas, and Trull (2016) focused on the impact of the training on the interveners' self-esteem and sense of belonging. Their analysis found that sixth-grade students who participated in the training reported an increase in self-esteem, while the control group (wait-listed students) reported a decrease in self-esteem. The impact on self-esteem was not significant for the other grade levels (fourth or fifth), and the training had no significant effect on sense of school belonging.

Bystander intervention programs are dependent on witnesses' willingness to intervene. Thornberg, Landgren, and Wiman (2018) conducted qualitative semistructured interviews with seventeen junior high school students from four schools in Sweden and found that their motivation to intervene in a bullying situation was influenced by their perceptions of the seriousness of the bullying, their relationships with those involved, their sense of personal responsibility, their social status in relation to the bully, their perceptions of risk, and their level of self-efficacy. Similarly, Cappadocia et al. (2012) found that among the 108 children and youth (eight-to-sixteen-year-olds) attending a residential summer camp in Ontario, Canada, those who reported intervening during a bullying incident identified sense of social justice—the idea that no one deserves to be bullied—as a major motivating factor. Those who indicated they witnessed bullying but did not intervene identified a sense of fear and a perceived lack of responsibility as influencing their decision. Cappadocia et al. (2012) also found gender differences in factors determining bystander intervention.

Questions

1. Think of a time when you directly witnessed a school bullying incident. Did you intervene? If so, why? If not, why not? Do your reasons align with the research presented in this Policy Box related to why individuals do or do not intervene? How so?

2. Search the internet for an existing bystander intervention program and then respond to the following:

   a. In what ways does the bystander intervention program align with the core concepts from social learning and social control theories?

   b. How might the program result in unintended negative consequences from a labeling perspective?

   c. What, if any, changes would you propose to the program to increase its success?

correlation between playing violent video games and bullying among a sample of 377 children displaying clinically elevated attention deficit or depressive symptoms on the Pediatric Symptom Checklist. Their findings supported the general conclusion from the literature, in that "violent video games were associated with neither delinquent criminality nor bullying behaviors" among their sample (132).

More common in the bullying literature are studies that assess the link between observed behaviors within close/intimate relationships, particularly in the home, and the perpetration of bullying, a dynamic we touched on in chapter 3. Hong, Kim, and Piquero (2017) found that punitive parenting was both directly and indirectly related to bullying perpetration among their sample of South Korean adolescents. In a review of literature, Hong et al. (2012) found research supporting the link between parental physical discipline and bullying behavior among adolescents (see also, Espelage, Bosworth, and Simon 2000), as did Garby (2013) in a review of literature suggesting that bullying often manifests as mimicry of behavior of parents and other adults in children's lives. Lee and Wong (2009), however, found only a weak relationship between authoritarian parenting styles and bullying among a random sample of 778 students in schools across Hong Kong. They also noted that this effect was indirect, with peer pressure and harmonious school life moderating its effect.

In a robust systematic meta-analysis of the relationship between maltreatment, witnessing domestic violence, and bullying among South Korean youth, Go, Kong, and Kim (2018) found that "directly experienced maltreatment—including physical violence, verbal abuse, emotional abuse, and neglect—is more likely to be associated with youths exhibiting bullying behaviors than indirect experience through exposure to DV [domestic violence]" (22), but that both direct experience and indirect experience through exposure to DV are correlated with bullying perpetration (25). These studies are suggestive of imitation causing aggressive behavior. However, DV may act indirectly through a breakdown of familial attachments, which is a component of Hirschi's social bond theory, discussed in the next section. This is one of several examples from the bullying literature where different social process theories conceptualize the influence of social interactions differently.

CONTROL THEORIES

Grounded in the writing of Émile Durkheim, control theories argue that crime (and deviance) is a normal and natural condition of society that serves specific functions, including the establishment of boundaries related to appropriate behavior. Interactions with others serve as a mechanism through which behaviors deemed inappropriate (or illegal) are controlled, not learned. In one of criminology's earliest articulations of a control theory, Albert Reiss (1951) theorized that individuals would be more likely to engage in delinquent activity if they did not develop internal controls during childhood, if the internal controls they developed broke down, or if the rules provided by social groups such as the family, close others, or the school were not intact. This was followed by Jackson Toby's (1957) control theory, focused on **stakes in conformity**. According to Toby, people will be less likely to engage in delinquent behavior if they feel they have a great deal to lose. Toby argued that individuals who do well in school would have more to lose if they engage in delinquent behavior than those who do less well in school, although he recognized that school adjustment could be heavily influenced by the family and community. F. Ivan Nye (1958) developed a theory of delinquency based on the idea that the family is the most important source of social control. In this theory, Nye introduced the concepts of direct and indirect parental controls. Direct control is the use of punishment or supervision by parents in order to control the behavior of their children, and indirect control is the modification of behavior based on internalized feelings that the behavior will cause pain or embarrassment to the individual's parents or loved ones. Building on earlier work with Gresham Sykes related to techniques of neutralization, David Matza (1964) introduced the concept of **drift**, which occurs after individuals utilize one or more of the techniques of neutralization discussed earlier in this chapter. Once the individual is in this state of drift, they are then free (or uncontrolled) to respond to any situation that may arise, as deviant or conformist.

Building on all of this prior work, the best-known and empirically tested control theory is Travis Hirschi's (1969) **social bond theory**. Hirschi introduced four elements of the social bond that influence an individual's participation in delinquency:

- *attachment:* an individual's emotional connection to others, with a particular focus on familial, peer, and school contexts
- *commitment:* the individual's investment in conventional activities (e.g., school, work, and religion)
- *involvement:* the amount of time an individual spends participating in these conventional activities; the more time a person spends involved with conventional activities, the less time they will have to participate in delinquency
- *beliefs:* an individual's feelings about laws, social mores, and norms

As these bonds decrease or break down, an individual is freed to engage in delinquent or deviant behavior.

While his theory continues to be a significant focus for criminological researchers, Hirschi later collaborated with Michael Gottfredson to address the influence of self-control (see Gottfredson and Hirschi 1990; Hirschi and Gottfredson 1994). Like Akers's social learning theory, Gottfredson and Hirschi's theory of self-control was posited as a **general theory of crime**, suggesting that it can explain all individual differences in any type of crime/deviance across all ages and contexts (see Akers 2000). Their general theory of crime suggests that individuals develop an enduring predisposition to involvement in criminal/delinquent/deviant behavior after being exposed to negative childhood socialization experiences (see Grasmick et al. 1993). As we discuss below, research testing the applicability of low self-control tends to rely on a scale developed by Grasmick et al. (1993), either in its original form or through later adaptations. Grasmick et al. (1993, 8) identified six components of low self-control, based on Gottfredson and Hirschi's (1990) original articulation, including impulsivity, preference for simple tasks, risk seeking, preference for physical activity, self-centeredness, and temper. They then created and tested a twenty-four-item scale that measured the unidimensional construct of low self-control. Seeing as both Hirschi's social bond theory and Gottfredson and Hirschi's general theory of crime are the most widely applied control theories in criminology, we focus our analysis of the applicability of control theories to school bullying on these two theories.

BULLYING AND (A LACK OF) SOCIAL BONDING

Some of the school bullying research that tests social bond theory includes combined measures of a general sense of bonding across multiple contexts. For instance, employing a measure of social support that assessed relationships with peers, parents, and teachers, Kwak and Oh (2017) assessed the connection between low social support and cyberbullying perpetration among Korean elementary, middle, and high school students and found that low social support significantly predicted cyberbullying. A few researchers have also tested specific components of Hirschi's theory, such as beliefs. In two studies of male students in China, researchers Chan and Chui (2013, 2015) found that a decrease in an individual's belief in the legal system correlated with increased perpetration of nonviolent and violent offending, as well as bullying. Similarly, Burton, Florell and Wygant (2013) found that among the 850 US students in grades six through eight who completed their survey, those who were categorized as bullies and bully-victims in terms of both traditional and cyberbullying held more positive normative beliefs about aggression compared to victims and uninvolved students.

Other researchers have looked at bonds in particular contexts, such as within the family or among peers. In their analysis of ethnic differences in cyberbullying, Shapka and Law (2013) found that both parenting behaviors and the degree to which youth feel comfortable talking with their parents about their experiences correlated with likelihood of engaging in cyberbullying behavior. In their extensive review of the literature, Hong et al. (2012) identified multiple studies that suggest a link between familial bonding and bullying. Citing Baldry and Farrington (2005), they noted that "youth whose parents were characterized as punitive, or with whom youth had a conflictual relationship, were at a heightened risk of bullying and victimization, while those with supportive and authoritative parents were less likely to be involved in bullying and victimization" (Hong et al. 2012, 176). Weak family attachments have been found to be associated with both bullying perpetration and victimization among students in China (Chan and Wong 2015). In their analysis of data from 504 primary school children in Crete, researchers Mitsopoulou and Giovazolias (2013) found "boys who perceived their mothers as less caring had lower empathic responses and this resulted in a higher tendency to bully other children" (10). Interestingly, Hoeve et al.'s (2009) meta-analysis of studies analyzing the relationship between parenting and delinquency found "fewer than 20% of the studies focused on parenting behavior of fathers, despite the fact that the effect of poor support by fathers was larger than poor maternal support, particularly for sons" (749).

Studies of the relationship between peer bonding and bullying also suggest an important link. For instance, Cho and Lee (2018) found that youth who felt attached to peers were less likely to engage in physical, verbal, and social bullying. Similarly, Costello, Hawdon, and Cross (2017) found that among their sample of 647 US youth, strong peer bonds increased the likelihood that an individual would intervene online when witnessing cyberbullying. Finally, Burton, Florell, and Wygant (2013) found that students in grades six through eight who reported strong peer attachments were less likely to self-report both traditional and online bullying, either as perpetrators or victims. These studies suggest that attachment to prosocial peers can serve as a mechanism of informal social control for youth. As we noted earlier, this is in juxtaposition to social learning theory, which posits that association with peers who hold probullying definitions will increase the likelihood of engaging in bullying behaviors.

In assessing the influence of school bonds on bullying perpetration, some researchers focus on specific theoretical constructs, while others more commonly focus on an individual's general sense of their school experience. In both instances, research supports the influence of positive school bonding on reductions in bullying perpetration (see Beaudoin and Roberge 2015; Wang, Berry, and Swearer 2013).

An example of testing specific components of social bond theory is researchers who focus on the influence of students' attachment to teachers. Wang et al. (2015) analyzed data from 435 middle school students in the midwestern US and found that negative student-teacher relationships predicted higher involvement in bullying (231). They noted that both the bully and bully-victim groups experienced less positive relationships with their teachers, enjoyed school less, and held positive attitudes toward bullying, all of which likely contributed to their bullying perpetration (231). Similarly, Cho and Lee (2018) found that among their sample of 14,627 students who completed the Health Behavior in School-Aged Children survey, those who reported feeling attached to teachers were less likely to engage in both physical and verbal bullying. In their extensive review of bullying literature, Hong et al. (2012) concluded, "the quality of teacher-student relationships can also determine whether children are likely to engage in bullying at school" (177). Lenzi et al. (2014) found that among their sample of 662 Italian students aged between eleven and thirteen years, perceived teacher unfairness was positively correlated with bullying behaviors. In contrast, analyzing data from 415 elementary students in Turkey, researchers Duy and Yildiz (2014) found that those categorized as bullies had lower levels of school attachment compared to victims and bystanders, but they did not find any significant effect for attachment to teachers in particular.

Others have studied the influence of commitment to school, such as the degree to which students invest in school as a means to success. Ünal and Çukur (2011) found a significant negative association between delinquency (defined broadly) and school commitment (e.g., "school is helping me to be ready for my future") among a large random sample of high school students in Turkey. Pecjak and Pirc (2017) similarly found a connection between lower commitment to school and chronic bullying among a sample of 414 primary and secondary school students in Slovenia. In a review of literature on cyberbullying, Cesaroni, Downing, and Alvi (2012) noted that "studies that have examined predictors of (self-reported) cyber-bullying seem to share a consistent set of variables that include . . . low school commitment" (207).

As noted above, studies also employ composite measures that capture a general sense of the student's school bond, including a sense of school connectedness, perceptions of a positive or harmonious school climate, and feelings of belongingness. These constructs are usually measured across several dimensions. In a robust analysis of survey data from over two hundred thousand students in forty countries, Harel-Fisch et al. (2011) measured school perception based on academic achievement, student social relationships, teacher-student relations, rules and regulations, and general school perceptions. They found that "negative perceptions of school experience were strongly and consistently associated with bullying, with being a victim of bullying and being a bully-victim," noting that "this finding is consistent with research showing the centrality of school 'connectedness' and school 'bonding' as shown through feelings of attachment and commitment to school" (646). These researchers also categorized survey respondents as bullies, victims, and bully-victims and noted marked differences in which dimensions of school perceptions mattered for which group. They noted that student peer relationships were significantly related to victimization, but perpetration was more significantly related to teacher-student relationships as well as rules and regulations. They found that "being a bully-victim was associated with negative school perceptions in both the areas associated for bullies . . . and those associated with victims. . . . As such, it appears that being a bully-victim may be associated with the most negative school experience" (647).

Aldridge, McChesney, and Afari (2018) found a significant negative association between school connectedness and both bullying victimization and student delinquency among a sample of high school students in Australia. Lee and Wong (2009) similarly found that "students' experience of harmony in school is one of the important predictors of bullying behavior" (229) among 778 randomly selected students in Hong Kong. Finally, Vitoroulis and Georgiades (2017) found that among a sample of thirteen hundred grade five-to-eight students across thirty-six schools in Hamilton, Ontario, Canada, an "increased sense of school belongingness was associated with decreased odds of bullying involvement" (149) for immigrant and nonimmigrant students alike. These findings, along with the findings of the other studies described above (and in chapter 4), suggest that the relationship between school bonds and bullying behavior is not limited to US contexts or to particular groups of students.

One interesting caveat regarding the relationship between school bonding and bullying is the influence of involvement in school activities. In three studies of Chinese students, Chan and colleagues found that involvement increased the level of bullying perpetration and victimization as well as nonviolent and violent offending (Chan and Chui 2013, 2015; Chan and Wong 2015). While we recognize that this is only one set of studies conducted by the same lead researcher with the same dataset, it does point to a dynamic that may be at play in school contexts. Specifically, Hirschi's conception of involvement in school, which suggests that involvement in prosocial activities will reduce the likelihood of time spent on antisocial activities, conflicts with findings from tests of lifestyle/routine activity theories (as well as some subcultural theories discussed in chapter 4), which suggest that involvement in some school-based activities increases the likelihood of exposure to bullying.

LOW SELF-CONTROL AND BULLYING

Gottfredson and Hirschi's low self-control theory has garnered quite a bit of attention in relation to bullying, particularly among those interested in cyberbullying perpetration. Most tests of low self-control employ a similar measurement scale, originally developed by Grasmick et al. (1993). For instance, Holt, Bossler, and May (2012) used the Grasmick et al. (1993) scale in their study of cyberdeviance among 435 middle and high school students in central Kentucky, US. They found "low self-control was able to predict simple forms of cyberdeviance, like . . . harassing others online, as well as cybercrimes that require some knowledge of computer technology" (391). Similarly, Lianos and McGrath (2018) found that low self-control was related to cyberbullying perpetration among the 320 internet-active young adults they surveyed for their study. Chui and Chan (2015) found the same to be true among male students in Macau, noting that even after "controlling for participants' demographics, their risk-seeking behavior, self-centeredness, and volatile temper, as indicators for low-self-control, are found to have significant effects on their bullying perpetration" (1751). Numerous studies have been conducted in South Korea testing the applicability of low self-control to bullying behaviors, finding significant effects for online harassment (Baek, Losavio, and Higgins 2016; Choi, Lee, and Lee 2017; Lee 2018) and both traditional and online bullying (Kwak and Oh 2017; Lee 2010). It is worth noting, however, that while in their longitudinal analysis of data from 655 Korean youth, Moon, Hwang, and McCluskey (2011) found a significant relationship between low self-control and bullying in their bivariate analysis, but when they tested this relationship in a multivariate analysis that included constructs from other criminological theories, the relationship between low self-control and bullying disappeared. With this contradictory evidence in mind, there does appear to be some significant impact of low self-control on bullying behaviors across cultures, lending support to Gottfredson and Hirschi's claim that this theory can serve as a general theory.

CONTROL THEORIES AND VICTIMIZATION

Although control theories are not theories of victimization, researchers have found some evidence that breakdowns in an individual's social bond and an individual's low self-control are linked to increased likelihood of bullying victimization. For instance, Popp and Peguero (2012) found a negative association between school bonds (measured in terms of attachment, commitment, and beliefs) and school-based victimization. Similarly, Cho and Wooldredge (2018b) found that attachment to peers and between teachers and students was a protective factor for victimization among US students, as did Cecen-Celik and Keith (2016). Eliot et al. (2010) offered one potential explanation for these dynamics, suggesting "students who perceive their teachers as caring, respectful, and interested in them were more likely to assert that they would tell a teacher when they themselves or a classmate were being bullied" (546). It is not only school-based bonds that seem to have an influence on bullying victimization. Healy, Sanders, and Iyer (2015) found that both poor peer relationships and certain parenting practices were more common among children who experienced bullying at school, as did Mitsopoulou and Giovazolias (2013), at least in terms of parenting styles. Finally, in a series of studies analyzing data from the Korean Youth Panel Survey, Cho (2017b) and Cho and Wooldredge (2018a, 2018b) found a significant relationship between low self-control and victimization, even when controlling for factors related to lifestyle theory and routine activity theory. These findings support the importance of considering multiple factors from seemingly disparate theories when formulating a more complete picture of a phenomenon, an issue we discuss in more detail in chapter 7 and our overview of social-ecological approaches to school bullying.

SOCIAL REACTION/LABELING THEORIES

Social reaction, or labeling, theories generally focus on the process through which individuals are labeled and how society's formal imposition of these labels is a significant factor in determining future behavior. Frank Tannenbaum's (1938) work related to the labeling of youth as delinquent represents an early articulation of these types of theories. Tannenbaum's concept of **tagging** was used to explain what happens to individuals after being arrested, convicted, and sentenced. Tannenbaum suggested that once tagged, an individual experiences societal reactions that reinforce their identity as a delinquent. Society shifts from condemning the delinquent behavior to condemning the individual as a delinquent or bad person.

Edwin Lemert (1951) similarly focused on the effects of formal labeling. Lemert extended labeling theory by introducing two core concepts: primary and secondary deviance. Primary deviance refers to the initial or original deviant act, which may be caused by a variety of factors that occur in the context of a noncriminal self-image, and that leads to a societal response. Secondary deviance refers to subsequent acts resulting from official labeling and in the context of a criminal self-concept. Erving Goffman (1963) extended the notion of labeling to include the stigma associated with those who are discredited and labeled as something other than "normal." Goffman noted that individuals who are stigmatized engender negative reactions from others due to their stigmatized status. It is important to note that like other social reaction theorists, Goffman is describing the construction of individuals as stigmatized, not the individuals themselves. In other words, the stigma and the stigmatized are social constructions that result from often implicit expectations for and constructions of "normality" in a given social context.

Although not self-described as a criminologist (see Martin, Mutchnick, and Austin 1990), the most well-known contributor to criminological labeling theory is Howard Becker (1963). Similar to earlier articulations of labeling theory, Becker's argument was that deviance is a product of social construction, not a quality of the individual or even the deviant act itself. Both deviance and the deviant person are constructed by society through the process of formal responses to proscribed behaviors. Various social groups put forth efforts to define what is good or right behavior and have their definitions embodied in law, a process Becker refers to as the **moral enterprise**. Becker recognized that most deviance is transitory in nature, meaning that it is not likely to occur again. However, those who are labeled as deviant are significantly blocked from opportunities for conforming behavior. As an individual's access to opportunities for conforming behavior are cut off, they experience a push toward deviant opportunities and then seek out the acquisition of techniques necessary to successfully engage in further deviant behavior. This leads to the development of a deviant identity or self-concept and eventual membership in a deviant subgroup. Becker created a typology of deviants that included the **pure deviant**, the **falsely accused deviant**, and the **secret deviant**. Becker also introduced the notion of a **master status**, which represents the central traits through which an individual is identified by others. Once applied, society often engages in the process of **retrospective interpretation**, by which evidence from an individual's past is selectively emphasized in order to (re)construct them to fit their master status or label. As we will see in the discussion below, when young people in schools are labeled as "bullies," they may internalize their label and engage in secondary deviance, such as continued or escalating bullying or other forms of antisocial behavior.

Tests of labeling and its relationship to bullying perpetration are limited. In fact, we were unable to identify any studies that applied labeling as an explicit explanatory variable for bullying perpetration in our search of relevant literature. However, researchers have applied labeling as an analytic tool for understanding some aspects of bullying or analogous behaviors. For instance, Kramer (2015) employed labeling in critique of antibullying legislation at the state level, with a specific focus on New Jersey's Anti-Bullying Bill of Rights Act. Kramer (2015, 284) cited several studies that have applied labeling to explain both school-based and non-school-based phenomena and support the notion that both direct and perceived labeling have short- and long-term effects on the behavior and well-being of those labeled. Kramer (2015) noted the definition of bullying in the New Jersey statute, which includes single incidents of behavior, and the degree to which it applied the bully label indefinitely would need to change so as to reduce the negative impact of the bully label. Bansel et al. (2009) similarly advocated that schools move away from the labeling of bully and victim and toward an understanding of how school practices (including discipline) work to reinforce bullying as a mechanism of power.

Others have applied labeling to more specific behaviors that are, at least to some degree, analogous to bullying or cyberbullying. Voisin and Hong (2012) noted that "researchers posit that youth identified as aggressive may believe that aggressive acts enhance their reputation or self-image . . . which further reinforces their use of bullying behaviors" (485–86). Payne, Hawkins, and Xin (2019) employed labeling as an analytic lens for understanding cyber offending. Through content analysis of US Department of Justice (DOJ) press releases related to 119 cybercrime cases, they found that labeling principles were useful to understanding differences in how cybercrimes are defined and how they are prosecuted. Their analysis suggested that cybercrime may be labeled/defined as a male phenomenon, resulting in differential participation in cyber offending by females (females not seeing themselves as cybercriminals and therefore not participating in such behaviors) and differential patterns of punishment (e.g., more severe punishment for females who engage in cyber offending due to having violated gendered norms or labels related to such behavior). While not a direct parallel to traditional or even cyber bullying, this study suggests that the extent to which individuals, groups, and behaviors are differentially labeled/defined has implications for official responses and subsequent perpetration.

Quite a bit of research has assessed the degree to which the stigmatizing effects of labeling increase the likelihood of bullying victimization. As Thornberg (2015a) pointed out, "being negatively labeled as different becomes the dominant feature of the victim's social identity at school" (311; see also Thornberg 2018). Speaking to the influence of stigma on bullying victimization, Huggins (2016) similarly pointed out, "labeling identifies individuals and groups as 'other' and limits their access to power or resources. If persons or groups cannot be completely removed from access, they are depersonalized, or made invisible, and a powerless status is imposed on them" (180). This powerless status may increase the likelihood of bullying victimization because victimization occurs within a real or perceived power differential between the bully and the victim. In their interviews with fourteen adults who dropped out of school as children and had experiences as bully-victims, Haney, Thomas, and Vaugh (2011) also made note of the influence of a felt sense of invisibility and its relationship to the internalization of pejorative labels such as dumb, unlovable, inconvenient, or bad (61). As we point out in several other places in this book, being viewed as different or as having deviated from the established norms of the school or social group can place youth at risk for bullying victimization (see also Cohen and Brooks 2014).

Researchers have also analyzed the influence of constructs that align with labeling. For instance, there is quite a bit of research analyzing the influence of shame in bullying contexts. Shame is related to labeling in that it serves as one mechanism through which the bully label may be internalized and result in subsequent (secondary) bullying. Once a child is labeled, the degree to which they internalize the label of bully may be at least partially determined by the degree to which they experience shame and the way in which the shame they experience is handled. Jennifer and Cowie (2012) presented ten-to-eleven-year-olds in London with pictorial vignettes that depicted bullying events and asked them how they might have felt if they were one of the individuals depicted. They found that "shame was most commonly attributed to self in the role of bully, typically in terms of the bullying behaviours perpetrated against the victim. A number of participants mentioned that they would feel ashamed after the event" (235).

While Jennifer and Cowie (2012) did not address the impact of this felt sense of shame, others have. For instance, in an application of **reintegrative shaming theory** (see Braithwaite 1989), Lee and Kavanaugh (2015) found that "when the shaming in the context of schooling is conceived as reintegrative rather than stigmatizing, students are less likely to demonstrate antisocial attitude" (513). Pontzer (2010) also applied reintegrative shaming theory to bullying, with a focus on parenting practices as opposed to school discipline responses. Pontzer applied the notion of **parental stigmatization**, which includes abuse, neglect, and hostility, arguing that by treating a child as antisocial, parents "condition the child to self-conceptualize as antisocial" (261). Pontzer (2010) found among a sample of 527 university students that "exposure to parental stigmatization during childhood was positively associated with being a bully" (271). In a longitudinal analysis of data from 335 Australian children, Ahmed and Braithwaite (2012) were able to track movement over time between bullying roles (i.e., bully, victim, bully-victim, nonbully-nonvictim, and residual conflict groups). They noted that "bullies who became nonbully-nonvictims were distinctive in being able to manage shame more adaptively" (94).

These studies suggest that the manner in which those who bully are labeled and the degree to which they internalize and act upon that label may depend on their emotional response. This also suggests that the deleterious effects of the bully label can be offset by approaches that admonish the behavior without admonishing the individual, an important distinction implied by labeling theory. The results of a study by Garandeau et al. (2016) support this idea. These researchers randomly assigned schools to respond to bullying through either a confrontational approach that involved blaming the bully and condemning the behavior or a nonconfrontational approach that involved attempts to make them feel empathy for the victim. They found that it was particularly important to "distinguish between condemning the behavior and blaming the child. While condemning the behavior yields desirable effects, blaming the child does not" (1041). As one principal noted, "feeling shamed, we seek to hide, bury our face in our hands, crawl in a hole and disappear, causing harm to the self and to others. In such moments, we internalize the judgments of others and direct blame and rage at ourselves" (Frank 2013, 179). Taken together, the studies discussed in this section suggest that labeling of an individual as a bully may result in feelings of shame, which, if not framed in the context of care and reintegration or done in a supportive environment, can result in the internalization of the label and additional bullying perpetration as a form of living up to the label or as a means to reestablish a sense of power and self-worth.

POLICY IMPLICATIONS OF SOCIAL PROCESS THEORIES

Social process theories all take as their starting point the idea that individuals are inseparable from their social contexts and relationships, including the school, peers, and family. One approach to bullying prevention that aligns with the implications of social process theories is Positive Behavioral Interventions & Support (PBIS) programs. PBIS "trains teachers, school staff, and administrators to model, provide practice opportunities for, and reward and correct children in learning specific actions for stopping bullying behaviors" (Letendre, Ostrander, and Mickens 2016, 239). In their discussion of these programs, Letendre, Ostrander, and Mickens (2016) noted that the focus is placed on student behaviors, not the labels of bully and victim, and that "participants discuss, model, and practice effective responses for seeking assistance from others, accessing social support, and avoiding situations where bullying might occur" (239). A number of rigorous evaluation studies, including some randomized control trials, have found significant positive effects of these types of programs (see Good, McIntosh, and Gietz 2011).

The success of these programs may be partially the result of how they change the overall culture of a school in ways that (1) make it more conducive to the learning of prosocial behaviors, norms, and definitions; (2) increase the likelihood of informal social control through bystander intervention; and (3) reduce labeling. For instance, Ferráns and Selman (2014) noted that "rules of the culture [that] create safe, ordered, caring, and empowering environments can help adolescents fulfill their personal needs for safety, connection, and power and increase the chances that witnesses will take a stand against bullying and peer aggression" (185). Similarly, Jenkins and Fredrick (2017) found a "significant and positive relation between social capital and prosocial bystander behavior" (766). Their notion of social capital included peer support, teacher support, and social skills, all of which are aspects of PBIS. Finally, these types of programs may also increase the likelihood that witnesses and victims will report bullying incidents to adults in the school.

SIX

Critical Criminology and Restorative Justice

This chapter explores how bullying is constructed, how it presents itself differently among social identity groups, and how prevention and enforcement policies are sometimes ineffective or even counterproductive. The chapter describes and applies concepts of **critical criminology**, which represents not a single theory or set of theories, but a multitude of perspectives that attempt to center inequality, social structure, power, and control in their analysis. We discuss a range of theories generally framed as part of critical criminology, with a specific focus on cultural theories, feminist and queer theories, critical race theory, and peacemaking and restorative justice.

Critical criminology expands the often-ignored "imbalance of power" element away from the dyad emphasized by Olweus (1993) to include meso- and macro-level power differentials, in line with Alvi, Downing, and Cesaroni's (2015) suggestion that in relation to cyberbullying, researchers "need to refocus attention on what matters, including the underlying issues of racism, sexism, homophobia, derision of physical and mental abilities, sexual orientation, poverty, inequality, social exclusion and the like" (400). Thus, bullying is a social justice issue. Bullying functions as a form of oppression in society, in that it "may be considered the exercise of perceived authority or superiority in a cruel and unjust manner" (Polanin and Vera 2013, 305). As Polanin and Vera suggested, "without having to be directly taught messages of intolerance . . . children learn, by both participating in and witnessing bullying, that certain groups in society possess power based on inherent characteristics (e.g., nationality, race, ethnicity, etc.)" and "these groups can utilize their power to create physical and psychological threats towards those who do not have power" (305).

Thornberg's (2015a) ethnographic fieldwork examining six bullying cases in four classrooms in Sweden supports this idea. Thornberg's research "revealed complex interactional patterns creating stigma processes in which bullying was considered the natural thing to do, and was justified by dehumanizing and blaming the victim," while at the same time functioning "as a self-serving and socially inclusive ritual for the bullies, in which they co-constructed the 'normal us'" (318). These processes lead some members of school communities to be more vulnerable to bullying victimization. For instance, Farmer et al. (2015) found that "youth with disabilities are at greater risk for peer victimization because they may be considered to be different from their peers and so, may be viewed as outsiders to the peer group" (265; see also Dunn, Clark, and Pearlman 2017).

Moreover, these forms of exclusion that emerge at the classroom or individual level are influenced by macro forces such as economic inequality and cultural individualism. For example, Menzer and Torney-Purta (2012) conducted secondary analysis of data from fifteen different countries to assess the influence of individualism and socioeconomic diversity on rates of bullying. They found that Australia reported the highest levels of bullying and violence and also the highest level of individualism and second-most socioeconomically diverse schools. They concluded that their findings "corroborate previous findings that inequality among students is related to violence" (2012, 1291), a concept discussed in chapter 4. Similarly, cultural dynamics of power may work to construct status hierarchies within classrooms, which, in turn, serve to reinforce bullying. For instance, in their longitudinal analysis of data from 11,296 eighth- and ninth-grade students from seventy-one schools, Garandeau, Lee, and Salmivalli (2014) found that "higher levels of classroom status hierarchy were concurrently associated with higher levels of bullying at the end of the school year" (1123).

CULTURAL CRIMINOLOGY

Cultural criminology is difficult to capture in a single definitional statement. Cultural criminologists critique the sterile and abstract nature of mainstream criminology, noting that criminologists should "seek to unearth and capture the phenomenology of social life ... its anger and adrenaline, its pleasure and panic, its excitement and humiliation, its desperation, and its edgework" (Ferrell, Hayward, and Young 2008, 65). As Ferrell (2013) suggested, "cultural criminology ... must explore the situated 'seductions of crime'" (259; see Jack Katz's book *Seductions of Crime* [1988]). In this sense, among other foci, cultural criminologists are interested in uncovering the cultural meanings of everyday interactions and elucidating the emotional content of crime and deviance.

Several studies captured emotional dynamics in relation to bullying, offering an alternative narrative to the prevailing idea that bullying is purely deviant. For example, Kerbs and Jolley (2007) analyzed qualitative survey data from interviews with urban students in grades six through eight in a public middle school in Florida. They found that "a majority of children in [their] study reported enjoyable experiences with school-based violence . . . reporting incidents that were physiologically pleasurable in that they were 'excited,' 'energized,' and 'hyped' by student-on-student victimization" (24). Kerbs and Jolley also found that bystanders reported they "enjoyed their roles as witnesses and members of the observing crowd," concluding that "watching school-based violence is similar to watching violence on television or in the movies" (24). Similarly, in an analysis of students' desires in relation to bullying perpetration, Rigby (2012) proposed the likelihood of bullying increases when "the aggressor sees some entertainment value in putting the target under pressure" and "finds hurting or placing people under pressure pleasurable in itself" (344). Bansel et al. (2009) argued that individuals become "invested in excessive practices that lead to their recognition as a 'bully'" and that their overinvestment in these practices "may be linked to the pleasures of, and capacities for, power, the necessity of belonging and the possibility of leadership, the pleasure of wielding of control, and the desire to engage in the (sometimes violent and dangerous) normative regulation of others" (67).

FEMINIST AND QUEER THEORIES

While we write here about **feminist theory** in general, there are in fact multiple feminist theories that have made an impact in criminology, including liberal, socialist, Marxist, radical, and postmodern. Each of these feminisms differs in terms of its definition of, and solutions to, gender inequality and oppression. Similarly, what is loosely understood as **queer criminology** is really a complex array of critical perspectives that "share a common attitude of pushing against orthodox knowledges, politics, and ways of thinking— whether regarding crime and justice matters, or sexuality and gender issues" (Ball 2014, 22; see also Woods 2014).

As we discussed in chapter 1, large studies and meta-analyses have found sex-based differences in bullying victimization, including that girls are more likely to be victims of cyber, relational, and verbal forms of bullying, while boys are more likely to be victims of physical bullying (see Waasdorp and Bradshaw 2015). Research also suggests that there are gender differences in the correlates of bullying. In their longitudinal analysis of data from 1,222 students who participated in a school-based law-related education program, Carbone-Lopez, Esbensen, and Brick (2010) found that boys' and girls' experiences of "repeated indirect bullying victimization" (such as teasing) are influenced by different factors. For example, age and race influenced boys' risk of victimization but not girls', while delinquent involvement had "a greater impact on girls' likelihood of repeated indirect bullying" than boys' (341). Some researchers have also found links between gender and homophobic bullying and other forms of gender violence. Espelage et al. (2015) found support for the bully-sexual violence pathway theory, "which posits that adolescent bullies who also participate in homophobic name-calling towards peers are more likely to perpetrate sexual harassment over time" (2541). These researchers found that among their sample of 979 students from four middle schools in Illinois, "boys who reported bully perpetration at Time 1 were more likely to report [perpetration of] sexual harassment measured 2 years later" and that "boys who reported high levels of bullying behaviors and also reported concurrent high levels of homophobic teasing were more likely to report [perpetration of] sexual harassment over time" (2554). This points to the interrelationships between gender and sexuality and how bullying serves as one mechanism through which **heteromasculine gender norms** are replicated and reinforced.

Quantitative research has shown LGBTQ youth experience particularly high rates of bullying victimization (see Hall 2017; O'Malley Olsen et al. 2014). Analyzing data from 1,758 students collected through the Illinois Youth Risk Behavior Survey (YRBS) in 2009, Gayles and Garofalo (2012, S27) found that after controlling for gender, race, and geography, LGB youth were more than two times as likely to be bullied in school than their non-LGB peers. Several qualitative studies have also found that sexual orientation was an important factor in terms of increased vulnerability for cyberbullying victimization (see Reason, Boyd and Reason 2016; Varjas et al. 2013).

There is also research indicating that LGBT youth experience heightened negative impacts in relation to bullying victimization in school. Dunn, Clark, and Pearlman (2017) found that "among students who were bullied, sexual minority girls reported the highest odds of recent depression and suicidal ideation" and that "sexual minority boys who were bullied at school and/or electronically bullied were more likely to seriously consider attempting suicide . . . when compared with their heterosexual counterparts" (3511). They noted the need to better understand "how the social constructs of masculinity and femininity contribute to bullying victimization" (3510). Roberts et al. (2013) similarly found that abuse and bullying victimization accounted for approximately half the increased prevalence of depressive symptoms among both nonconforming and conforming youth in their national sample of 10,655 youth aged twelve to thirty years. Research also suggests that these negative effects follow LGBT individuals throughout life. Among their sample of 594 LGBT-identified adults, Greene, Britton, and Fitts (2014) found that "victimization of LGBT persons in school significantly contributed to the prediction of continued bullying victimization of LGBT adults over and above that accounted for by demographic characteristics" (413).

While it is important to keep in mind the very real and damaging short- and long-term impacts of gender- and sexuality-based bullying victimization, the focus of critical criminological theories is the larger social structures and dynamics of power that make particular individuals more or less vulnerable. In other words, feminist and queer theories, while centering gender and sexuality, do so with an eye toward the ways in which gendered and sexualized identities and bodies are constructed and how systems of power are implicated in these constructions.

Bullying and the Social Construction of Gender

In their analysis of the construction of bullying as a social problem, Cohen and Brooks (2014) noted that bullying serves as one mechanism through which essentialist notions of gender are reinforced by youth and the boundaries of heteronormativity are policed by peers (e.g., bullying) and institutions (e.g., the criminalization of bullying). Payne and Smith (2013) similarly suggested "that a majority of peer-to-peer aggression in U.S. public schools is some form of *gender policing*" and that "bullying must be redefined to account for relationships between peer targeting and structural inequalities" (1; emphasis in original). They went on to suggest that "the majority of bullying research has been 'gender-blind'—failing to look at the sociocultural context of bullying and the ways in which many bullying behaviors are rooted in reinforcing the 'rules' for 'appropriate' gender behavior" (20–21).

More recently, in their qualitative analysis of gendered bullying through a critical feminist lens, Christensen and Wright (2018) found that the parents they interviewed "recognize [gendered] bullying in terms that are in alignment with how critical feminist theory contends that hegemonic gender norms are maintained through bullying behaviors" (523). They also found that parents relied on stereotypical patriarchal gender norms when offering advice to their children on how to respond to bullying, such that boys were to respond by fighting back, while girls were expected to avoid conflict or show empathy. Relatedly, in interviews with ten women regarding their recollections of their responses to bullying victimization, Bouchard et al. (2018) found that "women's resistance was constrained and determined by . . . practices that dictate gender expectations of how girls can appropriately respond to bullying without being labeled as a gender deviant" (1154). These researchers concluded, "gender expectations for how girls ought to respond were in contrast to dominant constructions of resistance that privilege overt resistance or 'standing up,' leaving women in a double-bind when negotiating their resistance" (1154). In other words, girls employed relational aggression in retaliation for their own bullying victimization so as to both "deny their victimized status while complying with gendered expectations" (1154), including the expectation that relational aggression/bullying is appropriate, or at least normative, for girls.

Researchers have pointed to other double standards faced by girls in relation to bullying. In their longitudinal analysis of data from multiple waves of the Rhode Island version of the YRBS, Dunn, Clark, and Pearlman (2017) found that "heterosexual girls who were sexually active were significantly more likely to report being bullied whereas a nonsignificant relationship existed for their male, heterosexual counterparts" (3509). These researchers attributed this difference to the sexual double standard that women and girls are subjected to in a patriarchal society. While heterosexual boys are rewarded for their promiscuity, "sexually active heterosexual girls are often subject to relationship bullying, such as malicious rumors and innuendos, for appearing too 'sexually forward' or promiscuous" (3510). Moreover, Lehman (2017) examined a national sample of 8,377 students from 750 public and private schools across the United States, finding a double standard wherein "female students have reported being bullied in various ways in connection with pro-equality attitudes," while male students are rewarded for those attitudes (460).

Cohen and Brooks (2014) traced the development of the "mean girls" construction through popular discourse beginning in the 1990s, noting that "as time progressed, the mean girls construction became an accepted reality . . . suggesting inherent differences between girls' and boys' performances of bullying" (100–101). Crooks (2016) similarly noted that "the preoccupation with relational aggression beginning in the 1990s was built on a paternalistic historical framework of female violence that left female relational aggression under-researched and the assumption that females were uniquely conniving and manipulative unchallenged" (66). Through their reading of teacher resource materials within a feminist framework employing critical discourse analytic techniques, Bethune and Gonick (2017) argued that "the concept of mean girls is tied to a discursive legacy of ideas shaping and constructing our understandings of femininity, girlhood, and women's relationships to each other" (400). They went on to make note of a particular contradiction:

> On the one hand, [resource materials] reference the "mean girl" as a cultural symbol of social instability around changing norms of femininity. On the other hand, the treatment and resolution of the mean girl problem are almost always articulated in individualized and individualizing terms rather than social ones. (401)

For Bethune and Gonick, this is an extension of a "political, social, and educational climate increasingly characterized by neo-liberal values and beliefs, with an emphasis on individualism, personal responsibility, and choice" (401). Tracing the reemergence of the "mean girl" discourse in the scholarship of cyberbullying, Ging and O'Higgins Norman (2016) found suggestions that "girls, because of their 'natural' proclivity for indirect aggression, are more attracted to the 'indirect' nature of cyber conflict" (808). They go on to argue, "such biodeterminist theories of gender ignore the wider social and cultural contexts that play such a significant role in shaping young people's identities, behaviors, and relationships" (808).

Not only do feminist researchers challenge the construction of the "mean girl" as essentialist—by making relational bullying somehow inherent to femininity and femaleness—they also challenge the ways in which the "mean girl" discourse situates girls' use of physical bullying/aggression as abnormal and abhorrent. For instance, Barron and Lacombe (2005) suggested that "through distortion, exaggeration and statistical manipulation of data, as well as expert evidence, the media was able to construct a new breed of female, the Nasty Girl, who has become one of our current folk devils" (58). Framing the notion of the so-called "nasty girl" as a moral panic, Barron and Lacombe noted that media attention to female violence does not attend to the "considerable impact of structural factors, including institutional racism, and economic and social inequality in the life of young female offenders and their victims" (58). In addition, and in alignment with Cohen and Brooks (2014), Barron and Lacombe (2005) suggested, "the moral panic over the statistically insignificant Nasty Girl is a projection of a desire to retrieve a patriarchal social order characterized by gender conformity" (65).

Several feminist researchers have also approached their critique of the "mean girl" discourse from an intersectional lens, with a particular focus on the ways in which the "mean girl" is racialized. For instance, Crooks (2016) noted, "the moral panic around the 'mean girl' in mass media really concerns middle-class white girls who fit normative definitions of femininity" (67). Similarly, Bethune and Gonick (2017) noted that images in antibullying teacher resource materials "reveal the discourse of girls' aggression for the highly classed and racialized discourse it is" (397). Referencing other feminist scholars, Bethune and Gonick also noted, "while 'meanness' is constructed as normative of middle-class repressive and pathological femininity, girl violence is marked as lower class and racialized, and so deviant it transgresses all norms of femininity" (397).

Bullying and the Social Construction of Sexualities

Cohen and Brooks (2014) identified various problematic ways that LGBT youth are constructed in the popular discourse of bullying, including as suffering and suicidal, fragile, and both resilient and nonresilient. Each of these constructions serves to individualize the problem and place, at least to some extent, the responsibility for victimization on the victims themselves. Take, for instance, the construction of LGBT victims of bullying as resilient, a construction that, at least on its face, seems positive. In their qualitative study of bullying and resilience in a neoliberal framework, however, Sims-Schouten and Edwards (2018) noted how "notions of 'resilience' are used to an extent to place responsibility of dealing with bullying, and further mental health and well-being implications ... with the young person" who is victimized (1397). In a critique of dominant approaches to addressing homophobic bullying, Monk (2011) suggested, "if homophobic bullying is caused by homophobic bullies, [and] consequently is individualized, what gets overlooked are structural forms of homophobia" (196). Ullman (2018) made a similar point, noting that "framing trans/gender-diverse inclusivity as an anti-bullying initiative can provide a safe context for educators' work" to support students, but "an agenda of protection does little to challenge the power dynamics within a hetero/cisnormative positioning of who is othered/victimized/

pathologized and who is in a position to do the protecting" (506). Ullman interviewed thirty-one school staff members from nine public and independent schools located in the New York City metro region as part of a study of policies in support of gender and sexuality diversity (GSD) inclusivity and found that "the bullying discourse may constrain ... educators' curricular 'translation' of GSD-inclusive policies into concrete actions, since resource documents and associated professional development activities may fail to disrupt the hetero/cisnormative gender climate which sits at the heart of social marginalization" (507).

This conclusion may be particularly important from the perspective of critical criminologists, given their argument that failure to address meso-level homophobic norms will lead to continued homophobic bullying. For example, in a study of 863 students in grades nine to thirteen from forty-nine classes in ten Italian public high schools, Prati (2012) found "student observations of peer aggression toward perceived gay males exhibited by classmates was [sic] associated with class homophobic attitudes that, in turn, were related to self-reported homophobic aggression toward perceived gay males" (422). Similarly, Orue and Calvete (2018) conducted a longitudinal analysis of the relationship between homophobic attitudes and exposure to homophobic aggression among 723 adolescents in four educational centers in northern Spain. These researchers found "reciprocal longitudinal relations between homophobic attitudes and homophobic bullying" (101). They also found sex differences, noting for boys, homophobic attitudes predicted homophobic bullying, while for girls the perpetration of homophobic bullying predicted the adoption of homophobic attitudes. They concluded that "exposure to homophobic bullying at school, exposure to homophobic language at home, and social interaction with individuals who identify as LGBT all play a role in the prediction of homophobic attitudes and bullying" (100). Franklin (2013) critiqued legal responses to antigay harassment cases and similarly argued, "it appears that children construct a culture in which the victimized child becomes fair game for anyone who chooses to bully him or her, and when one culprit is punished, another steps up in his or her place" (175).

In their critique of research that focuses on school climate in relation to LGBTQ bullying, Payne and Smith (2013) noted, "the link between climate and anti-bullying divorces climate from culture [and] continues the limited focus on visible signs of a deeper cultural problem" (13). They go on to suggest, "bullying behaviors are not anti-social but rather highly social acts deeply entrenched in the perpetuation of cultural norms and values related to hetero-gender, sex, and sexuality" (21). Payne and Smith, like other queer and critical theorists, concern themselves with the ways in which the "cultural privileging of heterosexuality and gender normativity goes unquestioned, LGBTQ marginalization is reproduced and re-entrenched in new ways, and schools avoid responsibility for complicity in LGBTQ harassment" (1).

CRITICAL RACE THEORY

Critical race theory emerged as both an extension and critique of critical legal studies (Russell 1999). In particular, critical race theorists were concerned with the lack of attention that critical legal studies paid to the role of race in the US legal system. Accordingly, critical race theory centers race and the analysis of how systems maintain white supremacy and the subordination of people of color (see Crenshaw et al. 1995). While early critical race theory focused on African American experiences of racial oppression, more recent developments include analyses of whiteness and a broader range of racial and ethnic identities, including Latinx, Asian, and Indigenous (Russell 1999).

Bajaj, Ghaffar-Kucher, and Desai (2016) employed critical race theory to "explore the intersections of racism, xenophobia, and bullying" among South Asian American youth in US schools (483). They noted that "the normalization of xenophobic bullying is based on ideas about which bodies are seen as fully human and which bodies are seen as subhuman" (493). Similar to feminist and queer theorists, critical race theorists offer a critique of mainstream research on bullying. After finding repeated examples of "teachers espousing xenophobic views of South Asian American youth" (491), Bajaj, Ghaffar-Kucher, and Desai (2016) made the argument that "conventional bullying literature provides insufficient frames for analysis of the sometimes-harmful attitudes and roles of teachers in xenophobic bullying incidents and for tracing such attitudes back to larger discourses, media narratives, and discriminatory policies" (500). By employing critical race theory, Bajaj, Ghaffar-Kucher, and Desai identified forms of **xenophobic bullying** that are not captured by conventional studies of bullying, including attacks on families and communities grounded in racial and ethnic threats, such as being told to "go back where you came from," property damage to places of worship, and ridicule regarding foods students eat. They traced these forms of xenophobic bullying to "colonial discourses that have been exacerbated in the post-9/11 period, when anyone perceived to be Muslim is seen as a threat to security" (490).

Vitoroulis and Georgiades (2017) analyzed data from a random sample of 1,449 students across thirty-six schools in Hamilton, Ontario, Canada, in order to assess relationships between school immigrant concentration, perceived teacher support for cultural diversity and interethnic relationships, sense of belongingness, generational status, and bullying perpetration and victimization. They noted that prior research had indicated greater prevalence of ethnic/racial bullying victimization among visible minority students. Among their study sample, Vitoroulis and Georgiades (2017) found that in schools with higher concentrations of immigrant students, immigrant students experienced less bullying victimization and were less involved in bullying perpetration, suggesting that "the presence of peers who share similar characteristics (e.g., immigrant background) in schools may provide increased opportunities for positive peer relationships and social support networks that can protect students against bullying victimization" (148) and "a higher representation of immigrant students in schools may be associated with positive characteristics associated with immigrant status that may contribute to lower levels of bullying and aggression" (149). Interestingly, Vitoroulis and Georgiades (2017) also found that "perceived teacher support for cultural diversity was associated with decreased odds for [ethnic/racial] victimization" (149). This is in alignment with Bajaj, Ghaffar-Kucher, and Desai's (2016) finding that xenophobia among teachers can lead to increased bullying of Muslim students.

Sulkowski et al. (2014) analyzed data from 2,929 youth who participated in the Youth Voice Project and had reported being victimized two or more times per month. They found that youth who had immigrated within two years of the study "were more likely to report being victimized because of their race, religion, and family income when compared to their non-immigrant peers" (659–60). Sulkowski et al. linked these types of bullying to the social construction of the immigrant identity, which, at least in the United States, is highly racialized and classed, and draws on anti-Muslim tropes. These researchers also found that "youth from immigrant families were more likely to report that every employed response was less effective or more likely to result in things 'getting worse' for them" (661), suggesting that structures put in place in their schools are failing to provide a safe environment, or in some cases are making the experiences of immigrant youth worse.

Similar to the ways feminist and queer theorists suggest that bullying is employed as a mechanism through which the boundaries of heteromasculine norms are policed, critical race theorists argue that bullying also serves as a mechanism through which racial stereotypes are constructed and reinforced.

Some research supports this claim. For instance, Peguero and Williams (2013) analyzed a subsample of 10,440 cases from the 2002 Educational Longitudinal Study to assess the degree to which racial and ethnic stereotypes influence the likelihood of bullying victimization. They found that "Black/African American and Latino American youth, who are in families with higher SES [socioeconomic status], identify more incidences of bullying" (556). They note that this was not true for Asian American and white American students, suggesting that "family SES is a potential risk factor for bullying victimization among youth from stereotypical economically disadvantaged backgrounds" (556). Peguero and Williams (2013) also found that "interscholastic sports participation places Latino American and Asian American youth at greater risk for bullying victimization, whereas sports is a potential protective factor for White American and Black/African American youth from being bullied at school" (559). Again, these researchers linked this finding to racial and ethnic stereotypes and the degree to which playing sports either aligned with or violated those stereotypes for a particular racial/ethnic identity group. Peguero and Williams noted similar dynamics were at work in relation to educational success, suggesting "increased educational success and engagement may promote more bullying victimization if students' behaviors or characteristics deviate from certain imposed racial and ethnic stereotypes" (559). It is possible, however, that the influence of violating racial stereotypes may be moderated by school climate. For instance, in their analysis of data from 48,027 students in grades nine to twelve attending 323 high schools in Virginia, Konold et al. (2017) found "a positive school climate holds similar benefits of promoting student engagement and reducing victimization experiences across Black, Hispanic, and White groups" (1289). It is possible that creating a positive school climate could reduce racial stereotyping, thereby reducing the influence of violating stereotypes on likelihood of bullying victimization. Further research is likely needed in this area. Perhaps more important from a critical race theory perspective, however, are the ways in which racial stereotyping leads to disproportionate disciplinary action targeting students of color and members of other racialized groups.

Racial Disproportionality, School Discipline, and the School-to-Prison Pipeline

As was discussed in chapter 2, the application of zero tolerance policies and practices through a deterrence lens seems to be ineffective in reducing bullying.

From a critical race theory perspective, zero tolerance policies and practices grounded in the criminalization of schools also serve to further entrench **racial disproportionality** and contribute to the **school-to-prison pipeline**. As Simon (2007) points out, "the merging of school and penal systems has resulted in speeding the collapse of the progressive project of education and tilting the administration of schools towards a highly authoritarian and mechanistic model" (209). Youth of color are more likely to experience the criminalization of schools than white youth, as illustrated by the fact that over half of the nation's high schools with black and Latino student populations greater than 75 percent of the student body have sworn law enforcement officers (SLEOs; United States Department of Education 2016c), while the presence of SLEOs in predominantly white schools is lower. Moreover, "black youth are 2.2 times as likely to receive a referral to law enforcement or be subject to a school-related arrest compared to white students" (United States Department of Education 2016c, 3).

The intersection of multiple identities compounds the disproportionate application and collateral consequences of exclusionary discipline policies and practices. While boys in general are disproportionately impacted by these policies and practices, boys of color are at particular risk. Similarly, while girls in general are at lower risk for disproportionate application of these policies and practices, girls of color experience higher rates of discipline. In fact, race/ethnicity interacts with almost all other social identities in ways that lead to particularly problematic outcomes for students of color. The internalization of cultural ideologies related to race, gender, economic status, and (dis)ability among school administrators, teachers, parents, and the general public has long influenced the disproportionate application of school disciplinary policies and practices, leading to problematic behavioral and educational outcomes.

The increased criminalization of schools does not appear to be the result of actual increases in victimization, the stated reason for zero tolerance policies grounded in the criminalization of schools. According to the National Center for Education Statistics (NCES; 2016), "through nearly two decades of decline, the rate of nonfatal victimization of 12- to 18-year-old students at school fell from 181 victimizations per 1,000 students in 1992 to 33 per 1,000 students in 2014" (xxxiii). Not unlike the wide discrepancy between rates of crime and incarceration more broadly, the trend toward the criminalization of schools seems to be more the result of exaggerated fears of youth violence than well-thought-out responses to actual disciplinary problems.

The US Department of Education's Office for Civil Rights revised their Civil Rights Data Collection (CRDC) for the 2013–2014 school year to include additional measures of school disciplinary problems and responses (United States Department of Education 2016c). (The 2013–2014 school year was the most recent data available at the time of writing.) The resulting data reveal significant issues related to disproportionate treatment across race/ethnicity, gender, and (dis)ability. The CRDC collected data on out-of-school suspensions and expulsions without educational services, finding that "black preschool children are 3.6 times as likely to be suspended as are white preschool students" (United States Department of Education 2016c, 3). Similarly, "black students are 1.9 times as likely to be expelled from school without educational services as white students" (4). A closer look at these data reveals additional forms of disproportionate treatment across race/ethnicity. While black children represent 19 percent of preschool enrollment, they are 47 percent of preschool children receiving one or more out-of-school suspensions (3). This is in comparison to white children, who represent 41 percent of preschool enrollment but only 28 percent of preschool children who receive one or more out-of-school suspensions (3). These racial/ethnic disparities hold across gender as well. According to the CRDC, 6 percent of all K–12 students were suspended one or more times; however, 18 percent of black boys and 10 percent of black girls were suspended one or more times, while only 5 percent of white boys and 2 percent of white girls were (3).

Bullying researchers have pointed to the role of racial bias and fear in explaining the disproportionate impact of school disciplinary policies and practices. In their study of race, urbanicity, and bullying involvement, Goldweber, Waasdorp, and Bradshaw (2013) noted that their finding of increased likelihood of African American youth being labeled as bully-victims "must be interpreted in light of racial disproportionality—the perception held by teachers and peers, that African American youth are more aggressive" (215). They went on to suggest that racial biases "relate to disproportionate disciplinary actions in childhood and adolescence and disproportionate minority contact and confinement in adolescence and adulthood" (215).

Huang and Cornell (2017) used self-report surveys to collect data from a statewide sample of 38,398 students attending 236 racially diverse high schools in Virginia to test the **differential involvement hypothesis**, which "suggests that racial disproportionality is not a result of discrimination but a consequence of differences in attitudes and behaviors that lead to higher rates of misbehavior among Black students" (299). The results of Huang and Cornell's analysis did not "support the differential involvement hypothesis with regard to suspensions" (304). However, these researchers noted that their results "strengthen the concern that racial disparities are the result of differential decisions by school authorities" (304).

Peguero and Shekarkhar (2011) found similar dynamics at play in their analysis of data from a subsample of 7,250 students in 580 public schools who completed the 2002 Educational Longitudinal Study. The results showed "Latino/a students are being disproportionately punished for misbehaving at the same, or even less, levels as White male students" (65). They found specifically that first- and third-generation Latino and Latina students are more likely to be punished "even though first-generation Latino and Latina students are less likely to engage in school misbehavior in comparison to White males" and "third-generation Latino and Latina students have similar patterns of school misbehavior to White males" (65). These researchers concluded that "although zero tolerance is ideally a school policy to ameliorate violence within schools, it appears that this policy has only magnified the overrepresentation of racial and ethnic minority students who are being disciplined" (66). As Payne and Welch (2010) pointed out, "harsher outcomes for Black students are not merely a reflection of more violations . . . but also importantly involve the discretion of teachers and administrators" (1024).

The above described disparities negatively impact a variety of educational outcomes, since students who experience schools as a place where they are racialized, demonized, stigmatized, and criminalized are much less likely to experience schools as providing safe, supportive spaces aimed at helping them improve their lives. Both perceived and actual racial discrimination in disciplinary practices have been linked to lower self-esteem, higher degrees of anxiety and stress, and lower levels of academic engagement, curiosity, and persistence (Thompson and Gregory 2011). According to Skiba, Arredondo, and Williams (2014), "the experience of out-of-school suspensions or expulsion in and of itself increases student risk for school disengagement, poor school outcomes, dropout, and involvement with juvenile justice, especially among groups more likely to be disproportionately disciplined" (558).

RESTORATIVE JUSTICE THEORY

From a **restorative justice** (RJ) perspective, crime is understood as "a violation of people and of interpersonal relationships" that "creates obligations" of which the "central obligation is to put right the wrongs" that resulted from the crime (Zehr 2002, 19). From a criminal justice perspective, when a crime is committed, justice officials focus on what laws were broken, who broke them, and what punishment they deserve in response. From a RJ perspective, when a crime is committed, practitioners focus on who has been hurt, what needs they have, and who is obligated to address those needs. Zehr (1990) described crime as "a violation of people and relationships. It creates obligations to make things right. Justice involves the victim, the offender, and the community in a search for solutions which promote repair, reconciliation, and reassurance" (181). The philosophical underpinnings of restorative justice also align with the peacemaking tradition in criminology. According to Arrigo (1999), "peacemaking criminology endeavors to forge meaningful, humane relationships between victims and offenders, between friends and enemies within situations of conflict" (51). Braswell, Fuller, and Lozoff (2001) pointed to the potential for **peacemaking criminology** and restorative justice to operate across multiple domains, including the personal, social, and institutional. They suggested that how individuals feel about themselves in relation to others is a primary determinant of their behavior; in order for harm to be repaired, our interactions with others should be based on trust, fairness, kindness, and compassion. Although early articulations of restorative justice in North America drew distinct lines between restorative and retributive justice (i.e., punishment for punishment's sake), more recent developments acknowledge that the underlying principle of accountability is an important and central aspect of both restorative and retributive responses to crime (Van Ness and Heetderks Strong 2010). Thus, RJ should not be understood as an alternative *to* punishment, but rather as an alternative *form of* punishment that seeks to hold individuals accountable to their offending behaviors in ways that heal relationships and repair the harm they caused.

There is substantial research on the effectiveness of restorative justice policies and practices in North America and around the globe. In their analysis of empirical studies of RJ, Sherman and Strang (2007) noted significant positive outcomes for RJ processes in comparison to more traditional criminal justice system approaches. They limited their review to studies that conducted rigorous comparisons of RJ participants and comparison/control groups who went through traditional criminal justice processes. They found that RJ practices showed positive results across a number of outcomes, including substantially reduced repeat offending, increased effective use of diversion from criminal justice, reduced post-traumatic stress symptoms and desires for revenge among victims, and reduced criminal justice costs. In a meta-analysis of restorative diversion programs for youth, Wong et al. (2016)

In addition to challenging traditional approaches to researching bullying, critical criminologists highlight what they see as ineffective and counterproductive responses to bullying in schools. Instead of focusing on punishment and individual-level behavioral change, critical criminologists seek to challenge dominant discourses that support the criminalization of schools through "get tough" zero tolerance policies and the excessive use of exclusionary disciplinary practices. Of particular concern is the degree to which zero tolerance policies disproportionately impact youth of color and other marginalized student communities and support the school-to-prison pipeline. Thus, critical criminologists advocate policies and practices that respond to bullying through a harm-reduction lens, such as restorative school discipline.

In a series of case studies of schools that have implemented restorative discipline practices, González (2012) concluded that "the development of sustained school-based restorative justice programs can be an important educational policy solution aimed at eliminating the school-to-prison pipeline" 335). However, Schiff (2018) noted that while there is strong evidence for this, its effectiveness is dependent on the degree to which programs grounded in restorative justice attend to institutional and organizational racism. This aligns with critical criminologists' call for bullying researchers to attend to institutional and cultural dynamics of power that are replicated and reinforced through bullying behaviors and through disciplinary policies grounded in zero tolerance, exclusion, and criminalization.

As one example of the potential of restorative school discipline, the Oakland Unified School District (OUSD) has implemented a restorative justice initiative. According to OUSD, their restorative justice (RJ) initiative was "implemented through a 3-tier, school-wide model" that engages students, teachers, school administrators, families, and communities in school climate and discipline issues (www .ousd.org/Page/12324). As indicated on OUSD's website (www.ousd .org/Page/12326), the initiative includes the following:

1. Professional development and coaching support to almost forty RJ sites throughout the district.
2. Partnership with Catholic Charities of the East Bay to implement trauma-informed restorative practices at their six comprehensive high schools.

3. Integration of Positive Behavioral Supports, African American Male Achievement, and Social Emotional Learning at participating sites.

4. Inclusion of parents and families to engage them in school climate and discipline issues.

5. Alignment with City of Oakland's "Oakland Unite" programs, including community crisis response and support network, conflict mediation, street outreach, and Juvenile Justice re-entry to schools.

6. Engaging youth leadership in restorative practices through the Peer RJ program.

Questions

Visit OUSD's website at www.ousd.org/Page/12324 and review their materials, videos, and links to resources and research studies, then answer the following:

1. How is restorative justice theory, as described on OUSD's website, different from and similar to more traditional approaches to crime and deviance?

2. What aspects of restorative school discipline make it an effective tool for reducing racial disproportionality?

3. RJ emphasizes the harm caused to and needs of victims. What role should bullying victims play in the disciplinary process, if any?

found that "restorative approaches are a promising way to combat recidivism among youth and should continue to be implemented and evaluated" (1324).

POLICY IMPLICATIONS OF CRITICAL CRIMINOLOGY AND RESTORATIVE JUSTICE

Unlike other categories of theories we have discussed throughout this text, the implications that emerge from critical criminology tend to be turned inward on the discipline itself. Critical theories serve as a critique of "mainstream" criminology and aim to uncover how existing definitions of discipli-nary concepts (e.g., crime, deviance, bullying) are limited in their ability to capture dynamics of power and oppression, and, therefore, policies that emerge from mainstream criminology are limited in their effectiveness. For example, Polanin and Vera (2013) suggest that in order to address bullying behaviors in schools, we must understand bullying as "reinforced by genera-tions of attitudes supporting the notions of cultural superiority" (308). Without this acknowledgement, prevention efforts will fail to address the prejudices and cultural messages of inferiority that are used to construct the "other" and to justify bullying behaviors in schools. Other critical scholars have attempted to redefine bullying in the literature so as to better capture dynamics of institutional and structural power. In what is perhaps the clear-est articulation of a definition of bullying grounded in critical theory, Payne and Smith (2013) suggest a redefining of bullying that accounts for the influ-ence of structural inequalities:

> Bullying is overt verbal, physical, or technology-based ("cyber," text messag-ing, etc.) aggression that is persistently focused on targeted person(s) over time. This behavior is visible aggression that has escalated from a larger sys-tem of low-level or covert normalized aggression that polices the boundaries between "normal" and "different" in a specific social context. Targeted person(s) are victimized because they are perceived to be outside the bounda-ries of "normal" as culturally defined within a peer group. This aggression is a tool for acquiring higher social status in a peer group because by targeting others as "different," the aggressor claims a higher position in the social hier-archy and reinforces the social "rules" of acceptability. Peer-to-peer aggres-sion typically replicates structural inequality, and therefore patterns of tar-geting are likely to reflect systemic marginalization along lines of gender, sex, sexuality, race, (dis)ability, and class. (26)

Restorative justice scholars and practitioners attempt to address these power dynamics as well. According to Pranis (2001), "on a micro level, [RJ] can bridge social distance, affirm values of mutual responsibility, and real-locate power in individual cases of crime" (301). Pranis linked the microlevel to the macro, suggesting restorative justice "can provide a model for trans-forming relationships and power across multiple systems and structures" (301). When communities engage in consensus building and value the well-being and wholeness of all members of the community, individuals who tend to lack access to power or who are rarely given voice within criminal justice and educational institutions (e.g., victims, offenders, youth) are empowered to affirm their needs and responsibilities and given voice and respect. In affirming the worth of all individuals within the community, RJ practices have the potential to reduce marginalization, alienation, and isolation. Braswell, Fuller, and Lozoff (2001) pointed to the need to dismantle institutional and systemic forms of oppression, stating that "when we allow racism or sexual (or other kinds of) harassment to be tolerated in our schools and businesses, we invite reactions that may be violent" (40). This includes the application of exclusionary discipline policies that exert a form of structural violence through disproportionate application for youth of color. Restorative approaches to school discipline therefore have the potential to alleviate the suffering of marginalized students and break the cycle of violence that is generated by discriminatory and exclusionary school discipline policies.

A major threat to marginalized populations in school settings is the continued growth of the school-to-prison pipeline. According to Fania Davis, Executive Director of Restorative Justice for Oakland Youth (RJOY), "the school-to-prison pipeline refers to the alarming national trend of punishing and criminalizing our youth instead of educating and nurturing them" (2014, 40). In an extensive review of the literature on the application of restorative justice in schools within the United States, González (2012) noted that restorative school discipline practices can serve to mediate the relationship between school discipline and the school-to-prison pipeline. Findings from González's specific evaluation of the North High School Restorative Justice Program confirmed "that when schools adopt alternative processes to address discipline they can build a safer school culture, reduce entry into the school-to-prison pipeline, and positively impact educational performance" (335).

According to Englehart (2014), many of the current approaches to school discipline tend to miss the mark in terms of addressing the affective dimensions of harm. In discussing the need to address the affective, emotional aspects of school victimization, Englehart pointed to parents' desires to know that their children are safe and children's desires to see that adults at school are looking out for them (28). These needs suggest that there are benefits in engaging all school stakeholders (i.e., students, teachers, administrators, and parents) when addressing behavioral problems. As Margaret Thorsborne, a pioneer in the application of restorative justice in schools, has put it, "the adults in the school community are the ones who must take the lead and change their behavior first" (2013, 49).

Evaluations of restorative disciplinary practices in schools have highlighted the potential for positive outcomes related to bullying. In an extensive review of research, Fronius et al. (2019) found support for the effectiveness of RJ policies and practices to address bullying in schools across a number of studies. Wong et al. (2011) employed a longitudinal quasi-experimental design to study the effectiveness of a "Restorative Whole-school Approach (RWsA)" in reducing bullying in four Hong Kong public schools. One school had fully implemented RWsA, two schools had partially implemented RWsA, and one school did not implement RWsA at all (the comparison group). The results of the authors' longitudinal analysis showed significant decreases in bullying (both overall and across multiple forms, including physical and exclusionary) at both the RWsA and partial RWsA schools, while bullying at the non-RWsA school worsened over the study period. In fact, "almost half (49.9%) of students who had bullied others at the RWsA school had reduced their bullying behaviors, [while] 51% of students at the non-RWsA school had increased their bullying behaviors" (2011, 853–54).

Restorative justice programs also have effects on other factors related to school bullying. For example, Alkhalayleh and Newlyn (2015) outlined how restorative justice programming in schools could be implemented to break the link between domestic violence experienced in the home and school bullying, a correlation we discussed in more detail in chapters 2 and 4. In a mixed-methods evaluation of the RJ-based Responsible Citizenship Program in an Australian primary school, Morrison (2002) found that students' feelings of safety significantly increased over the course of the year in which the program was implemented. Perhaps more importantly, "the use of maladaptive shame management skills decreased significantly, in terms of both feelings of rejection by others and displacement of wrongdoing onto others" (2002, 5). Reductions in maladaptive shame management and increases in feelings of safety can lead to positive outcomes for youth, including a reduction in problematic behaviors such as bullying and increases in academic success.

SEVEN

Integrationist, Life Course, and Developmental Theories

Chapters 2 through 6 of this book focused on particular categories of criminological theory and their associated unit theories. These chapters introduced each unit theory (e.g., Hirschi's social bond theory, Agnew's general strain theory, etc.), then tested them as a competing explanation of crime, delinquency, and/or deviance. Even though in many instances these theories draw on the same constructs or measures, the theorists who developed them and the researchers who tested their applicability tend to argue that the theory they are testing is distinct and often incompatible with other theories. This is true even when theories use the same constructs. For instance, measures of "peer association" are used to test constructs associated with social control, social learning, opportunity, and subcultural theories. Each theory posits an arguably unique, yet overlapping influence of peer associations depending on the basic tenets of the theory and its perspective on the fundamental drivers of human behavior.

INTEGRATIONIST PERSPECTIVES

Alternatively, some researchers and theorists have taken on the challenge of theoretical integration, arguing that theoretical constructs from seemingly competing theories can in fact be combined to more fully explain the complexity of human behavior. Williams and McShane (2010) identified two models of theory integration in criminology. The first, the **fully integrated model**, involves the incorporation of "concepts from several theories without regard to either the assumptions or the general thrust of the theories" (217). The second, the **end-to-end model**, involves "[putting] theories together in a sequential, straight-line fashion" (217).

Fully Integrated Models

One of the more prominent and established fully integrated models of criminological theory is Elliott et al.'s (1979) integrated theory, which combines elements of social control, social learning, and strain. Menard and Grotpeter (2011) noted that Elliott et al.'s integrated theory draws on Agnew's (1992) early work on general strain theory, the constructs of external and internal controls articulated by Reiss (1951) and Nye (1958), and elements of Sutherland's (1947) theory of differential association (all of which we covered in earlier chapters). As an example of how a fully integrated model may ignore the original formulation of the theory from which it borrows constructs, Elliott et al. (1979) posited that it is the development of internal bonds (attitudes/beliefs) that make one more or less likely to associate with conforming or deviant peer groups. This is in opposition to Sutherland's (1947) original formulation, which posits that definitions (attitudes/beliefs) are learned within the context of existing peer associations. In other words, Elliott et al. reverse the causal order of the relationship between definitions (or internal controls) and peer associations proposed by differential association theory.

In order to test the integrated theory in relation to bullying-related behaviors, Menard and Grotpeter (2011) analyzed data from 3,497 elementary school students in Colorado. Menard and Grotpeter included measures of constructs from social control theory, including external controls (relationships with parents and other adults) and internal controls (attitudes toward aggression and violence). Their measure of social learning constructs included friends' attitudes toward aggression and violence as a measure of deviant peer association. Finally, to assess the effects of strain, Menard and Grotpeter included a measure of school performance, arguing that poor school performance represents a failure of achievement that would induce strain. Interestingly, they also used respondents' self-reported attitudes toward aggressive behavior as a measure of offender motivation, a construct borrowed from routine activity theory (covered in chapter 2).

According to Menard and Grotpeter (2011), their results are "consistent with the integrated theory, and with the components extracted from Routine Activity Theory, but less so with self-control theory" (198). Specifically, Menard and Grotpeter found that "peer group is consistently a statistically significant and relatively strong predictor of perpetration of physical aggression" (195). They also found that external controls did not have a direct influence on physical aggression but may act indirectly through internal controls and peer association. In terms of relational aggression, Menard and Grotpeter found that "perpetration is most strongly and consistently influenced by one's own attitudes toward aggression, followed by one's peers' attitudes toward aggression" (196). They also note that for relational aggression, external controls in the form of family bonding have both an indirect and direct effect.

Menard and Grotpeter (2011) also looked at the influence of these constructs on victimization. They found that for physical aggression victimization, "exposure to friends whose attitudes are favorable toward aggression increases one's own risk of being a victim of aggression" (196). They noted inconsistent findings related to the direct influence of external controls (i.e., familial bonding) on both physical and relational aggression victimization but added that "family bonding appears to have an impact on the peer group climate (peer attitudes), and hence an indirect impact, via peer attitudes toward aggression, on physical and relational aggression victimization" (196). These findings should not be interpreted as establishing a causal relationship, given the limitations of the repeated cross-sectional design of the study.

Kulig et al. (2017) tested the applicability of an integrated low self-control and risky lifestyles explanation of victimization by analyzing data from 1,901 middle school students in the city of Roanoke, Virginia. Specifically, Kulig et al. asked whether "engaging in various forms of risky behaviors effectively mediates the link between low self-control and bullying victimization" (892). They argued that individuals with "low levels of self-control . . . are more likely to self-select into [risky behaviors] because they provide the kind of immediate gratification that those who lack self-control crave" (893), which makes individuals more vulnerable to victimization. While the authors generally supported this integrated theory, they also expressed skepticism of its applicability to bullying victimization for two reasons: (1) "victims of bullying may have little or no control over where they go to school and who their classmates are" (895), and (2) "bullying generally involves a power differential between the bully and the victim" meaning that "the individual does not have to engage in any particular behavior (risky or otherwise) to attract a bully; they could be simply singled out due to their stature or vulnerability" (895). These researchers found that "after controlling for other factors, engaging in risky lifestyles . . . does not appear to put youths at risk of bullying victimization" (904). They also found that "even after accounting for risky lifestyles, low self-control maintained a direct effect on all forms of bullying victimization with the exception of social victimization" (904). Finally, they noted that in addition to low self-control, the presence of physical limitations (measured through a single item asking respondents "if they had any physical problems that kept them from doing things they wanted to do" [898]) increased the risk of victimization, and youths with strong parental attachments (a form of guardianship) were less likely to experience bullying victimization.

Cho and Lee (2018) conducted a study that assessed an integrated approach that included lifestyle/routine activity theories, but with social control as opposed to self-control. Drawing from the Health Behavior in School-Aged Children (HBSC) survey, Cho and Lee analyzed data from a sample of 12,642 students who completed the 2009–2010 survey. They examined the "direct impacts of risk factors (delinquent peer associations) and mediating effects of social controls on three types of bullying status: bullies, victims, and bully-victims in each of the following: physical, verbal, and social bullying" (379). Their measure of the lifestyle/routine activity construct of *exposure* was delinquent peer associations. Their measures of social controls, which were hypothesized to mediate (e.g., serve as protective factors) the relationship between exposure and bullying, were parental attachment, peer attachment, and teacher attachment. Cho and Lee found that "adolescents who associated with delinquent peers were more likely to be bullies, victims, and bully-victims in physical, verbal, and social bullying" and that "the social controls had direct and mediating effects on bullies, victims, and bully-victims by three subtypes of bullying" (379). Based on these findings, they concluded that "social controls are highly influential during adolescence" and "effective parenting practices influenced adolescent's friendship choices and engagement in bullying-related behaviors" (379).

While these studies set out to explicitly test established integrated theories, other bullying researchers have conducted studies that test the relationship between constructs from distinct unit theories without explicitly grounding the analysis in a specific integrated theoretical framework. Williams and McShane (2010) referred to this as "research-produced theory" (218), which occurs when integrative theory is developed through the conduct of research testing existing theoretical constructs. For instance, Moon and Alarid (2015) tested a model that included constructs from self-control theory and opportunity theory. These researchers analyzed data from 296 adolescents who completed surveys while attending two schools in a single school district. Moon and Alarid employed multiple measures of opportunity, including association with bullies, parental supervision and monitoring, negative school environment, and teachers' negative feedback. They also employed Grasmick et al.'s (1993) twenty-four-item scale (described in chapter 5) to measure each respondent's level of self-control. Moon and Alarid (2015) analyzed the relationship between these opportunity factors and self-control, and a combined measure of physical and psychological bullying perpetration. While their analysis showed a significant relationship between low self-control and bullying perpetration, they also noted that "the influence of self-control weakened when opportunity measures were introduced into the model" (850). They concluded that "researchers should consider opportunity factors when testing low self-control theory, as low self-control by itself may not be as strong a predictor for school bullying as it was for other forms of more serious crime" (851).

Unnever and Cornell (2003) also conducted a study to test the relationship between self-control and bullying, but with a focus on the additional influence of attention deficit hyperactivity disorder (ADHD). Drawing data from 2,472 middle school students from six public schools in the city of Roanoke, Virginia, researchers Unnever and Cornell analyzed the relationships among measures of bullying perpetration, bullying victimization, self-reported ADHD diagnosis, and self-control. They found that "middle-school students who reported taking medication for ADHD were both more likely to report bullying others and more likely to report being victimized by bullies" (141). They also found that self-control fully mediated the influence of ADHD on bullying perpetration, meaning that "students with ADHD were more likely to engage in bullying because of their problems in self-control" (142), not because of their diagnosis alone.

Researchers have also conducted tests of constructs from two theories that operate at different explanatory levels. For example, Holt, Turner, and Exum (2014) designed a study to "investigate the effects of individual-level and neighborhood-level factors on the prevalence of bully victimization" (349). Using self-report data from 2,562 middle and high school students in a single North Carolina school system, Holt, Turner, and Exum analyzed the "predictive properties of both low self-control and neighborhood disorder on bullying victimization" (351–52). They measured self-control using a six-item scale and neighborhood disorder using a seven-item index. Similar to Moon and Alarid (2015), Holt, Turner, and Exum found a significant relationship between low self-control and all forms of bullying victimization they measured. They also found that neighborhood disorder was significantly related to all forms of bullying victimization. In their analytic model including both self-control and neighborhood disorder, both remained significantly associated with bullying victimization, but neighborhood disorder also moderated the relationship between self-control and victimization (352). This means that neighborhood disorder has some influence on the relationship between low self-control and risk of bullying victimization. Interestingly, Holt, Turner, and Exum (2014) also employed full models that included a measure of polyvictimization. In other words, they included measures of verbal and physical bullying victimization in relation to cyberbullying, cyber and physical in relation to verbal, and verbal and cyber in relation to physical. When these measures of polyvictimization were included in the model, the effect of self-control on bullying victimization disappeared, but the effect of neighborhood disorder on bullying victimization remained significant. Drawing on routine activity theory, Holt, Turner, and Exum interpreted this finding as support for the idea that "self-control may have an indirect relationship to bullying victimization through exposure to motivated offenders" (353). Finally, based on their analysis, Holt, Turner, and Exum (2014) concluded that "there is a need to consider how broader environmental conditions may affect the risk of harm from bullying" (353).

While these tests of fully integrated theoretical models are important in terms of identifying how seemingly competing theoretical constructs can fit together, they suffer from a consistent limitation. Specifically, all of these studies rely on cross-sectional data, which means they are unable to establish temporal ordering, a required element for establishing causality.

End-to-End Models

There are not many examples of end-to-end models of integration in the bullying literature. However, Cho (2017a) conducted a statistically sophisticated longitudinal analysis of the integrated theory of lifestyles and routine activities (LRAT) and self-control in order to assess the time-ordered relationship between bullying perpetration and victimization. As Cho points out, a major thrust of this integrated theory is that "individuals with low self-control are more likely to willingly engage in risky lifestyles that may, in turn, place themselves at higher odds of being victimized" (281). Cho also noted that "despite a large body of research examining the offending-victimization association, little is known about the time-ordered relationship between offending and victimization" (282). Cho analyzed data from five waves of the Korean Youth Panel Survey, which began in 2004 ($n = 2,844$) and included annual follow-up interviews/surveys with the same participants. Cho's dependent variable, bullying victimization, included three items that measured collective bullying victimization (a significant issue in South Korea), severe teasing or bantering, and severe beating, respectively. Independent variables included bullying perpetration, association with bullies (as a measure of exposure to motivated offenders), parent-youth relationships (as a measure of guardianship), and low self-control (using parts of Grasmick et al.'s scale). The results of the analysis "demonstrated that youth who bullied others were generally at higher risk of bullying victimization (a reciprocal effect) among the three different bullying models" (285). Additionally, "youth who had associated with bullies during the previous year were more likely to have subsequent risk of future bullying victimization (a time ordered relationship), except for physical bullying" (285). This finding is consistent with lifestyle and routine activity theories, which consider association with bullies to be an indicator of exposure to motivated offenders. Cho also found that low self-control was significantly associated with verbal bullying, even when controlling for measures of lifestyle and routine activities. Based on this analysis, Cho (2017a) drew several conclusions, including that "for collective bullying, risky lifestyles may be a more significant factor predicting victimization compared to individual trait characteristics or verbal bullying" (288) and that "the integrated approach of both LRAT and self-control theory can be used to explain bullying victimization" (288). Cho cautioned that studies that omit individual trait characteristics (e.g., self-control) "may mislead the relationships between lifestyle factors and bullying victimization" (285).

While not a pure example of an end-to-end integration model, Cho's (2017a) longitudinal analysis does align with the need for research that is able to assess temporal ordering and causal relationships. If the theoretical argument is that low self-control leads to risky lifestyles, which in turn lead to increased odds of victimization, researchers must be able to establish the time ordering of these phenomena among their study samples. This becomes even more important as integrated theories attempt to explain changes over more prolonged periods.

DEVELOPMENTAL AND LIFE COURSE THEORIES

Developmental and life course (DLC) theories both examine continuation and changes in patterns of offending over time—respectively, "persistence" and "desistance"—but they each have a different focus. Developmental theories rely more on psychological processes, while life course theories look more at influences from social structure. Nevertheless, each focuses on the individual, including intrapersonal change and interpersonal difference (Boman and Mowen 2018) rather than, say, explaining crime rates across geographic areas. The key areas DLC theories seek to explain include the onset of delinquency, versatility, escalation, co-offending, persistence, and desistance (Farrington 2003). DLC theories thus hypothesize different pathways to offending by examining "the development of offending and antisocial behavior, risk factors at different ages, and the effects of life events on the course of development" (Farrington 2003, 221). Many of them are highly integrative, borrowing from an assortment of theories, including those based in strain and control. Their empirical beginnings can be traced to early longitudinal research by Glueck and Glueck (1950, 1968) and to the "criminal career" research of the 1980s (Blumstein 1986). Because of the limited populations of most DLC studies, "findings and theories apply to [conventional] offending by lower class urban males in Western industrialized societies," and so their application to other types of offending and other persons (and in other places) remains to be seen (Farrington 2003, 223). This includes, of course, school bullying.

Prominent DLC Theories

Age-graded theory is a type of life course criminology developed by Sampson and Laub (1993, 1997, 2005) that was at first based on reconstructed data from Glueck and Glueck (1950, 1968). Glueck and Glueck's data came from a longitudinal study of male adolescent and adult criminal offending that began in 1940. Age-graded theory stresses the importance of informal social controls, beginning with parenting styles and attachment to parents, then attachment to school and peers, and finally marital stability and employment (Sampson and Laub 2005, 15). The theory thus focuses on various "turning points" in late adolescence and early adulthood that "[1] 'knife off' the past from the present, . . . [2] provide both supervision and monitoring as well as new opportunities of social support and growth, . . . [3] change and structure routine activities . . . [and] [4] provide the opportunity for identity transformation" (Sampson and Laub 2005, 17–18, citing to Laub and Sampson 2003). Because the theory focuses on positive social bonds and desistance, it does not fully explain what processes *encourage* offending (Farrington 2003).

Moffitt (2017) developed an influential theory that suggests that there are two distinct types of offenders: **adolescent-limited** (AL) and **life-course-persisting** (LCP). LCP persons experience early neuropsychological deficits that result in hyperactivity, impulsivity, low self-control, and difficult temperament in childhood. The LCP person fails to learn prosocial behavior because of the negative interactions between the individual and the social environment. LCP people show stability of antisocial behavior over time because "they become ensnared in an antisocial lifestyle by the consequences of offending, such as dropping out of school and incarceration" (Farrington 2003, 242). In contrast, AL offending is temporary, fueled by social mimicry and peer influence. It stops in late adolescence or early adulthood when persons enter legitimate adult roles and the costs of antisocial behavior begin to outweigh its benefits, a concept found in deterrence theories.

The **social development model** (SDM), proposed by Catalano and Hawkins (1996), integrates social learning theory, social control theory, and differential association theory to explain the causes and course of delinquency (Bishop et al. 2017). The SDM recognizes that individuals "will be prosocial and/or antisocial depending on the degree of association with and bonding to prosocial and antisocial individuals and the adoption of associated beliefs" (Bishop et al. 2017, 278). The SDM specifies several "submodels" that explain phases of development from childhood through adolescence. It also allows for the inclusion of individual factors, such as cognitive ability; exogenous factors, such as race; and external constraints, including parental control over behavior.

Developmental Research on School Bullying

Some of the earliest bullying research examined the relationship between bullying and later criminality (e.g., Olweus 1980, 1991), and researchers have continued longitudinal or prospective research that examines whether childhood involvement in bullying roles is related to later antisocial behavior, such as drug use (e.g., Ttofi, Farrington, Lösel et al. 2016). However, most of this research has not drawn from developmental *theories*, and thus we know relatively little about individual trajectories of victimization or perpetration over the course of schooling (Zych, Ttofi et al. 2020). While researchers have demonstrated that rates of bullying and victimization generally decline with age, research delineating individual pathways to perpetration and victimization is inconsistent, showing peaks and valleys in different grade levels, with different patterns of persistence and desistance (Skrzypiec et al. 2018). In addition, many studies are methodologically hampered by following students only over short periods or by using single-item questions about bullying and/or victimization (Zych, Ttofi et al. 2020).

Questions that appear relevant here include the following:

- What is the overall pattern of bullying involvement over the K–12 span, and which individual and or situational factors explain it?
- Are there particular inflection points, such as school transitions, where involvement tends to increase or decrease?
- What factors explain why some children become chronic perpetrators or chronic victims (or both) while others' involvement is more transitory?
- To what extent does involvement in various types of bullying (physical, verbal, relational, and cyber) have different trajectories?
- How is the type, severity, and development of internalizing and externalizing symptoms related to the trajectory of victimization and perpetration?
- Does participation in bullying roles predict later involvement in those or other roles?
- Do the effects of risk and protective factors remain constant or change over time?
- What is the trajectory of the bully-victim (i.e., what percentage begin as a bully or a victim, and why and when do they take on the new role)?
- Are trajectories different for different groups of victims (e.g., sexual minority youth, students with disabilities)?

We have at least partial answers to most of these questions, although we explore only a few of them here given space limitations, first focusing on developmental aspects of victimization and then on bullying perpetration. We do not discuss bully-victims separately because there is little research about their developmental processes (for two exceptions, see Ettekal and Ladd 2020; Sung et al. 2018). There is also little extant research on development of bystander behaviors (e.g., Mazzone, Camodeca, and Salmivalli 2018).

Developmental Aspects of Victimization. Victimization is transient among young children but becomes more stable for middle elementary school students (Hymel and Swearer 2015). However, as time intervals increase, victimization patterns becomes less consistent (Hymel and Swearer 2015). Some studies have also found that the *seriousness* of victimization declines throughout high school (e.g., Ladd, Ettekal, and Kochenderfer-Ladd 2017).

Research shows that the victimization role is relatively stable (Bishop et al. 2017). Even though the *frequency* of victimization steadily declines throughout high school, the *percentage* of victims stays relatively constant (Troop-Gordon 2017). Most research attempts to explain this stability based on a personality trait or internalizing/externalizing behaviors rather than theorizing a developmental process. For instance (and as noted in chapter 3), victims may develop "maladaptive schemas" (unhealthy ways of thinking and feeling) that tend to entrench their victimization (Calvete et al. 2018). Measurement issues have hindered research on developmental aspects of bullying. Most bullying measures yield a composite score that reflects how many types of bullying a student has experienced; this overall "exposure score" thus combines types of victimization but not the temporal intensity of it (Randa, Reyns, and Nobles 2019). Because of this, Randa, Reyns, and Nobles (2019) noted, "there is a particular lack of clarity regarding the effects of *limited victimization* experiences versus prolonged, persistent, or repeated victimization experiences" (393, emphasis in original).

Continuity, Desistance, and Noninvolvement Researchers have identified different victim subtypes, typically according to (1) the intensity of victimization and (2) whether victimization increases, declines, or stays the same. They have mostly measured victimization from a two-year to a four-year interval and have tended to focus on particular grade ranges. Thus, we know more about the periods of both grades K through five and seven through eight, and less about other periods, such as grades nine through twelve (Ladd, Ettekal, and Kochenderfer-Ladd 2017). However, even when examining students in the same grade range, research has been inconsistent. For instance, one study that followed children from grade three through grade six identified three distinct trajectories, while another that followed students over the same grades identified five trajectories (see Ladd, Ettekal, and Kochenderfer-Ladd 2017). Research by Ladd, Ettekal, and Kochenderfer-Ladd (2017) is one of the few studies to follow the same group of students from kindergarten through grade twelve. The authors reported that the percentage of severe victims declined nearly every year of the study, while moderate victimization increased slightly from kindergarten through grade three and dropped off markedly from grade six to grade seven. Contrary to many other studies, this study did not find that victimization increased across school transitions (i.e., elementary to middle school or middle school to high school).

Ladd, Ettekal, and Kochenderfer-Ladd (2017) noted, "as of yet, no theory speaks to developmental vicissitudes in peer victimization" (837). The authors offered several possibilities, including "changes in children's maturity (e.g., growth in moral reasoning, perspective taking, empathy, etc.), social environments (e.g., movement toward selective peer environments, peer niche seeking at later grade levels), and socialization processes (e.g., increasing sanctions against bullying and aggression)" (837). It may also be that there is increasing equity in peer structures over time and that youth learn how to avoid their aggressors and develop advanced cognitive skills and a more sophisticated sense of identity (Troop-Gorden 2017). Ladd, Ettekal, and Kochenderfer-Ladd (2017) also noted that two victim classes experienced moderate to high victimization that practically ceased by high school, and these groups warrant further study because they could provide clues as to how to reduce victimization because some children may "possess certain psychological or social resources that allow them to overcome early victimization experiences" (837).

A more age-limited study of more than three thousand Australian students in grades eight through twelve reported involvement in *any* bullying role in grade seven greatly increased the chances of becoming a victim in high school (Skrzypiec et al. 2018). It also found that new victims emerged throughout high school. Skrzypiec et al. (2018) offered some hypotheses about this pattern. It may be that relational aggression increases during high school as popularity becomes more salient or that sexual harassment increases as students mature. The study also found that the bully-victim role became more prevalent through the high school years, perhaps due to either social modeling (victims began to bully others as they had been bullied) or because bullying perpetrators "became victims of bullying as the limitations of their self-regulatory and emotional capabilities were manifested" (575).

Researchers have also examined victimization trajectories for different groups of students, such as those of sexual minority youth (Sterzing et al. 2018). Further research is needed to determine if and how trajectories are different for students in specific identified groups versus students overall.

Coping and Internalizing and Externalizing Behaviors Randa, Reyns, and Nobles (2019) analyzed a nationally representative US sample of more than thirty-five hundred youth and found among students in the persistent victimization group "a greater proportion of individuals experiencing fear of future victimization, ... avoiding places at school, and ... reporting carrying a weapon for protection" (409). Research by Erath, Kaeppler, and Tu (2019) suggests that there may be differences in coping strategies according to both developmental period and context, such as school transition. Studies have shown that children and adolescents can "recover" once victimization ends; for instance, academic performance can rebound (Bowes et al. 2013; Ladd, Ettekal, and Kochenderfer-Ladd 2017).

Developmental Aspects of Bullying Perpetration. Research has shown that bullying perpetration is less common than victimization. Most studies have shown that bullying behaviors increase during middle school and also before and during transition between schools (see discussion in Merrin et al. 2018). Research suggests forms of peer aggression, including bullying and homophobic teasing, are related to the formation and maintenance of peer networks. A longitudinal study of 190 middle school students in Illinois "found evidence that youth were influenced by their friends' homophobic teasing behaviors and over time adopted similar behaviors of their friends" (Merrin et al. 2018, 613). The authors concluded that prevention efforts ought to target the dynamics of peer groups as well as individual behaviors.

Continuity, Desistance, and Noninvolvement Just as with victimization, researchers have identified various subtypes of perpetrator trajectories. For instance, one study followed 871 Canadian children over seven years, starting when students were ten to twelve years old (Pepler et al. 2008). Pepler et al. (2008) reported four distinct developmental trajectories based on whether bullying occurred, and if it did, how frequent it was and whether it desisted. Another study tracked students only through high school and found that the total percentage of perpetrators did not change over time but that new perpetrators emerged year to year and old ones either desisted or became bully-victims or victims (Skrzypiec et al. 2018). The authors did not collect data designed to answer the question *why* students begin or stop bullying in high school and suggested "longitudinal studies with measures of social competence, popularity and different forms of peer aggression (e.g., physical and relational) would enlighten our understanding of this complex issue" (Skrzypiec et al. 2018, 574).

Risk and Protective Factors Pepler et al. (2008) found "adolescents who were at high risk on moral disengagement and on physical aggression were 16 times more likely to be in the high-bullying group than the never [having bullied] group. Those who were at high risk on relational aggression were 10.5 times more likely to be in the high-bullying trajectory group than the never group" (334). Similarly, students who reported problems in relationships with their parents were two to four times more likely to be in the high-bullying group, and the risk was three to six times higher for students reporting problems with peers. However, the study did not attempt to explicate the potential cause and effect pathways. It is possible that relationship difficulties (poor social bonds) cause bullying. However, it could also be that problematic relationships lead to bullying or that aggression leads to both parental relationship problems and peer bullying.

Relationship to Trajectories of Externalizing Behaviors As discussed above and in previous chapters, bullying behaviors in childhood and adolescence have been linked to a variety of externalizing behaviors (EB; e.g., drug use, delinquency), even into adulthood. However, few studies have investigated whether specific trajectories of bullying make EB more or less likely. One hypothesis is that the earlier bullying begins and the more intense it is, the higher the level of EB. Lee, Liu, and Watson (2016) analyzed data from a sample of 440 mother-child dyads in Springfield, Massachusetts, and found four different trajectories: the noninvolved, early desisters, late onsetters, and persisters. They found (unsurprisingly) that the noninvolved had the lowest levels of EB and the persisters had the highest level. They also reported that the early desisters showed little increase in EB, supporting the "cessation effect" or "recovery effect," while the late onsetters showed a greater increase, suggesting an "onset effect" (2790–91). The authors noted that prior research had shown that childhood bullying was related to later EB in adolescence and adulthood; however, much of that research had not distinguished among various trajectories, including early desistance. This finding has important implications for prevention, suggesting that early intervention can reduce later EB in children and adolescents, and thus theoretically in adults as well.

A SOCIAL-ECOLOGICAL APPROACH

The final integrated theory we address in this chapter is a social-ecological model originally developed by Bronfenbrenner (1979, 2005) as a bioecological theory. Bronfenbrenner's model includes six dimensions (see figure 3). Five of these dimensions are levels of analysis, while the sixth dimension represents

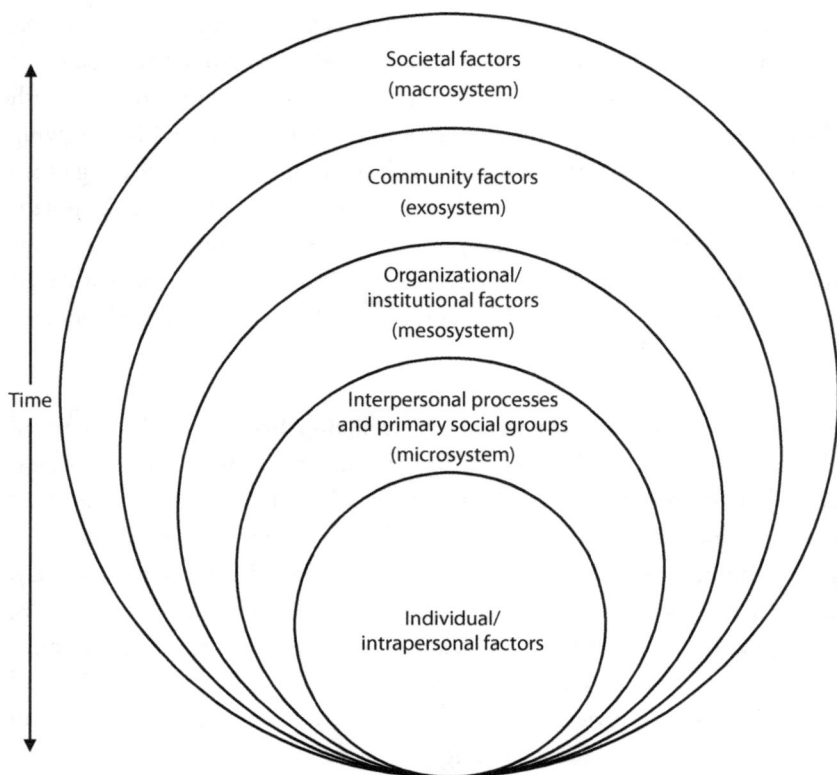

FIGURE 3. An adaptation of Bronfenbrenner's bioecological model.

the influence of time. The five levels of analysis include the individual/intra-personal, interpersonal, organizational/institutional, community, and soci-etal (see Hayes, O'Toole, and Halpenny 2017).

The **individual/intrapersonal level** addresses characteristics, identities, and other aspects of individuals, such as sex, age, health, and race/ethnicity. Factors operating at the **interpersonal level** include aspects of an individu-al's immediate relationships, such as interactions within primary social groups, such as the family, coworkers, and peer networks. In the bullying literature, Espelage (2014) and others refer to this as the **microsystem**, which represents "structures or locations where children have direct contact," including "peers, family, community, and schools" (258). The **organiza-tional/institutional level** addresses interconnections between two or more settings. This would include the interactive effects of family and coworkers or friendship networks and schools. In the bullying literature this represents the **mesosystem** and might include the effects of "parental involvement in their child's school" (Espelage 2014, 258). **Community-level factors** are often less visible and represent more distant influences on the individual, including settings that influence the individual but in which the individual does not directly participate. This might include policy-making bodies, institutional management structures, informal social networks, social and mass media, and neighborhood conditions. As Espelage (2014) explains, this **exosystem** "is the social context with which the child does not have direct contact, but which affects him or her indirectly through the microsystem" (258). Finally, the **societal level** includes cultural and structural factors, such as sociocultural belief systems, cultural attitudes, and public policy. This **macrosystem** "is commonly regarded as a cultural blueprint, which may determine the social structures and activities in the various levels" (Espelage 2014, 258). The sixth dimension, which Bronfenbrenner referred to as the **chronosphere**, refers to the impact of sociohistorical conditions and time. As illustrated in figure 3, this dimension of the model operates across the other five levels. For instance, at the individual level, time might emerge as a consideration of the influence of age on behavior, while at the societal level time might emerge as a consideration of the influence of the current rise in overt (white) nationalism in the United States and the global West in relation to the criminalization of immigrants and refugees. As Espelage (2014) explains, the chronosystem "includes consistency or change (e.g., historical or life events) of the individual and the environment over the life course (e.g., changes in family structure through divorce, displacement, or death)" (258).

As a form of theory integration, this social-ecological framework has garnered significant attention within the bullying literature (see, for instance, Hong and Espelage 2012) and has been applied and tested by a number of bullying scholars who draw on constructs from multiple theories and ground them in the six levels described above. For instance, Hong et al. (2016) conducted a study to test the social-ecological model in which they analyzed data from "7,533 adolescents in grades 6–10 in public and private schools in the United States" collected through "the 2005 to 2006 Health Behavior in School-Aged Children (HBSC) study" (643). They included multiple measures of individual-level factors, family context, friend/peer context, and school context. Using a series of statistical models, Hong et al. (2016) "evaluated the unique effects of a wider social-ecological context after controlling for more proximal contextual effects" (647). These researchers concluded that "there are important similarities and differences across these contexts in their association with victimization and that those relationships are similar or different depending on whether victimization is face-to-face or taking place in cyberspace" (653–54). More specifically, Hong et al. found that "parents are important contributors to the development of their children's peer relations ... [and] ... adolescents who report parental monitoring and peer groups accepted by parents are at a lower risk of face-to-face bullying" (654) and cyberbullying victimization. This was also the case for school context, as measured in this study. However, friend/peer context had differing effects for face-to-face victimization than cyberbullying victimization, decreasing the likelihood of the former but not the latter.

Lee (2011) also conducted an analysis of bullying behaviors among 485 middle school students in a single school district in a southern US state, with an explicit focus on Bronfenbrenner's social-ecological model. Lee found that "individual traits, particularly individual tendency for aggression and fun seeking, have the most important influence on bullying behaviors" (1685), which is consistent with self-control theory. Lee also found indirect effects of individual tendency for aggression and fun seeking, noting that "individual tendency has a direct and strong influence on bullying behaviors, but it also influences peer interactions, which influences school climate. School climate, in turn, influences bullying behaviors" (1685). This finding points to the importance of conducting analyses that can identify the interactive effects of variables operating at different levels of influence.

In another study, Lee collaborated with Song (2012) to conduct a similar test of this social-ecological theoretical framework among a sample of 1,238 South Korean middle school students, using a randomized multistage cluster sampling model. Lee and Song were interested in the effects of individual traits, family interactions, school climate, and parental involvement on relational, verbal, and physical bullying perpetration. Similar to Lee's (2011) study, Lee and Song (2012) found that "individual traits have the most important influence on bullying behaviors" (2449). They also found "no direct relationship between family interactions and bullying at school" (2456) but did note that "family interactions is negatively related to the individual traits, indicating that negative experiences in the family (e.g., authoritarian parenting, witnessing domestic abuse, etc.) would decrease the negative individual traits" (2457). Lee and Song also found that "the more negative individual traits children have, the more bullying behaviors they commit, and the more their parents would contact teachers and friends at schools" (2457). Finally, applying a social-ecological lens, Lee and Song concluded that factors operating at different levels interact in ways that make bullying more or less likely, including that "parental involvement with teachers, peers, and school boards would influence formation of more positive and academic environments in schools, resulting in reduced bullying behaviors within schools" (2458).

Mann et al. (2015) conducted a similar analysis using data from the 2009 Youth in Iceland survey, which included a sample of 7,084 ninth- and tenth-grade students enrolled in 140 of the 146 secondary schools in Iceland. Mann et al. looked at the influence of parental, school, peer group, and community factors on both bullying perpetration and victimization. These researchers found that "higher levels of community and family connection, closure [defined as intergenerational connections between adults and youth in community], and support reduced the odds of young people choosing group bullying behaviors and experiencing victimization" (481). They also found that the magnitude of these relationships increased as the odds of group bullying and victimization increased. Moreover, Mann et al. found that peer connections were negatively associated with bullying behavior, while peer support served as a protective factor for those experiencing victimization (482).

While each of these studies evaluated the degree to which factors operating at different levels of the social-ecological model influence bullying perpetration and victimization, other researchers have employed the social-ecological model to specifically explore the power element of bullying. Similar to those who adopt a critical criminological theoretical lens to explore power differentials, these researchers use the social-ecological model to identify how dynamics of power at the mesosystemic and macrosystemic levels interact with the individual and microsystem to influence bullying perpetration and victimization experiences. Schumann, Craig, and Rosu (2014) conducted a study with two main objectives: "(a) to investigate the extent to which individual characteristics predict bullying victimization and (b) to examine the extent to which the built social characteristics of the community are associated with bullying victimization" (850). They utilized data from 17,777 students in grades six to ten collected as part of the 2009–2010 Health Behavior in School-aged Children Survey in Canada to measure individual characteristics and geographical information systems (GIS) data covering a five-kilometer buffer around each school to measure the built social environment (850). Their individual-level variables included age, gender, socioeconomic status (SES), social capital (i.e., involvement in clubs and organizations), recreational opportunity (i.e., students' perception of availability of recreational spaces in their community), and collective efficacy (how students felt about the safety, cooperation, and trust that existed in their neighborhoods) (852). At the community level, Schumann and colleagues included measures of community SES, community-built social capital (i.e., counts of certain types of buildings in a five-kilometer buffer zone around the school), recreation (i.e., counts of community and shopping centers in a five-kilometer radius of the school), community stability (i.e., residential mobility, homeownership), and population density within a five-kilometer buffer of each school (852–53).

Consistent with other research we have discussed in this book, Schumann, Craig, and Rosu (2014) found that "individual factors such as age, gender, SES, and individual social inclusion factors such as individual social capital, recreation, and collective efficacy contribute to the power differential in bullying" (857). Also consistent with research we discussed earlier in this book, they found that "relationships with others are another source of social power" and that "those with low collective efficacy were more likely to be victimized, either in person or electronically, than those with high collective efficacy" (857). They also found that "environmental factors have the potential to affect the power differential between individuals and influence the likelihood of victimization" (857). They specifically noted that "the most important community factor was increased recreational opportunities (access to shopping centers, community centers, etc.), which was related to decreased victimization" (857). These findings led Schumann, Craig, and Rosu to conclude that "supporting the social ecological theory, we found that both individual sociodemographic and social inclusion factors along with community built environment factors affected the prevalence of victimization" but that the significance of community-built environment factors was limited (856).

Thornberg (2018) also applied the social-ecological model to understand how dynamics of power operating at multiple levels influence bullying experiences. Thornberg specifically "adopts a social-ecological perspective on bullying, which states that bullying has to be understood as a social phenomenon which is established and perpetuated over time as a result of the complex interplay between individual and contextual factors" (145). Thornberg focused on the microsystem, described as the "peer ecology in the school classes" (145), and the macro system, described as "cultural norms, social categories, power structures, and ideologies" (145). Interestingly, Thornberg adopted the "modified ecological model in which the social-ecological theory has been integrated with symbolic interactionism and the new sociology of childhood" (145). Through the conduct of ethnographic fieldwork in three public schools in

A WHOLE-SCHOOL APPROACH TO BULLYING PREVENTION AND INTERVENTION

Throughout this book, we have included a Policy Box at the end of each chapter. Each of these Policy Boxes offered an opportunity to reflect on the implications of various criminological theories for prevention and intervention efforts related to school bullying. In chapter 1, you explored the efficacy of charging youth criminally for bullying-related behaviors that result in death by suicide. In chapter 2, you considered the physical environment and whether changes to the design of schools might help to decrease school bullying. In chapter 3, you reflected on the moral, ethical, and instrumental implications of biologically based interventions. In chapter 4, you debated the imposition of mandatory school uniforms and its implications for school climate and bullying. In chapter 5, you addressed bystander intervention programs that also target school cultures and interactions among students, teachers, and staff. Finally, in chapter 6 you considered the utility of restorative responses to bullying that serve to challenge prevailing cultural discourses and eliminate the disproportionate impact of exclusionary discipline policies on students of color and other marginalized students. After reflecting on your responses to the questions in each of the preceding Policy Boxes, consider the following:

1. What would an effective whole-school approach to bullying prevention look like?
   a. What types of policies, programs, and practices would you recommend?
   b. How would these policies, programs, and practices align with the six levels articulated in the social-ecological framework described in this chapter?
2. How would you go about evaluating the effectiveness of your whole-school approach?
   a. What would success look like?
   b. What types of data would you collect, from whom, and how?
3. How does your whole-school approach to prevention align with the various criminological theories discussed in this book?
   a. Which theories inform which aspects of your approach?
   b. What research evidence exists to support the elements of your approach?

Sweden, Thornberg found a "huge overlap between bullying and discrimination" (155). In line with dominant critical criminological critiques, Thornberg concluded, "there is a widespread and predominant bully discourse deployed in school policy and practice in which bullying is conceptualized as caused by bullies' and victims' individual characteristics. This predominant discourse not only makes teachers and others blind to gender norms, heteronormativity, racism and a range of other oppressions taking place in bullying, but will fail to offer an appropriate knowledge base on how to counteract and reduce bullying" (155). Similar to Schumann, Craig, and Rosu (2014), by adopting a social-ecological lens, Thornberg was able to identify the interplay of power dynamics across microsystems and macrosystems.

The Social-Ecological Model as Metatheory

Bronfenbrenner's model can also be understood and applied as a **metatheory**. As Williams and McShane (2010) noted, "metatheories tell us how to put unit theories together, or they specify the things that should be included in unit theories about a particular subject" (224). By this point, the astute reader is probably already thinking that the social-ecological model described here offers a holistic picture of how the various unit theories discussed throughout this book might fit together. As we mentioned in the introduction, the social-ecological framework served as a grounding for the presentation of these criminological theories as applied to school bullying. In the introduction to their 2004 edited book titled *Bullying in American Schools: A Social-Ecological Perspective on Prevention and Intervention*, Swearer and Espelage argue convincingly for a social-ecological approach to bullying, urging researchers to recognize that "bullying has to be understood across individual, family, peer, school, and community contexts. Bullying and victimization are ecological phenomena that are established and perpetuated over time as the result of the complex interplay between inter- and intra-individual variables" (1). Thornberg (2015b) has similarly argued for "the necessity of dialogue between different theoretical perspectives and the inclusive potential of the social-ecological framework to create a meeting point of theories in order to develop a more comprehensive understanding of school bullying" (161). Since the publication of Swearer and Espelage's edited volume, scholars have taken up this call, not only through the conduct of the research described above, but also by conducting numerous reviews of the bullying literature in order to show how existing research findings can be better understood when placed within a social-ecological framework or metatheory (see, for instance, Hong et al. 2014; McGuckin and Minton 2014; Rose, Nickerson, and Stormont 2015; Swearer and Hymel 2015a).

The adoption of the social-ecological framework as a metatheory within the study of school bullying has led to a series of important insights. First, and as already alluded to, in order to understand more fully the complexity of human phenomena such as bullying perpetration and victimization, we must employ multiple theoretical perspectives that address different explanatory levels. This can be achieved through the development of integrated theories or through the consideration of findings from multiple studies, each grounded in a different unit theory. Second, as Swearer and Espelage (2004) point out, "assessment of [the] bullying phenomenon must utilize multiple methods of assessment, use multiple informants, and include assessments across contexts" (4). Whether this occurs within specific studies or through the combining of interrelated findings from multiple studies, bullying scholars will need to incorporate both qualitative and quantitative methodologies; collect data from students, teachers, school staff, parents, community members, and others; and attend to differing spatial, geographic, sociocultural, political and other contexts within which school bullying occurs. Finally, in order to be effective in the long term, intervention and prevention efforts must attend to the individual, microsystem, mesosystem, exosystem, macrosystem, and chronosystem.

REFERENCES

Agnew, Robert. 1992. "Foundation for a General Strain Theory of Crime and Delinquency." *Criminology* 30 (1): 47–88.

———. 1999. "A General Strain Theory of Community Differences in Crime Rates." *Journal of Research in Crime and Delinquency* 36 (2): 123–55.

———. 2001. "Building on the Foundation of General Strain Theory: Specifying the Types of Strain Most Likely to Lead to Crime and Delinquency." *Journal of Research in Crime and Delinquency* 38 (4): 319–61.

———. 2006. *Pressured into Crime: An Overview of General Strain Theory.* Los Angeles: Roxbury.

———. 2010. "A General Strain Theory of Terrorism." *Theoretical Criminology* 14 (2): 131–53.

Ahmed, Eliza, and Valerie Braithwaite. 2012. "Learning to Manage Shame in School Bullying: Lessons for Restorative Justice Interventions." *Critical Criminology* 20 (1): 79–97.

Ainsworth, Mary, and John Bowlby. 1991. "An Ethological Approach to Personality Development." *American Psychologist* 46 (4): 333–41.

Akers, Ronald. 1973. *Deviant Behavior: A Social Learning Approach.* Belmont, CA: Wadsworth.

Akers, Ronald. 2000. *Criminological Theories: Introduction, Evaluation, and Application.* 3rd ed. Los Angeles: Roxbury.

Albertson, Alicia. 2014. "Criminalizing Bullying: Why Indiana Should Hold the Bully Responsible." *Indiana Law Review* 48 (1): 243–71.

Aldridge, Jill, Katrina McChesney, and Ernest Afari. 2018. "Relationships between School Climate, Bullying and Delinquent Behaviours." *Learning Environments Research* 21 (2): 153–72.

Alhafez, Laila, and Amira Masri. 2019. "School Bullying: An Increasingly Recognized Etiology for Psychogenic Non-Epileptic Seizures: Report of Two Cases." *International Journal of Pediatrics and Adolescent Medicine* 6 (4): 155–57. https://doi.org/10.1016/j.ijpam.2019.05.007.

Alikasifoglu, Mujgan, Ethem Erginoz, Oya Ercan, Omer Uysal, and Deniz Albayrak-Kaymak. 2007. "Bullying Behaviours and Psychosocial Health: Results from a Cross-Sectional Survey among High School Students in Istanbul, Turkey." *European Journal of Pediatrics* 166 (12): 1253–60.

Alipan, Alexandra, Jason Skues, Stephen Theiler, and Lisa Wise. 2015. "Defining Cyberbullying: A Multiple Perspectives Approach." In *Annual Review of Cybertherapy and Telemedicine*, edited by Brenda K. Wiederhold, Giuseppe Riva, and Mark D. Wiederhold, 9–13. Amsterdam: IOS Press.

Alkhalayleh, Hesham, and David Newlyn. 2015. "Domestic Violence and School Bullying: An Examination of the Inextricable Link Between the Two and the Use of Restorative Justice to Break the Cycle." *International Journal of Business, Economics and Law* 8 (4): 147–54.

Allison, Stephen, Leigh Roeger, Bradley Smith, and Linda Isherwood. 2014. "Family Histories of School Bullying: Implications for Parent-Child Psychotherapy." *Australasian Psychiatry* 22 (2): 149–53.

Alvi, Shahid, Steven Downing, and Carla Cesaroni. 2015. "The Self and the 'Selfie': Cyber-Bullying Theory and the Structure of Late Modernity." *Contemporary Perspectives in Family Research* 9:383–406.

American Educational Research Association. 2013. *Prevention of Bullying in Schools, Colleges, and Universities: Research Report and Recommendations*. Washington, DC: American Educational Research Association.

American Psychiatric Association. 2013. *Diagnostic and Statistical Manual of Mental Disorders (DSM-5)*. 5th. ed. Arlington, VA: American Psychiatric Association.

Amir, Menachem. 1967. "Victim-Precipitated Forcible Rape." *Journal of Criminal Law, Criminology, and Police Science* 58:493–502.

Appelbaum, Paul, and Nicholas Scurich. 2014. "Impact of Behavioral Genetic Evidence on the Adjudication of Criminal Behavior." *Journal of the American Academy of Psychiatry and the Law* 42 (1): 91–100.

Arana, Allyson, Erin Boyd, Maria Guarneri-White, Priya Iyer-Eimerbrink, Angela Liegey Dougall, and Lauri Jensen-Campbell. 2018. "The Impact of Social and Physical Peer Victimization on Systemic Inflammation in Adolescents." *Merrill-Palmer Quarterly* 64 (1): 12–40.

Ard, Kerry. 2015. "Trends in Exposure to Industrial Air Toxins for Different Racial and Socioeconomic Groups: A Spatial and Temporal Examination of Environmental Inequality in the US from 1995 to 2004." *Social Science Research* 53:375–90.

Arnarsson, Arsaell, and Thoroddur Bjarnason. 2018. "The Problem with Low-Prevalence of Bullying." *International Journal of Environmental Research and Public Health* 15 (7): 1535. https://doi.org/10.3390/ijerph15071535.

Arnout, Boshra A., Abeer S. Alshehri, Aeshah M. Assiri, and Fatma Y. Al-Qadimi. 2020. "Diagnostic Criteria for Postbullying Disorder: A Phenomenological Research Design of Bullying Victims." *Journal of Public Affairs*: e2063. Published ahead of print, January 10, 2020. https://doi.org/10.1002/pa.2063.

Arrigo, Bruce. 1999. *Social Justice/Criminal Justice: The Maturation of Critical Theory in Law, Crime, and Deviance*. Belmont, CA: Wadsworth.

Averdijk, Margit, Tina Malti, Manuel Eisner, Denis Ribeaud, and David Farrington. 2016. "A Vicious Cycle of Peer Victimization? Problem Behavior Mediates Stability in Peer Victimization over Time." *Journal of Developmental and Life-Course Criminology* 2 (2): 162–81.

Ayers, Stephanie, M. Alex Wagaman, Jennifer Mullins Geiger, Monica Bermudez-Parsai, and E.C. Hedberg. 2012. "Examining School-Based Bullying Interventions Using Multilevel Discrete Time Hazard Modeling." *Prevention Sciences* 13:539–50.

Azeredo, Catarina Machado, Ana Elisa Madalena Rinaldi, Claudia Leite de Moraes, Renata Bertazzi Levy, and Paulo Rossi Menezes. 2015. "School Bullying: A Systematic Review of Contextual-Level Risk Factors in Observational Studies." *Aggression and Violent Behavior* 22:65–76.

Azurmendi, Aitziber, Francisco Braza, Ainhoa García, Paloma Braza, José M. Muñoz, and José Sánchez-Martín. 2006. "Aggression, Dominance, and Affiliation: Their Relationships with Androgen Levels and Intelligence in 5-Year-Old Children." *Hormones and Behavior* 50 (1): 132–40.

Baams, Laura, Craig Talmage, and Stephen Russell. 2017. "Economic Costs of Bias-Based Bullying." *School Psychology Quarterly* 32 (3): 422–33.

Baek, Hyunin, Michael Losavio, and George Higgins. 2016. "The Impact of Low Self-Control on Online Harassment: Interaction with Opportunity." *Journal of Digital Forensics, Security and Law* 11 (3): 27–42.

Bain, Marc. 2018. "More US School Kids than Ever Are Wearing Uniforms This Fall." *Quartz*, September 11, 2018. https://qz.com/quartzy/1382336/school-uniforms-are-rapidly-on-the-rise-at-us-public-schools/.

Bajaj, Monisha, Ameena Ghaffar-Kucher, and Karishma Desai. 2016. "Brown Bodies and Xenophobic Bullying in US Schools: Critical Analysis and Strategies for Action." *Harvard Educational Review* 86 (4): 481–505.

Baldasare, Angela, Sheri Bauman, Lori Goldman, and Alexandra Robie. 2012. "Cyberbullying? Voices of College Students." In *Misbehavior Online in Higher Education*, edited by Laura A. Wankel and Charles Wankel, 127–55. Bingley, UK: Emerald.

Baldry, Anna, and David Farrington. 2005. "Protective Factors as Moderators of Risk Factors in Adolescence Bullying." *Social Psychology of Education* 8 (3): 263–84.

Ball, Harriet, Louise Arseneault, Alan Taylor, Barbara Maughan, Avshalom Caspi, and Terrie Moffitt. 2008. "Genetic and Environmental Influences on Victims, Bullies and Bully-Victims in Childhood." *Journal of Child Psychology and Psychiatry* 49 (1): 104–12.

Ball, Matthew. 2014. "Queer Criminology, Critique, and the 'Art of Not Being Governed'." *Critical Criminology* 22 (1): 21–34.

Bandura, Albert. 1973. *Aggression: A Social Learning Analysis*. Englewood Cliffs, NJ: Prentice-Hall.

———. 1990. "Selective Activation and Disengagement of Moral Control." *Journal of Social Issues* 46 (1): 27–46.

Bansel, Peter, Bronwyn Davies, Cath Laws, and Sheridan Linnell. 2009. "Bullies, Bullying and Power in the Contexts of Schooling." *British Journal of Sociology of Education* 30 (1): 59–69.

Barlett, Christopher, and Sarah Coyne. 2014. "A Meta-Analysis of Sex Differences in Cyber-Bullying Behavior: The Moderating Role of Age." *Aggressive Behavior* 40 (5): 474–88.

Barlett, Christopher, Sara Prot, Craig Anderson, and Douglas Gentile. 2017. "An Empirical Examination of the Strength Differential Hypothesis in Cyberbullying Behavior." *Psychology of Violence* 7 (1): 22–32.

Barnes, Amy, Donna Cross, Leanne Lester, Lydia Hearn, Melanie Epstein, and Helen Monks. 2012. "The Invisibility of Covert Bullying among Students: Challenges for School Intervention." *Journal of Psychologists and Counsellors in Schools* 22 (2): 206–26.

Barnes, J.C., and Ryan Motz. 2018. "Reducing Racial Inequalities in Adulthood Arrest by Reducing Inequalities in School Discipline: Evidence from the School-to-Prison Pipeline." *Developmental Psychology* 54 (12): 2328.

Barron, Christie, and Dany Lacombe. 2005. "Moral Panic and the Nasty Girl." *Canadian Review of Sociology* 42 (1): 51–69.

Battistich, Victor, and Allen Hom. 1997. "The Relationship between Students' Sense of Their School as a Community and Their Involvement in Problem Behaviors." *American Journal of Public Health* 87 (12): 1997–2001.

Bazelon, Emily. 2010. "The Untold Story of Her Suicide and the Role of the Kids Who Have Been Criminally Charged for It." *Slate*, July 20, 2010. https://slate.com/human-interest/2010/07/what-really-happened-to-phoebe-prince-the-untold-story-of-her-suicide-and-the-role-of-the-kids-who-have-been-criminally-charged-for-it-1.html.

———. 2012. "A Big Win: The Landmark Settlement in a Minnesota Bullying Case and How It Could Help Gay Students Everywhere." *Slate*, March 7, 2012. https://slate.com/news-and-politics/2012/03/the-anoka-hennepin-settlement-a-big-win-in-the-fight-against-gay-bashing-bullies.html.

Beaty, Lee A., and Erick B. Alexeyev. 2008. "The Problem of School Bullies: What the Research Tells Us." *Adolescence* 43 (169): 1–11.

Beaudoin, Huguette, and Ginette Roberge. 2015. "Student Perceptions of School Climate and Lived Bullying Behaviours." *Procedia—Social and Behavioral Sciences* 174 (C): 321–30.

Beaver, Kevin, Brian Boutwell, J.C. Barnes, Michael Vaughn, and Matt DeLisi. 2017. "The Association between Psychopathic Personality Traits and Criminal Justice Outcomes: Results from a Nationally Representative Sample of Males and Females." *Crime & Delinquency* 63 (6): 708–30.

Becker, Howard. 1963. *Outsiders: Studies in the Sociology of Deviance*. New York: Free Press.

Bellair, Paul, Thomas McNulty, and Alex Piquero. 2016. "Verbal Ability and Persistent Offending: A Race-Specific Test of Moffitt's Theory." *Justice Quarterly* 33 (3): 455–80.

Bender, Patrick, Courtney Plante, and Douglas Gentile. 2018. "The Effects of Violent Media Content on Aggression." *Current Opinion in Psychology* 19:104–8.

Berryessa, Colleen. 2017. "Jury-Eligible Public Attitudes toward Biological Risk Factors for the Development of Criminal Behavior and Implications for Capital Sentencing." *Criminal Justice and Behavior* 44 (8): 1073–1100.

Besemer, Sytske, Shaikh Ahmad, Stephen Hinshaw, and David Farrington. 2017. "A Systematic Review and Meta-Analysis of the Intergenerational Transmission of Criminal Behavior." *Aggression and Violent Behavior* 37:161–78.

Bethune, Jennifer, and Marnina Gonick. 2017. "Schooling the Mean Girl: A Critical Discourse Analysis of Teacher Resource Materials." *Gender and Education* 29 (3): 389–404.

Bezdjian, Serena, Laura Baker, and Catherine Tuvblad. 2011. "Genetic and Environmental Influences on Impulsivity: A Meta-Analysis of Twin, Family and Adoption Studies." *Clinical Psychology Review* 31 (7): 1209–23.

Billings, Stephen, and Kevin Schnepel. 2018. "Life after Lead: Effects of Early Interventions for Children Exposed to Lead." *American Economic Journal: Applied Economics* 10 (3): 315–44.

Binik, Oriana, Adolfo Ceretti, Roberto Cornelli, Hans Schadee, Alfredo Verde, and Uberto Gatti. 2019. "Neighborhood Social Capital, Juvenile Delinquency, and Victimization: Results from the International Self-Report Delinquency Study-3 in 23 Countries." *European Journal on Criminal Policy and Research* 25 (3): 241–58.

Bishop, Asia, Karl Hill, Amanda Gilman, James Howell, Richard Catalano, and J. David Hawkins. 2017. "Developmental Pathways of Youth Gang Membership: A Structural Test of the Social Development Model." *Journal of Crime and Justice* 40 (3): 275–96

Blanco-Castilla, Elena, and Juan Cano-Galindo. 2019. "School Bullying and Teen Suicide in the Spanish Press: From Journalistic Taboo to Boom." *Revista Latina de Comunicación Social* 74:937–49.

Blau, Judith, and Peter Blau. 1982. "The Cost of Inequality: Metropolitan Structure and Violent Crime." *American Sociological Review* 47 (1): 114–29.

Blumstein, Alfred, ed. 1986. *Criminal Careers and "Career Criminals."* Vol. 1. Washington, DC: National Academies.

Boge, Cecilie, and Anna Larsson. 2018. "Understanding Pupil Violence: Bullying Theory as Technoscience in Sweden and Norway." *Nordic Journal of Educational History* 5 (2): 131–49.

Boman, John, and Thomas Mowen. 2018. "The Role of Turning Points in Establishing Baseline Differences between People in Developmental and Life-Course Criminology." *Criminology* 56 (1): 191–224.

Booth, Alan, David Johnson, Douglas Granger, Ann Crouter, and Susan McHale. 2003. "Testosterone and Child and Adolescent Adjustment: The Moderating Role of Parent-Child Relationships." *Developmental Psychology* 39 (1): 85–98.

Borgwald, Kristin, and H. Theixos. (2013). "Bullying the Bully: Why Zero-Tolerance Policies Get a Failing Grade." *Social Influence* 8 (2–3): 149–60.

Bossler, Adam, Thomas Holt, and David May. 2012. "Predicting Online Harassment Victimization among a Juvenile Population." *Youth & Society* 44 (4): 500–23.

Bouchard, Karen, Camilla Forsberg, J. David Smith, and Robert Thornberg. 2018. "Showing Friendship, Fighting Back, and Getting Even: Resisting Bullying Victimization within Adolescent Girls' Friendships." *Journal of Youth Studies* 21 (9): 1141–58.

Bouffard, Leana, and Maria Koeppel. 2014. "Understanding the Potential Long-Term Physical and Mental Health Consequences of Early Experiences of Victimization." *Justice Quarterly* 31 (3): 568–87.

Bowes, Lucy, Barbara Maughan, Harriet Ball, Sania Shakoor, Isabelle Ouellet-Morin, Avshalom Caspi, Terrie Moffitt, and Louise Arseneault. 2013. "Chronic Bullying Victimization across School Transitions: The Role of Genetic and Environmental Influences." *Development and Psychopathology* 25 (2): 333–46.

Bowlby, John. 1988. *A Secure Base: Parent-Child Attachment and Healthy Human Development.* New York: Basic Books.

Bradshaw, Catherine, Tracy Evian Waasdorp, and Sarah Lindstrom Johnson. 2015. "Overlapping Verbal, Relational, Physical, and Electronic Forms of Bullying in Adolescence: Influence of School Context." *Journal of Clinical Child & Adolescent Psychology* 44 (3): 494–508.

Braithwaite, John. 1981. "The Myth of Social Class and Criminality Reconsidered." *American Sociological Review* 46 (1): 36–57.

———. 1989. *Crime, Shame, and Reintegration.* Cambridge, UK: Cambridge University Press.

———. 2006. "Doing Justice Intelligently in Civil Society." *Journal of Social Issues* 62 (2): 393–409.

Branson, Christopher, and Dewey Cornell. 2009. "A Comparison of Self and Peer Reports in the Assessment of Middle School Bullying," *Journal of Applied School Psychology* 25 (1): 5–27.

Braswell, Michael, John Fuller, and Bo Lozoff. 2001. *Corrections, Peacemaking, and Restorative Justice: Transforming Individuals and Institutions.* Cincinnati: Anderson.

Brezina, Timothy, Alex Piquero, and Paul Mazerolle. 2001. "Student Anger and Aggressive Behavior in School: An Initial Test of Agnew's Macro-Level Strain Theory." *Journal of Research in Crime and Delinquency* 38 (4): 362–86.

Broll, Ryan, and Laura Huey. 2015. "'Just Being Mean to Somebody Isn't a Police Matter': Police Perspectives on Policing Cyberbullying." *Journal of School Violence* 14:155–76.

Bronfenbrenner, Urie. 1979. *The Ecology of Human Development.* Cambridge, MA: Harvard University Press.

———. 2005. *Making Human Beings Human: Bioecological Perspectives on Human Development.* Thousand Oaks, CA: SAGE.

Brook, Michael, Matthew Panizzon, David Kosson, Elizabeth Sullivan, Michael Lyons, Carol Franz, Seth Eisen, and William Kremen. 2010. "Psychopathic Personality Traits in Middle-Aged Male Twins: A Behavior Genetic Investigation." *Journal of Personality Disorders* 24 (4): 473–86.

Brookshire, Attillah. 2016. "The Impact of School Uniforms on School Climate." PhD diss., Walden University. https://scholarworks.waldenu.edu/cgi/viewcontent .cgi?article=3352&context=dissertations.

Bruening, Rebecca, Rosaura Orengo-Aguayo, Angela Onwuachi-Willig, and Marizen Ramirez. 2018. "Implementation of Antibullying Legislation in Iowa Schools: A Qualitative Examination of School Administrators' Perceived Barriers and Facilitators." *Journal of School Violence* 17 (3): 284–97.

Brunsma, David, ed. 2005. *Uniforms in Public Schools: A Decade of Research and Debate*. Lanham, MD: Rowman and Littlefield.

Burraston, Bert, James McCutcheon, and Stephen Watts. 2018. "Relative and Absolute Deprivation's Relationship with Violent Crime in the United States: Testing an Interaction Effect between Income Inequality and Disadvantage." *Crime & Delinquency* 64 (4): 542–60.

Burton, Alex, Dan Florell, and Dustin Wygant. 2013. "The Role of Peer Attachment and Normative Beliefs About Aggression on Traditional Bullying and Cyberbullying." *Psychology in the Schools* 50 (2): 103–15.

Burton, Patrick, and Lezanne Leoschut. 2013. *School Violence in South Africa: Results of the 2012 National School Violence Study*. Cape Town, South Africa: Center for Justice and Crime Prevention.

Calvete, Esther, Liria Fernández-González, Joaquín González-Cabrera, and Manuel Gámez-Guadix. 2018. "Continued Bullying Victimization in Adolescents: Maladaptive Schemas as a Mediational Mechanism." *Journal of Youth and Adolescence* 47 (3): 650–60.

Cantone, Elisa, Anna Piras, Marcello Vellante, Antonello Preti, Sigrun Daníelsdóttir, Ernesto D'Aloja, Sigita Lesinskiene, Mathhias Angermeyer, Mauro Carta, and Dinesh Bhugra. 2015. "Interventions on Bullying and Cyberbullying in Schools: A Systematic Review." Supplement, *Clinical Practice and Epidemiology in Mental Health* 11 (S1 M4): 58–76.

Cappadocia, Catherine, Debra Pepler, Joanne Cummings, and Wendy Craig. 2012. "Individual Motivations and Characteristics Associated with Bystander Intervention during Bullying Episodes among Children and Youth." *Canadian Journal of School Psychology* 27 (3): 201–16.

Carbone-Lopez, Kristin, Finn-Aage Esbensen, and Bradley Brick. 2010. "Correlates and Consequences of Peer Victimization: Gender Differences in Direct and Indirect Forms of Bullying." *Youth Violence and Juvenile Justice* 8 (4): 332–50.

Carney, JoLynn, Yanhong Liu, and Richard Hazler. 2018. "A Path Analysis on School Bullying and Critical School Environment Variables: A Social Capital Perspective." *Children and Youth Services Review* 93:231–39.

Carpenter, David, and Rick Nevin. 2010. "Environmental Causes of Violence." *Physiology & Behavior* 99 (2): 260–68.

Cascardi, Michele, Cathy Brown, Melinda Iannarone, and Norma Cardona. 2014. "The Problem with Overly Broad Definitions of Bullying: Implications for the Schoolhouse, the Statehouse, and the Ivory Tower." *Journal of School Violence* 13 (3): 253–76.

Casper, Deborah, Diana Meter, and Noel Card. 2015. "Addressing Measurement Issues Related to Bullying Involvement." *School Psychology Review* 44 (4): 353–71.

Catalano, Richard, and J. David Hawkins. 1996. "The Social Development Model: A Theory of Antisocial Behavior." In *Delinquency and Crime: Current Theories*, edited by J. David Hawkins, 149–97. Cambridge, MA: Cambridge University Press.

Cecen-Celik, Hatice, and Shelley Keith. 2016. "Analyzing Predictors of Bullying Victimization with Routine Activity and Social Bond Perspectives." *Journal of Interpersonal Violence* 32 (18): 3807–32.

Cesaroni, Carla, Steven Downing, and Shahid Alvi. 2012. "Bullying Enters the 21st Century? Turning a Critical Eye to Cyber-Bullying Research." *Youth Justice* 12 (3): 199–211.

Chan, Heng, and Choon Chui. 2013. "Social Bonds and School Bullying: A Study of Macanese Male Adolescents on Bullying Perpetration and Peer Victimization." *Child & Youth Care Forum* 42 (6): 599–616.

———. 2015. "Social Bond and Self-Reported Nonviolent and Violent Delinquency: A Study of Traditional Low Risk, At-Risk, and Adjudicated Male Chinese Adolescents." *Child & Youth Care Forum* 44 (5): 711–30.

Chan, Heng, and Choon Wong. 2015. "The Overlap between School Bullying Perpetration and Victimization: Assessing the Psychological, Familial, and School Factors of Chinese Adolescents in Hong Kong." *Journal of Child and Family Studies* 24 (11): 3224–34.

Chance, Susan E., Ronald Brown, James Dabbs, and Robert Casey. 2000. "Testosterone, Intelligence and Behavior Disorders in Young Boys." *Personality and Individual Differences* 28 (3): 437–45.

Chandler, Tara. 2018. "Impact of a Varied Understanding of School Bullying." *Journal of Aggression, Conflict and Peace Research* 10 (1): 36–45.

Chaux, Enrique, and Melisa Castellanos. 2015. "Money and Age in Schools: Bullying and Power Imbalances." *Aggressive Behavior* 41 (3): 280–93.

Chaux, Enrique, Andrés Molano, and Paola Podlesky. 2009. "Socio-Economic, Socio-Political and Socio-Emotional Variables Explaining School Bullying: A Country-Wide Multilevel Analysis." *Aggressive Behavior: Official Journal of the International Society for Research on Aggression* 35 (6): 520–29.

Chen, Guanghui, Yanhong Kong, Kirby Deater-Deckard, and Wenxin Zhang. 2018. "Bullying Victimization Heightens Cortisol Response to Psychosocial Stress in Chinese Children." *Journal of Abnormal Child Psychology* 46 (5): 1051–59.

Cho, Sujung. 2017a. "Explaining the Overlap between Bullying Perpetration and Bullying Victimization: Assessing the Time-Ordered and Correlative Relationships." *Children and Youth Services Review* 79:280–90.

———. 2017b. "Self-Control and Risky Lifestyles in Context: Cross-Level Integration between Opportunity and Collective Efficacy in the Study of Peer Victimization among South Korean Youth." *Journal of Child and Family Studies* 26 (1): 67–79.

Cho, Sujung, Jun Sung Hong, Dorothy Espelage, and Kyung-Shick Choi. 2017. "Applying the Lifestyle Routine Activities Theory to Understand Physical and Nonphysical Peer Victimization." *Journal of Aggression, Maltreatment & Trauma* 26 (3): 297–315.

Cho, Sujung, and Jeoung Lee. 2018. "Explaining Physical, Verbal, and Social Bullying among Bullies, Victims of Bullying, and Bully-Victims: Assessing the Integrated Approach between Social Control and Lifestyles-Routine Activities Theories." *Children and Youth Services Review* 91:372–82.

Cho, Sujung, and John Wooldredge. 2018a. "Direct and Indirect Effects of Low Self-Control on the Personal Victimization of South Korean Youth." *Journal of Youth Studies* 21 (7): 958–82.

———. 2018b. "Lifestyles, Informal Controls, and Youth Victimization Risk in South Korea and the United States." *Journal of Youth Studies* 27:958–82.

Cho, Sujung, John Wooldredge, and Cheong Sun Park. 2016. "Lifestyles/Routine Activities and Bullying among South Korean Youths." *Victims & Offenders* 11:285–314.

Choi, Kyung-Shick, Shea Cronin, and Heather Correia. 2016. "The Assessment of Capable Guardianship Measures against Bullying Victimization in the School Environment." *Police Practice and Research* 17 (2): 149–59.

Choi, Kyung-Shick, Kevin Earl, Jin Ree Lee, and Sujung Cho. 2019. "Diagnosis of Cyber and Non-Physical Bullying Victimization: A Lifestyles and Routine Activities Theory Approach to Constructing Effective Preventative Measures." *Computers in Human Behavior* 92:11–19.

Choi, Kyung-Shick, Seong-Sik Lee, and Jin Ree Lee. 2017. "Mobile Phone Technology and Online Sexual Harassment among Juveniles in South Korea: Effects of Self-Control and Social Learning." *International Journal of Cyber Criminology* 11 (1): 110–27.

Choy, Olivia, Farah Focquaert, and Adrian Raine. 2020. "Benign Biological Interventions to Reduce Offending." *Neuroethics* 13: 29–41.

Christensen, Candace, and Rachel Wright. 2018. "'I Didn't Raise a D#@k!' How Parents Perceive and Address Gendered Bullying with Children." *Journal of Human Behavior in the Social Environment* 28 (4): 509–27.

Chui, Wing, and Hong Chan. 2015. "Self-Control, School Bullying Perpetration, and Victimization among Macanese Adolescents." *Journal of Child and Family Studies* 24 (6): 1751–61.

Cicchetti, Dante, and Fred Rogosch. 1996. "Equifinality and Multifinality in Developmental Psychopathology." *Development and Psychopathology* 8 (4): 597–600.

Clarke, Ronald, and Derek Cornish. 1985. "Modeling Offenders' Decisions: A Framework for Research and Policy." *Crime and Justice* 6:147–85.

Cloward, Richard, and Lloyd Ohlin. 1960. *Delinquency and Opportunity: A Study of Delinquent Gangs.* New York: Free Press.

Coburn, Cynthia. 2016. "What's Policy Got to Do with It? How the Structure-Agency Debate Can Illuminate Policy Implementation." *American Journal of Education* 122 (3): 465–75.

Cohen, Albert. 1955. *Delinquent Boys: The Culture of the Gang.* New York: Free Press.

Cohen, Jeffrey W., and Robert A. Brooks. 2014. *Confronting School Bullying: Kids, Culture, and the Making of a Social Problem.* Boulder, CO: Lynne Rienner Press.

Cohen, Jonathan, Libby McCabe, Nicholas Michelli, and Terry Pickeral. 2009. "School Climate: Research, Policy, Practice, and Teacher Education." *Teachers College Record* 111 (1): 180–213.

Cohen, Lawrence, and Marcus Felson. 1979. "Social Change and Crime Rate Trends: A Routine Activity Approach." *American Sociological Review* 44 (4): 588–608.

Cohen, Lawrence, James Kluegel, and Kenneth Land. 1981. "Social Inequality and Predatory Criminal Victimization: An Exposition and Test of a Formal Theory." *American Sociological Review* 46 (5): 505–24.

Collier, Kate, Gabriel Van Beusekom, Henny Bos, and Theo Sandfort. 2013. "Sexual Orientation and Gender Identity/Expression Related Peer Victimization in Adolescence: A Systematic Review of Associated Psychosocial and Health Outcomes." *Journal of Sex Research* 50 (3–4): 299–317.

Connolly, Eric, and Kevin Beaver. 2016. "Considering the Genetic and Environmental Overlap between Bullying Victimization, Delinquency, and Symptoms of Depression/Anxiety." *Journal of Interpersonal Violence* 31 (7): 1230–56.

Conrad, Peter. 2017. *Identifying Hyperactive Children: The Medicalization of Deviant Behavior.* Expanded ed. Oxon, England: Routledge.

Constantino, John, Daniel Grosz, Paul Saenger, Donald Chandler, Reena Nandi, and Felton Earls. 1993. "Testosterone and Aggression in Children." *Journal of the American Academy of Child & Adolescent Psychiatry* 32 (6): 1217–22.

Cook, Philip, Denise Gottfredson, and Chongmin Na. 2010. "School Crime Control and Prevention." *Crime and Justice,* 39 (1): 313–440.

Copeland, William, Cynthia Bulik, Nancy Zucker, Dieter Wolke, Suzet Tanya Lereya, and Elizabeth Jane Costello. 2015. "Does Childhood Bullying Predict Eating Disorder Symptoms? A Prospective, Longitudinal Analysis." *International Journal of Eating Disorders* 48 (8): 1141–49.

Corcoran, Lucie, Conor McGuckin, and Garry Prentice. 2015. "Cyberbullying or Cyber Aggression?: A Review of Existing Definitions of Cyber-Based Peer-to-Peer Aggression." *Societies* 5 (2): 245–55.

Cornell, Dewey, and Sharmila Bandyopadhyay. 2010. "The Assessment of Bullying." In *Handbook of Bullying in Schools: An International Perspective,* edited by Shane R. Jimerson, Susan M. Swearer, and Dorothy L. Espelage, 265–76. New York: Routledge.

Cornell, Dewey, Anne Gregory, Francis Huang, and Xitao Fan. 2013. "Perceived Prevalence of Teasing and Bullying Predicts High School Dropout Rates." *Journal of Educational Psychology* 105 (1): 138–49.

Cornell, Dewey, and Francis Huang. 2016. "Authoritative School Climate and High School Student Risk Behavior: A Cross-Sectional Multi-Level Analysis of Student Self-Reports." *Journal of Youth and Adolescence* 45:2246–59.

Cornell, Dewey, and Susan Limber. 2015. "Law and Policy on the Concept of Bullying at School." *American Psychologist* 70 (4): 333–43.

Cornell, Dewey, Kathan Shulka, and Timothy Konold. 2016. "Authoritative School Climate and Student Academic Engagement, Grades, and Aspirations in Middle and High Schools." *AERA Open* 2, no. 2 (April–June): 1–18.

Costello, Matthew, James Hawdon, and Amanda Cross. 2017. "Virtually Standing Up or Standing By? Correlates of Enacting Social Control Online." *International Journal of Criminology and Sociology* 6:16–28.

Craig, Wendy, and Debra Pepler. 1998. "Observations of Bullying and Victimization in the School Yard." *Canadian Journal of School Psychology* 13 (2): 41–59.

Craig, Wendy, Debra Pepler, and Rona Atlas. 2000. "Observations of Bullying in the Playground and in the Classroom." *School Psychology International* 21 (1): 22–36.

Crenshaw, Kimberlé, Neil Gotanda, Gary Peller, and Kendall Thomas. 1995. *Critical Race Theory: The Key Writings That Formed the Movement.* New York: New Press.

Cressey, Donald. 1960. "Epidemiology and Individual Conduct: A Case from Criminology." *Sociological Perspectives* 3 (2): 47–58.

Crick, Nicki, and Kenneth Dodge. 1994. "A Review and Reformulation of Social Information-Processing Mechanisms in Children's Social Adjustment." *Psychological Bulletin* 115 (1): 74–101.

Cron, Alan. 2016. "From Legislation to Implementation: A Distributed Leadership View of One District's Response to the Massachusetts Anti-Bullying Law of 2010." *Journal of Educational Administration* 54 (1): 75–91.

Crooks, Hayley. 2016. "An Intersectional Feminist Review of the Literature on Gendered Cyberbullying: Digital Girls." *Jeunesse: Young People, Texts, Cultures* 8 (2): 62–73.

Cullen, David. 2010. *Columbine.* New York: Twelve.

Cullen, Francis, James Unnever, Jennifer Hartman, Michael Turner, and Robert Agnew. 2008. "Gender, Bullying Victimization, and Juvenile Delinquency: A Test of General Strain Theory." *Victims and Offenders* 3 (4): 346–64.

Cullingford, Cedric, and Jenny Morrison. 1995. "Bullying as a Formative Influence: The Relationship between the Experience of School and Criminality." *British Educational Research Journal* 21 (5): 547–60.

Cunningham, Charles, Cailin Mapp, Heather Rimas, Lesley Cunningham, Stephanie Mielko, Tracy Vaillancourt, and Madalyn Marcus. 2016. "What Limits the Effectiveness of Antibullying Programs? A Thematic Analysis of the Perspective of Students." *Psychology of Violence* 6 (4): 596–606.

Cunningham, Charles, Heather Rimas, Stephanie Mielko, Cailin Mapp, Lesley Cunningham, Don Buchanan, Tracy Vaillancourt, Yvonne Chen, Ken Deal, and Madalyn Marcus. 2016. "What Limits the Effectiveness of Antibullying

Programs? A Thematic Analysis of the Perspective of Teachers." *Journal of School Violence* 15 (4): 460–82.

Cunningham, Twylla, Katrina Hoy, and Ciaran Shannon. 2016. "Does Childhood Bullying Lead to the Development of Psychotic Symptoms? A Meta-Analysis and Review of Prospective Studies." *Psychosis* 8 (1): 48–59.

Curtis, Lynn. 1974. "Victim-Precipitation and Violent Crimes." *Social Problems* 21:594–605.

Davies, Bronwyn. 2011. "Bullies as Guardians of the Moral Order or an Ethic of Truths?" *Children & Society* 25 (4): 278–86.

Davis v. Monroe County Board of Education, 526 U.S. 629 (1999).

Davis, Fania. 2014. "Discipline with Dignity: Oakland Classrooms Try Healing Instead of Punishment." *Reclaiming Children and Youth* 23 (1): 38–41.

Davis, Jordan, Katherine Ingram, Gabriel Merrin, and Dorothy Espelage. 2020. "Exposure to Parental and Community Violence and the Relationship to Bullying Perpetration and Victimization among Early Adolescents: A Parallel Process Growth Mixture Latent Transition Analysis." *Scandinavian Journal of Psychology* 61 (1): 77–89.

Dayton, John, and Anne Proffitt Dupre. 2009. "A Child's Right to Human Dignity: Reforming Anti-Bullying Laws in the United States." *Irish Educational Studies* 28 (3): 333–50.

DeCamp, Whitney, and Brian Newby. 2015. "From Bullied to Deviant: The Victim–Offender Overlap among Bullying Victims." *Youth Violence and Juvenile Justice* 13 (1): 3–17.

Della Cioppa, Victoria, Amy O'Neil, and Wendy Craig. 2015. "Learning from Traditional Bullying Interventions: A Review of Research on Cyberbullying and Best Practice." *Aggression and Violent Behavior* 23:61–68.

Delprato, Marcos, Kwame Akyeampong, and Máiréad Dunne. 2017. "The Impact of Bullying on Students' Learning in Latin America: A Matching Approach for 15 Countries." *International Journal of Educational Development* 52:37–57.

Dick, Danielle M., Fazil Aliev, Robert F. Krueger, Alexis Edwards, Arpana Agrawal, Michael Lynskey, Pinpin Lin et al. 2011. "Genome-Wide Association Study of Conduct Disorder Symptomatology." *Molecular Psychiatry* 16 (8): 800–808.

DiLalla, Lisabeth Fisher. 2017. "Behavior Genetics of Aggression in Children: Review and Future Directions." In *Biosocial Theories of Crime*, edited by Kevin M. Beaver and Anthony Walsh, 153–82. New York: Routledge.

Dorio, Nicole, Kelly Clark, Michelle Demaray, and Elyse Doll. 2019. "School Climate Counts: A Longitudinal Analysis of School Climate and Middle School Bullying Behaviors." *International Journal of Bullying Prevention*. Published ahead of print, September 2, 2019. https://doi.org/10.1007/s42380-019-00038-2.

Douglas, Thomas. 2014. "Criminal Rehabilitation through Medical Intervention: Moral Liability and the Right to Bodily Integrity." *Journal of Ethics* 18 (2): 101–22.

Dragone, Mirella, Concetta Esposito, Grazia De Angelis, Gaetana Affuso, and Dario Bacchini. 2020. "Pathways Linking Exposure to Community Violence,

Self-Serving Cognitive Distortions and School Bullying Perpetration: A Three-Wave Study." *International Journal of Environmental Research and Public Health* 17 (1): 188.

Drydakis, Nick. 2014. "Bullying at School and Labour Market Outcomes." *International Journal of Manpower* 35 (8): 1185–1211.

Due, Pernille, Juan Merlo, Yossi Harel-Fisch, Mogens Trab Damsgaard, Bjørn Holstein, Jørn Hetland, Candace Currie, Saoirse Nic Gabhainn, Margarida Gaspar de Metos, and Jon Lynch. 2009. "Socioeconomic Inequality in Exposure to Bullying during Adolescence: A Comparative, Cross-Sectional, Multilevel Study in 35 Countries." *American Journal of Public Health* 99 (5): 907–14.

Duncan, Laramie, Alisha Pollastri, and Jordan Smoller. 2014. "Mind the Gap: Why Many Geneticists and Psychological Scientists Have Discrepant Views about Gene–Environment Interaction (GxE) Research." *American Psychologist* 69 (3): 249–68.

Dunn, Hailee, Melissa Clark, and Deborah Pearlman. 2017. "The Relationship between Sexual History, Bullying Victimization, and Poor Mental Health Outcomes among Heterosexual and Sexual Minority High School Students: A Feminist Perspective." *Journal of Interpersonal Violence* 32 (22): 3497–519.

Du Plessis, Mieke, Sanny Smeekens, Antonius Cillessen, Sarah Whittle, and Berna Güroğlu. 2019. "Bullying the Brain? Longitudinal Links between Childhood Peer Victimization, Cortisol, and Adolescent Brain Structure." *Frontiers in Psychology* 9:2706.

Duy, Baki, and Mehmet Yildiz. 2014. "School Attachment and Loneliness in Early Adolescents with Different Bully Status." *Egitim Ve Bilim* 39 (174): 173–88.

Eastman, Meridith, Brad Verhulst, Lance Rappaport, Melanie Dirks, Chelsea Sawyers, Daniel Pine, Ellen Leibenluft, Melissa Brotman, John Hettema, and Roxann Roberson-Nay. 2018. "Age-Related Differences in the Structure of Genetic and Environmental Contributions to Types of Peer Victimization." *Behavior Genetics* 48 (6): 421–31.

Edmondson, Lynne, and Laura Dreuth Zeman. 2011. "Making School Bully Laws Matter." *Reclaiming Children and Youth* 20 (1): 33–38.

Edwards, Oliver, and Gordon Taub. 2017. "Children and Youth Perceptions of Family Food Insecurity and Bullying." *School Mental Health* 9 (3): 263–72.

Efron, Daryl, Michell Wijaya, Philip Hazell, and Emma Sciberras. 2018. "Peer Victimization in Children with ADHD: A Community-Based Longitudinal Study." *Journal of Attention Disorders*. Published ahead of print, September 7, 2018. https://doi.org/10.1177/1087054718796287.

Efstathopoulos, Paschalis, Filip Andersson, Philippe A. Melas, Liu L. Yang, J. Carlos Villaescusa, Joëlle Rüegg, Tomas J. Ekström, Yvonne Forsell, Maria Rosaria Galanti, and Catharina Lavebratt. 2018. "NR3C1 Hypermethylation in Depressed and Bullied Adolescents." *Translational Psychiatry* 8 (1): 1–8.

Elgar, Frank, Kate Pickett, William Pickett, Wendy Craig, Michal Molcho, Klaus Hurrelmann, and Michela Lenzi. 2013. "School Bullying, Homicide and Income Inequality: A Cross-National Pooled Time Series Analysis." *International Journal of Public Health* 58 (2): 237–45.

Eliot, Megan, Dewey Cornell, Anne Gregory, and Xitao Fan. 2010. "Supportive School Climate and Student Willingness to Seek Help for Bullying and Threats of Violence." *Journal of School Psychology* 48 (6): 533–53.

Elliott, Delbert, Suzanne Ageton, Rachelle Canter, James Short, and Travis Hirschi. 1979. "An Integrated Theoretical Perspective on Delinquent Behavior." *Journal of Research in Crime and Delinquency* 16 (1): 3–27.

Ellis, Bruce, Anthony Volk, Jose-Michael Gonzalez, and Dennis Embry. 2016. "The Meaningful Roles Intervention: An Evolutionary Approach to Reducing Bullying and Increasing Prosocial Behavior." *Journal of Research on Adolescence* 26 (4): 622–37.

Endresen, Inger, and Dan Olweus. 2005. "Participation in Power Sports and Anti-social Involvement in Preadolescent and Adolescent Boys." *Journal of Child Psychology and Psychiatry* 46 (5): 468–78.

Englander, Elizabeth, Edward Donnerstein, Robin Kowalski, Carolyn Lin, and Katalin Parti. 2017. "Defining Cyberbullying." Supplement, *Pediatrics* 140 (2): S148–51.

Englehart, Joshua. 2014. "Attending to the Affective Dimensions of Bullying: Necessary Approaches for the School Leader." *Planning and Changing* 45 (1–2): 19–30.

Erath, Stephen, Alexander Kaeppler, and Kelly Tu. 2019. "Coping with Peer Victimization Predicts Peer Outcomes across the Transition to Middle School." *Social Development* 28 (1): 22–40.

Eriksen, Ingunn Marie. 2018. "The Power of the Word: Students' and School Staff's Use of the Established Bullying Definition." *Educational Research* 60 (2): 157–70.

Espelage, Dorothy. 2014. "Ecological Theory: Preventing Youth Bullying, Aggression, and Victimization." *Theory Into Practice* 53 (4): 257–64.

———. 2018. "Understanding the Complexity of School Bully Involvement." *The Chautauqua Journal* 2 (1): 1–23.

Espelage, Dorothy, Kathleen Basile, Lisa De La Rue, and Merle Hamburger. 2015. "Longitudinal Associations among Bullying, Homophobic Teasing, and Sexual Violence Perpetration among Middle School Students." *Journal of Interpersonal Violence* 30 (14): 2541–61.

Espelage, Dorothy, Kris Bosworth, and Thomas Simon. 2000. "Examining the Social Context of Bullying Behaviors in Early Adolescence." *Journal of Counseling & Development* 78 (3): 326–33.

Ettekal, Idean, and Gary W. Ladd. 2020. "Development of Aggressive-Victims from Childhood through Adolescence: Associations with Emotion Dysregulation, Withdrawn Behaviors, Moral Disengagement, Peer Rejection, and Friendships." *Development and Psychopathology* 32 (1): 271–91.

Evans, Caroline, and Paul Smokowski. 2016. "Theoretical Explanations for Bullying in School: How Ecological Processes Propagate Perpetration and Victimization." *Child and Adolescent Social Work Journal* 33 (4): 365–75.

Evans, Caroline, Paul Smokowski, and Katie Cotter. 2014. "Cumulative Bullying Victimization: An Investigation of the Dose–Response Relationship between Victimization and the Associated Mental Health Outcomes, Social Supports, and School Experiences of Rural Adolescents." *Children and Youth Services Review* 44:256–64.

Fanti, Kostas, and Eva Kimonis. 2013. "Dimensions of Juvenile Psychopathy Distinguish 'Bullies,' 'Bully-Victims,' and 'Victims'." *Psychology of Violence* 3 (4): 396–409.

Faris, Robert, & Diane Felmlee. 2011a. *Social Networks and Aggression at the Wheatley School*. Special report, University of California at Davis, Department of Sociology. http://i2.cdn.turner.com/cnn/2011/images/10/10/findings.from.the .wheatley.school.pdf.

———. 2011b. "Status Struggles: Network Centrality and Gender Segregation in Same-and Cross-Gender Aggression." *American Sociological Review* 76 (1): 48–73.

———. 2014. "Casualties of Social Combat: School Networks of Peer Victimization and Their Consequences." *American Sociological Review* 79 (2): 228–57.

Farmer, Thomas W., Robert A. Petrin, Dylan L. Robertson, Mark W. Fraser, Cristin M. Hall, Steven H. Day, and Kimberly Dadisman. 2010. "Peer Relations of Bullies, Bully-Victims, and Victims: The Two Social Worlds of Bullying in Second-Grade Classrooms." *Elementary School Journal* 110 (3): 364–92.

Farmer, Thomas, Traci Wike, Quentin Alexander, Philip Rodkin, and Meera Mehtaji. 2015. "Students with Disabilities and Involvement in Peer Victimization: Theory, Research, and Considerations for the Future." *Remedial and Special Education* 36 (5): 263–74.

Farrell, Albert, Terri Sullivan, Elizabeth Goncy, and Anh-Thuy Le. 2016. "Assessment of Adolescents' Victimization, Aggression, and Problem Behaviors: Evaluation of the Problem Behavior Frequency Scale." *Psychological Assessment* 28 (6): 702–14.

Farrington, David. 1993. "Understanding and Preventing Bullying." *Crime and Justice* 17:381–458.

———. 2003. "Developmental and Life-Course Criminology: Key Theoretical and Empirical Issues—The 2002 Sutherland Award address." *Criminology* 41 (2): 221–55.

Farrington, David, and Anna Baldry. 2010. "Individual Risk Factors for School Bullying." *Journal of Aggression, Conflict and Peace Research* 2 (1): 4–16.

Farrington, David, Jeremy Coid, and Donald West. 2009. "The Development of Offending from Age 8 to Age 50: Recent Results from the Cambridge Study in Delinquent Development." *Monatsschrift für Kriminologie und Strafrechtsreform (Journal of Criminology and Penal Reform)* 92 (2–3): 160–73.

Ferguson, Christopher. 2015. "Do Angry Birds Make for Angry Children? A Meta-analysis of Video Game Influences on Children's and Adolescents' Aggression, Mental Health, Prosocial Behavior, and Academic Performance." *Perspectives on Psychological Science* 10 (5): 646–66.

Ferguson, Christopher, and Cheryl Olson. 2014. "Video Game Violence Use among 'Vulnerable' Populations: The Impact of Violent Video Games on Delinquency and Bullying among Children with Clinically Elevated Depression or Attention Deficit Symptoms." *Journal of Youth and Adolescence* 43:127–36.

Fergusson, David, Nicola Swain-Campbell, and John Horwood. 2004. "How Does Childhood Economic Disadvantage Lead to Crime?" *Journal of Child Psychology and Psychiatry* 45 (5): 956–66.

Ferráns, Silvia Diazgranados, and Robert Selman. 2014. "How Students' Perceptions of the School Climate Influence Their Choice to Upstand, Bystand, or Join Perpetrators of Bullying." *Harvard Educational Review* 84 (2): 162–87.

Ferrara, Pietro, Giorgia Bottaro, Costanza Cutrona, Fabio Quintarelli, Giulia Spina, Maria Amato, Annamaria Sbordone, Antonio Chiaretti, Giovanni Corsello, and Riccardo Riccardi. 2015. "School Bullying: An International Public Health Emergency Correlated to Psychosomatic Problems as Long-Term Sequelae." *Minerva Psichiatrica* 56 (3): 103–8.

Ferrell, Jeff. 2013. "Cultural Criminology and the Politics of Meaning." *Critical Criminology* 21 (3): 257–71.

Ferrell, Jeff, Keith Hayward, and Jock Young. 2008. *Cultural Criminology*. Los Angeles: SAGE.

Festl, Ruth, and Thorsten Quandt. 2013. "Social Relations and Cyberbullying: The Influence of Individual and Structural Attributes on Victimization and Perpetration via the Internet." *Human Communication Research* 39 (1): 101–26.

Ficks, Courtney, and Irwin Waldman. 2014. "Candidate Genes for Aggression and Antisocial Behavior: A Meta-Analysis of Association Studies of the 5HTTLPR and MAOA-Uvntr." *Behavior Genetics* 44 (5): 427–44.

Fink, Elian, Praveetha Patalay, Helen Sharpe, and Miranda Wolpert. 2018. "Child- and School-Level Predictors of Children's Bullying Behavior: A Multilevel Analysis in 648 Primary Schools." *Journal of Educational Psychology* 110 (1): 17–26.

Fisher, Benjamin, Thomas Mowen, and John Boman. 2018. "School Security Measures and Longitudinal Trends in Adolescents' Experiences of Victimization." *Journal of Youth and Adolescence* 47 (6): 1221–37.

Focquaert, Farah. 2019. "Neurobiology and Crime: A Neuro-Ethical Perspective." *Journal of Criminal Justice* 65 (November–December). https://doi.org/10.1016/j.jcrimjus.2018.01.001.

Fonagy, Peter, Stuart Twemlow, Eric Vernberg, Jennifer Mize Nelson, Edward Dill, Todd D. Little, and John A. Sargent. 2009. "A Cluster Randomized Controlled Trial of Child-Focused Psychiatric Consultation and a School Systems-Focused Intervention to Reduce Aggression." *Journal of Child Psychology and Psychiatry* 50 (5): 607–16.

Forbes, Miriam, Sally Fitzpatrick, Natasha Magson, and Ronald Rapee. 2019. "Depression, Anxiety, and Peer Victimization: Bidirectional Relationships and Associated Outcomes Transitioning from Childhood to Adolescence." *Journal of Youth and Adolescence* 48 (4): 692–702.

Forsberg, Camilla. 2019. "The Contextual Definition of Harm: 11- to 15-Year-Olds' Perspectives on Social Incidents and Bullying." *Journal of Youth Studies* 22 (10): 1378–92. https://doi.org/10.1080/13676261.2019.1580351.

Foucault, Michel. 1977. *Discipline and Punish: The Birth of the Prison*. New York: Vintage.

Fram, Sheila, and Ellyn Dickman. 2012. "How the School Built Environment Exacerbates Bullying and Peer Harassment." *Children, Youth and Environments* 22 (1): 227–49.

Frank, Daniel. 2013. "A Principal Reflects on Shame and School Bullying." *Psychoanalytic Inquiry* 33 (2) 174–80.

Franklin, Kris. 2013. "'Baton Bullying': Understanding Multi-Aggressor Rotation in Anti-Gay Harassment Cases." *National Lawyers Guild Review* 70 (3): 174–87.

Freud, Sigmund. (1923) 1989. "The Ego and the Id (1923)." *TACD Journal* 17 (1): 5–22.

Fronius, Trevor, Sean Darling-Hammond, Hannah Persson, Sarah Guckenburg, Nancy Hurley, and Anthony Petrosino. 2019. *Restorative Justice in U.S. Schools: An Updated Research Review.* San Francisco: WestEd. https://files.eric.ed.gov/fulltext/ED595733.pdf.

Gaffney, Hannah, David Farrington, Dorothy Espelage, and Maria Ttofi. 2019. "Are Cyberbullying Intervention and Prevention Programs Effective? A Systematic and Meta-Analytical Review." *Aggression and Violent Behavior* 45 (March–April): 134–53.

Gaffney, Hannah, David Farrington, and Maria Ttofi. 2019. "Examining the Effectiveness of School-Bullying Intervention Programs Globally: A Meta-Analysis." *International Journal of Bullying Prevention* 1 (1): 14–31.

Garandeau, Claire, F. Lee, and Ihno Salmivalli. 2014. "Inequality Matters: Classroom Status Hierarchy and Adolescents' Bullying." *Journal of Youth and Adolescence* 43 (7): 1123–33.

Garandeau, Claire, and Christina Salmivalli. 2019. "Can Healthier Contexts Be Harmful? A New Perspective on the Plight of Victims of Bullying." *Child Development Perspectives* 13 (3): 147–52.

Garandeau, Claire, F. Vartio, Annina Poskiparta, and Elisa Salmivalli. 2016. "School Bullies' Intention to Change Behavior Following Teacher Interventions: Effects of Empathy Arousal, Condemning of Bullying, and Blaming of the Perpetrator." *Prevention Science* 17 (8): 1034–43.

Garby, Lisa. 2013. "Direct Bullying: Criminal Act or Mimicking What Has Been Learned?" *Education* 133 (4): 448–50.

Gardella, Joseph, Benjamin Fisher, and Abbie Teurbe-Tolon. 2017. "A Systematic Review and Meta-Analysis of Cyber-Victimization and Educational Outcomes for Adolescents." *Review of Educational Research* 87 (2): 283–308.

Gayles, Travis, and Robert Garofalo. 2012. "Bullying and School-Based Violence in LGBT Teenage Populations." *Journal of Adolescent Health* 50 (2): S27.

Gendron, Martin, and Eric Frenette. 2016. "Peer Aggression in Soccer (Football) in Quebec among U12 to U18 Elite Players of Sport Study Programs: Differences According to Age and Player's Role." *Staps* 2:49–66.

Georgiou, Stelios. 2008. "Bullying and Victimization at School: The Role of Mothers." *British Journal of Educational Psychology* 78 (1): 109–25.

Georgiou, Stelios, Kyriaki Fousiani, Michalis Michaelides, and Panayiotis Stavrinides. 2013. "Cultural Value Orientation and Authoritarian Parenting as Parameters of Bullying and Victimization at School." *International Journal of Psychology* 48 (1): 69–78.

Gerlinger, Julie, and James Wo. 2016. "Preventing School Bullying: Should Schools Prioritize an Authoritative School Discipline Approach over Security Measures?" *Journal of School Violence* 15:133–57.

Ging, Debbie, and James O'Higgins Norman. 2016. "Cyberbullying, Conflict Management or Just Messing? Teenage Girls' Understandings and Experiences of Gender, Friendship, and Conflict on Facebook in an Irish Second-Level School." *Feminist Media Studies* 16 (5): 805–21.

Gini, Gianluca, Paolo Albiero, Beatrice Benelli, and Gianmarco Altoè. 2008. "Determinants of Adolescents' Active Defending and Passive Bystanding Behavior in Bullying." *Journal of Adolescence* 31 (1): 93–105.

Gini, Gianluca, Noel Card, and Tiziana Pozzoli. 2018. "A Meta-Analysis of the Differential Relations of Traditional and Cyber-Victimization with Internalizing Problems." *Aggressive Behavior* 44 (2): 185–98.

Gini, Gianluca, and Tiziana Pozzoli. 2009. "Association between Bullying and Psychosomatic Problems: A Meta-Analysis." *Pediatrics* 123 (3): 1059–65.

Gini, Gianluca, Tiziana Pozzoli, Francesco Borghi, and Lara Franzoni. 2008. "The Role of Bystanders in Students' Perception of Bullying and Sense of Safety." *Journal of School Psychology* 46 (6): 617–38.

Gini, Gianluca, Tiziana Pozzoli, and Shelley Hymel. 2014. "Moral Disengagement among Children and Youth: A Meta-Analytic Review of Links to Aggressive Behavior." *Aggressive Behavior* 40 (1): 56–68.

Gini, Gianluca, Tiziana Pozzoli, Michela Lenzi, and Alessio Vieno. 2014. "Bullying Victimization at School and Headache: A Meta-Analysis of Observational Studies." *Headache: The Journal of Head and Face Pain* 54 (6): 976–986.

Giumetti, Gary, and Robin Kowalski. 2016. "Cyberbullying Matters: Examining the Incremental Impact of Cyberbullying on Outcomes over and above Traditional Bullying in North America." In *Cyberbullying across the Globe: Gender, Family, and Mental Health*, edited by Raúl Navarro, Santiago Yubero, and Elisa Larrañaga, 117–30. Switzerland: Springer International.

Gladden, R. Matthew, Alana Vivolo-Kanter, Merle Hamburger, and Coery Lumpkin. 2014. *Bullying Surveillance among Youths: Uniform Definitions for Public Health and Recommended Data Elements, Version 1.0.* Atlanta, GA: National Center for Injury Prevention and Control, Centers for Disease Control and Prevention, and US Department of Education. https://www.cdc.gov/violenceprevention/pdf/bullying-definitions-final-a.pdf.

Glenn, Andrea, and Adrian Raine. 2014. "Neurocriminology: Implications for the Punishment, Prediction and Prevention of Criminal Behaviour." *Nature Reviews Neuroscience* 15 (1): 54–63.

Glueck, Sheldon, and Eleanor Touroff Glueck. 1950. *Unraveling Juvenile Delinquency.* Cambridge, MA: Harvard University Press.

———. 1968. *Delinquents and Nondelinquents in Perspective.* Cambridge, MA: Harvard University Press.

Go, Eun Joo, Jung Won Kong, and Ko Eun Kim. 2018. "A Meta-Analysis of the Correlation between Maltreatment, Witnessing Domestic Violence, and

Bullying among Youths in South Korea." *Social Work in Public Health* 33 (1): 17–30.

Goffman, Erving. 1963. *Stigma: Notes on the Management of Spoiled Identity.* Englewood Cliffs, NJ: Prentice-Hall.

Gofin, Rosa, and Malka Avitzour. 2012. "Traditional versus Internet Bullying in Junior High School Students." *Maternal and Child Health Journal* 16 (8): 1625–35.

Goldweber, Asha, Tracy Waasdorp, and Evian Bradshaw. 2013. "Examining Associations Between Race, Urbanicity, and Patterns of Bullying Involvement." *Journal of Youth and Adolescence* 42 (2): 206–19.

Gómez-Ortiz, Olga, Eva María Romera, and Rosario Ortega-Ruiz. 2016. "Parenting Styles and Bullying: The Mediating Role of Parental Psychological Aggression and Physical Punishment." *Child Abuse & Neglect* 51:132–43.

González, Thalia. 2012. "Keeping Kids in Schools: Restorative Justice, Punitive Discipline, and the School to Prison Pipeline." *Journal of Law & Education* 41 (2): 281–335.

González-Cabrera, Joaquin, Esther Calvete, Ana León-Mejía, Carlota Pérez-Sancho, and José Peinado. 2017. "Relationship between Cyberbullying Roles, Cortisol Secretion and Psychological Stress." *Computers in Human Behavior* 70:153–60.

Good, Chris, Kent McIntosh, and Carmen Gietz. 2011. "Integrating Bullying Prevention into Schoolwide Positive Behavior Support." *Teaching Exceptional Children* 44 (1): 48–56.

Gorman, Emma, Colm Harmon, Silvia Mendolia, Anita Staneva, and Ian Walker. 2019. "The Causal Effects of Adolescent School Bullying Victimisation on Later Life Outcomes." Discussion Paper No. 12241, IZA Institute of Labor Economics, Bonn, Germany. http://ftp.iza.org/dp12241.pdf.

Gottfredson, Michael, and Michael Hindelang. 1981. "Sociological Aspects of Criminal Victimization." *Annual Review of Sociology* 7:107–28.

Gottfredson, Michael, and Travis Hirschi. 1990. *A General Theory of Crime.* Stanford, CA: Stanford University Press.

Gower, Amy, Molly Cousin, and Iris Borowsky. 2017. "A Multilevel, Statewide Investigation of School District Anti-Bullying Policy Quality and Student Bullying Involvement." *Journal of School Health* 87 (3): 174–81.

Granberg-Rademacker, J. Scott, Jeffrey Bumgarner, and Avra Johnson. 2007. "Do School Violence Policies Matter? An Empirical Analysis of Four Approaches to Reduce School Violence." *Southwest Journal of Criminal Justice* 4 (1): 3–29.

Grant, Nickholas, Gabriel Merrin, Matthew King, and Dorothy Espelage. 2019. "Examining Within-Person and Between-Person Associations of Family Violence and Peer Deviance on Bullying Perpetration among Middle School Students." *Psychology of Violence* 9 (1): 18–27.

Grasmick, Harold, Charles Tittle, Robert Bursik, and Bruce Arneklev. 1993. "Testing the Core Empirical Implications of Gottfredson and Hirschi's General Theory of Crime." *Journal of Research in Crime and Delinquency* 30 (1): 5–29.

Green, Jennifer Greif, Michael Furlong, and Erika Felix. 2017. "Defining and Measuring Bullying across the Life Course." In *Handbook on Bullying Prevention: A Life Course Perspective*, edited by Catherine P. Bradshaw, 7–20. Washington, DC: NASW Press.

Greene, Darrell, Paula Britton, and Brian Fitts. 2014. "Long-Term Outcomes of Lesbian, Gay, Bisexual, and Transgender Recalled School Victimization." *Journal of Counseling and Development* 92 (4): 406–17.

Gregory, Anne, Dewey Cornell, Xitao Fan, Peter Sheras, Tse-Hua Shih, and Francis Huang. 2010. "Authoritative School Discipline: High School Practices Associated with Lower Bullying and Victimization." *Journal of Educational Psychology* 102 (2): 483–96.

Greitemeyer, Tobias, and Christina Sagioglou. 2017. "Increasing Wealth Inequality May Increase Interpersonal Hostility: The Relationship between Personal Relative Deprivation and Aggression." *Journal of Social Psychology* 157 (6): 766–76.

Grigg, Dorothy Wunmi. 2010. "Cyber-Aggression: Definition and Concept of Cyberbullying." *Journal of Psychologists and Counsellors in Schools* 20 (2): 143–16.

Grinshteyn, Erin, and Y. Tony Yang. 2017. "The Association between Electronic Bullying and School Absenteeism among High School Students in the United States." *Journal of School Health* 87 (2): 142–49.

Groß, Eva, Andreas Hövermann, and Steven Messner. 2018. "Marketized Mentality, Competitive/Egoistic School Culture, and Delinquent Attitudes and Behavior: An Application of Institutional Anomie Theory." *Criminology* 56 (2): 333–69.

Grob-Plante, Stephie. 2017. "The Impossible Question of Public School Uniforms." *Racked*, May 3, 2017. https://www.racked.com/2017/5/3/15518542/public-school-uniforms-education-policy.s

Gumpel, Thomas, Vered Zioni-Koren, and Zvi Bekerman. 2014. "An Ethnographic Study of Participant Roles in School Bullying." *Aggressive Behavior* 40 (3): 214–28.

Guy, Alexa, Kirsty Lee, and Dieter Wolke. 2017. "Differences in the Early Stages of Social Information Processing for Adolescents Involved in Bullying." *Aggressive Behavior* 43 (6): 578–87.

Hagan, Frank. 2011. *Introduction to Criminology: Theories, Methods, and Criminal Behavior.* 7th ed. Thousand Oaks, CA: SAGE.

Hall, Wayne. 2013. "Did the Elimination of Lead from Petrol Reduce Crime in the USA in the 1990s?" *F1000Research* 2:156. https://dx.doi.org/10.12688%2Ff1000research.2-156.v2.

Hall, William. 2017. "The Effectiveness of Policy Interventions for School Bullying: A Systematic Review." *Journal of the Society for Social Work & Research* 8 (1): 45–69.

Hall, William, and Mimi Chapman. 2018. "Fidelity of Implementation of a State Antibullying Policy with a Focus on Protected Social Classes." *Journal of School Violence* 17 (1): 58–73.

Hamburger, Merle, Kathleen Basile, and Alana Vivolo. 2011. *Measuring Bullying Victimization, Perpetration, and Bystander Experiences: A Compendium of Assess-*

ment Tools. Atlanta: Centers for Disease Control and Prevention, National Center for Injury Prevention and Control.

Han, Ziqiang, Guirong Zhang, and Haibo Zhang. 2017. "School Bullying in Urban China: Prevalence and Correlation with School Climate." *International Journal of Environmental Research and Public Health* 14 (10): 1116.

Haney, Kimberly, Joy Thomas, and Courtney Vaughn. 2011. "Identity Border Crossings within School Communities, Precursors to Restorative Conferencing: A Symbolic Interactionist Study." *School Community Journal* 21 (2): 55–80.

Harbin, Shannon Marie, Mary Lou Kelley, Jennifer Piscitello, and Seandra Walker. 2019. "Multidimensional Bullying Victimization Scale: Development and Validation." *Journal of School Violence* 18 (1): 146–61.

Harcourt, Susan, Vanessa Green, and Chris Bowden. 2015. "'It Is Everyone's Problem': Parents' Experiences of Bullying." *New Zealand Journal of Psychology* 44 (3): 4–17.

Harcourt, Susan, Marieke Jasperse, and Vanessa Green. 2014. "'We Were Sad and We Were Angry': A Systematic Review of Parents' Perspectives on Bullying." *Child & Youth Care Forum,* 43 (3): 373–91.

Harel-Fisch, Yossi, Sophie D. Walsh, Haya Fogel-Grinvald, Gabriel Amitai, William Pickett, Michal Molcho, Pernille Due, Margarida Gaspar de Matos, and Wendy Craig. 2011. "Negative School Perceptions and Involvement in School Bullying: A Universal Relationship across 40 Countries." *Journal of Adolescence* 34 (4): 639–52.

Harris, Monica. 2009. "Taking Bullying and Rejection (Inter) Personally: Benefits of a Social Psychological Approach to Peer Victimization." In *Bullying, Rejection, and Peer Victimization: A Social Cognitive Neuroscience Perspective,* edited by Monica J. Harris, 3–23. New York: Springer.

Hart, Stephen, and Robert Hare. 1997. "Psychopathy: Assessment and Association with Criminal Conduct." In *Handbook of Antisocial Behavior,* edited by David Stoff, James Breiling, and Jack Maser, 2–35. Hoboken, NJ: John Wiley & Sons.

Hatzenbuehler, Mark, Laura Schwab-Reese, Shabbar Ranapurwala, Marci Hertz, and Marizen Ramirez. 2015. "Associations between Antibullying Policies and Bullying in 25 States." *JAMA Pediatrics* 169 (10): e152411.

Hay, Carter, Ryan Meldrum, and Karen Mann. 2010. "Traditional Bullying, Cyber Bullying, and Deviance: A General Strain Theory Approach." *Journal of Contemporary Criminal Justice* 26 (2): 130–47.

Hayes, Nóirín, Leah O'Toole, and Ann Marie Halpenny. 2017. *Introducing Bronfenbrenner: A Guide for Practitioners and Students in Early Years Education.* London: Taylor and Francis.

Hazler, Richard, JoLynn Carney, and Douglas Granger. 2006. "Integrating Biological Measures into the Study of Bullying." *Journal of Counseling & Development* 84 (3): 298–307.

Healy, Karyn, Matthew Sanders, and Aarti Iyer. 2015. "Parenting Practices, Children's Peer Relationships and Being Bullied at School." *Journal of Child and Family Studies* 24 (1): 127–40.

Heberle, Amy, and Alice Carter. 2015. "Cognitive Aspects of Young Children's Experience of Economic Disadvantage." *Psychological Bulletin* 141 (4): 723–46.

Henry, Jeffrey, Jean-Baptiste Pingault, Michel Boivin, Frühling Rijsdijk, and Essi Viding. 2016. "Genetic and Environmental Aetiology of the Dimensions of Callous-Unemotional Traits." *Psychological Medicine* 46 (2): 405–14.

Hindelang, Michael, Michael Gottfredson, and James Garofalo. 1978. *Victims of Personal Crime: An Empirical Foundation for a Theory of Personal Victimization.* Cambridge, MA: Ballinger.

Hinduja, Sameer, and Justin Patchin. 2013. "Social Influences on Cyberbullying Behaviors among Middle and High School Students." *Journal of Youth and Adolescence* 42:711–22.

———. 2015. *Cyberbullying Legislation and Case Law: Implications for School Policy and Practice.* Fact sheet, Cyberbullying Research Center, updated January 2015. https://cyberbullying.org/cyberbullying-legal-issues.pdf.

———. 2019. "Connecting Adolescent Suicide to the Severity of Bullying and Cyberbullying." *Journal of School Violence* 18 (3): 333–46.

Hirschi, Travis. 1969. *Causes of Delinquency.* Berkeley: University of California Press.

Hirschi, Travis, and Michael Gottfredson. 1994. *The Generality of Deviance.* New Brunswick, NJ: Transaction.

Hirschi, Travis, and Michael Hindelang. 1977. "Intelligence and Delinquency: A Revisionist Review." *American Sociological Review* 42 (4): 571–87.

Hoeve, Machteld, Judith Semon Dubas, Veroni Eichelsheim, Peter van der Laan, Wilma Smeenk, and Jan Gerris. 2009. "The Relationship between Parenting and Delinquency: A Meta-Analysis." *Journal of Abnormal Child Psychology* 37 (6): 749–75.

Holben, Diane, and Perry Zirkel. 2014. "School Bullying Litigation: An Empirical Analysis of the Case Law." *Akron Law Review* 47:299–328.

Holfeld, Brett, and Bonnie Leadbeater. 2017. "Concurrent and Longitudinal Associations between Early Adolescents' Experiences of School Climate and Cyber Victimization." *Computers in Human Behavior* 76:321–28.

Holt, Melissa K., Alana M. Vivolo-Kantor, Joshua R. Polanin, Kristin M. Holland, Sarah DeGue, Jennifer L. Matjasko, Misty Wolfe, and Gerald Reid. 2015. "Bullying and Suicidal Ideation and Behaviors: A Meta-Analysis." *Pediatrics* 135 (2): e496–e509.

Holt, Thomas, Adam Bossler, and David May. 2012. "Low Self-Control, Deviant Peer Associations, and Juvenile Cyberdeviance." *American Journal of Criminal Justice* 37 (3): 378–95.

Holt, Thomas, Michael Turner, and M. Lyn Exum. 2014. "The Impact of Self Control and Neighborhood Disorder on Bullying Victimization." *Journal of Criminal Justice* 42 (4): 347–55.

Hong, Irene K., Weijun Wang, Debra J. Pepler, and Wendy M. Craig. 2020. "Peer Victimization through a Trauma Lens: Identifying Who Is at Risk for Negative Outcomes." *Scandinavian Journal of Psychology* 61 (1): 6–16.

Hong, Jun Sung, and Dorothy Espelage. 2012. "A Review of Research on Bullying and Peer Victimization in School: An Ecological System Analysis." *Aggression and Violent Behavior* 17 (4): 311–22.

Hong, Jun Sung, Dorothy Espelage, Andrew Grogan-Kaylor, and Paula Allen-Meares. 2012. "Identifying Potential Mediators and Moderators of the Association between Child Maltreatment and Bullying Perpetration and Victimization in School." *Educational Psychology Review* 24 (2): 167–86.

Hong, Jun Sung, Dong Ha Kim, and Alex Piquero. 2017. "Assessing the Links between Punitive Parenting, Peer Deviance, Social Isolation and Bullying Perpetration and Victimization in South Korean Adolescents." *Child Abuse & Neglect* 73:63–70.

Hong, Jun Sung, Jungup Lee, Dorothy L. Espelage, Simon C. Hunter, Desmond Upton Patton, and Tyrone Rivers Jr. 2016. "Understanding the Correlates of Face-to-Face and Cyberbullying Victimization among U.S. Adolescents: A Social-Ecological Analysis." *Violence and Victims* 31 (4): 638–63.

Hong, Jun, Chang-Hun Lee, Jungup Lee, Na Lee, and James Garbarino. 2014. "A Review of Bullying Prevention and Intervention in South Korean Schools: An Application of the Social–Ecological Framework." *Child Psychiatry & Human Development* 45 (4): 433–42.

Horn, David M. 2000. *Bruised Inside: What Our Children Say about Youth Violence, What Causes It, and What We Need to Do about It—A Report of the National Association of Attorneys General (NAAG)*. Washington, DC: National Association of Attorneys General.

Hövermann, Andreas, Eva M. Groß, Andreas Zick, and Steven Messner. 2015. "Understanding the Devaluation of Vulnerable Groups: A Novel Application of Institutional Anomie Theory." *Social Science Research* 52:408–21.

Huang, Francis, and Dewey Cornell. 2017. "Student Attitudes and Behaviors as Explanations for the Black-White Suspension Gap." *Children and Youth Services Review* 73:298–308.

Huggins, Michael. 2016. "Stigma Is the Origin of Bullying." *Journal of Catholic Education* 19 (3): 166–96.

Hughes, Robert, and Jay Coakley. 1991. "Positive Deviance among Athletes: The Implications of Overconformity to the Sport Ethic." *Sociology of Sport Journal* 8 (4): 307–25.

Hymel, Shelley, Robyn Mcclure, Miriam Miller, Ellen Shumka, and Jessica Trach. 2015. "Addressing School Bullying: Insights from Theories of Group Processes." *Journal of Applied Developmental Psychology* 37 (1): 16–24.

Hymel, Shelley, and Susan Swearer. 2015. "Four Decades of Research on School Bullying: An Introduction." *American Psychologist* 70 (4): 293–99.

Innes, Martin. 2004. "Signal Crimes and Signal Disorders: Notes on Deviance as Communicative Action." *British Journal of Sociology* 55 (3): 335–55.

Isen, Joshua. 2010. "A Meta-Analytic Assessment of Wechsler's P>V Sign in Antisocial Populations." *Clinical Psychology Review* 30 (4): 423–35.

Jack, Alexander, and Vincent Egan. 2018. "Childhood Bullying, Paranoid Thinking and the Misappraisal of Social Threat: Trouble at School." *School Mental Health* 10 (1): 26–34.

Jackson, Dylan. 2016. "The Link between Poor Quality Nutrition and Childhood Antisocial Behavior: A Genetically Informative Analysis." *Journal of Criminal Justice* 44:13–20.

Jackson, Dylan, and Michael Vaughn. 2018. "The Bully-Victim Overlap and Nutrition among School-Aged Youth in North America and Europe." *Children and Youth Services Review* 90:158–65.

James, Lois, Natalie Todak, and Joanne Savage. 2018. "Unnecessary Force by Police: Insights from Evolutionary Psychology." *Policing: A Journal of Policy and Practice.* https://doi.org/10.1093/police/pay025.

Jang, Hyunseok, Juyoung Song, and Ramhee Kim. 2014. "Does the Offline Bully-Victimization Influence Cyberbullying Behavior among Youths? Application of General Strain Theory." *Computers in Human Behavior* 31:85–93.

Jansen, Pauline, Marina Verlinden, Anke Dommisse-van Berkel, Cathelijne Mieloo, Jan van der Ende, René Veenstra, Frank C. Verhulst, Wilma Jansen, and Henning Tiemeier. 2012. "Prevalence of Bullying and Victimization among Children in Early Elementary School: Do Family and School Neighbourhood Socioeconomic Status Matter?" *BMC Public Health* 12 (1): 494.

Jasper, James, and Jane Poulsen. 1995. "Recruiting Strangers and Friends: Moral Shocks and Social Networks in Animal Rights and Anti-Nuclear Protests." *Social Problems* 42 (4): 493–512.

Jenkins, Lyndsay, and Stephanie Fredrick. 2017. "Social Capital and Bystander Behavior in Bullying: Internalizing Problems as a Barrier to Prosocial Intervention." *Journal of Youth and Adolescence* 46 (4): 757–71.

Jennifer, Dawn, and Helen Cowie. 2012. "Listening to Children's Voices: Moral Emotional Attributions in Relation to Primary School Bullying." *Emotional and Behavioural Difficulties* 17 (3–4): 229–41.

Jessor, Richard, and Shirley Jessor. 1977. *Problem Behavior and Psychosocial Development: A Longitudinal Study of Youth.* New York: Academic Press.

Jiang, Jiang, Yan Zhang, Yannan Ke, Skyler Hawk, and Hui Qiu. 2015. "Can't Buy Me Friendship? Peer Rejection and Adolescent Materialism: Implicit Self-Esteem as a Mediator." *Journal of Experimental Social Psychology* 58:48–55.

Jiménez-Barbero, José Antonio, Alejandro Jiménez-Loaisa, David González-Cutre, Vicente J. Beltrán-Carrillo, Laura Llor-Zaragoza, and José Antonio Ruiz-Hernández. 2020. "Physical Education and School Bullying: A Systematic Review." *Physical Education and Sport Pedagogy* 25 (1): 79–100.

Johnston, April, Aida Midgett, Diana Doumas, and Steve Moody. 2018. "A Mixed Methods Evaluation of the 'Aged-Up' STAC Bullying Bystander Intervention for High School Students." *Professional Counselor* 8 (1): 73–87.

Jolliffe, Darrick, and David Farrington. 2004. "Empathy and Offending: A Systematic Review and Meta-analysis." *Aggression and Violent Behavior* 9 (5): 441–76.

Kalia, Divya, and Sheema Aleem. 2017. "Cyber Victimization among Adolescents: Examining the Role of Routine Activity Theory." *Journal of Psychosocial Research* 12 (1): 223–32.

Katz, Jack. 1988. *Seductions of Crime: Moral and Sensual Attractions in Doing Evil.* New York: Basic Books.

Kaufman, Tessa M. L., Gijs Huitsing, and René Veenstra. 2020. "Refining Victims' Self-Reports on Bullying: Assessing Frequency, Intensity, Power Imbalance, and Goal-Directedness." *Social Development* 29 (2): 375–90.

Keith, Shelley. 2018. "How Do Traditional Bullying and Cyberbullying Victimization Affect Fear and Coping among Students? An Application of General Strain Theory." *American Journal of Criminal Justice* 43 (1): 67–84.

Kelly, Erin, Nicola Newton, Lexine Stapinski, Tim Slade, Emma Barrett, Patricia J. Conrod, and Maree Teesson. 2015. "Suicidality, Internalizing Problems and Externalizing Problems among Adolescent Bullies, Victims and Bully-Victims." *Preventive Medicine* 73:100–105.

Kerbs, John, and Jennifer Jolley. 2007. "The Joy of Violence: What about Violence Is Fun in Middle-School?" *American Journal of Criminal Justice* 32 (1–2): 12–29.

Kim, Namei, and Insoo Oh. 2017. "Analysis of Stakeholders' Perceptions of Zero Tolerance Policy for School Violence in South Korea." *KEDI Journal of Educational Policy* 14 (1): 61–78.

King, Keith. 1998. "Should School Uniforms Be Mandated in Elementary Schools?" *Journal of School Health* 68 (1): 32–37.

Kirk, David. 2009. "Unraveling the Contextual Effects on Student Suspension and Juvenile Arrest: The Independent and Interdependent Influences of School, Neighborhood, and Family Social Controls." *Criminology* 47 (2): 479–520.

Kliewer, Wendy, Ashley Dibble, Kimberly Goodman, and Terri Sullivan. 2012. "Physiological Correlates of Peer Victimization and Aggression in African American Urban Adolescents." *Development and Psychopathology* 24 (2): 637–50.

Klomek, Anat Brunstein, Andre Sourander, and Henrik Elonheimo. 2015. "Bullying by Peers in Childhood and Effects on Psychopathology, Suicidality, and Criminality in Adulthood." *Lancet Psychiatry* 2 (10): 930–41.

Knaappila, Noora, Mauri Marttunen, Sari Fröjd, Nina Lindberg, and Riittakerttu Kaltiala-Heino. 2018. "Socioeconomic Trends in School Bullying among Finnish Adolescents from 2000 to 2015." *Child Abuse & Neglect* 86:100–108.

Koh, Jun-Bin, and Jennifer Wong. 2017. "Survival of the Fittest and the Sexiest: Evolutionary Origins of Adolescent Bullying." *Journal of Interpersonal Violence* 32 (17): 2668–90.

Kohlberg, Lawrence, and Richard Hersh. 1977. "Moral Development: A Review of the Theory." *Theory into Practice* 16 (2): 53–59.

Kolbert, Jered, and Laura Crothers. 2003. "Bullying and Evolutionary Psychology: The Dominance Hierarchy among Students and Implications for School Personnel." *Journal of School Violence* 2 (3): 73–91.

Kollerová, Lenka, Pavlína Janošová, and Pavel Říčan. 2014. "Moral Disengagement from Bullying: The Effects of Gender and Classroom." *New Educational Review* 37 (3): 280–91.

Konold, Timothy, Dewey Cornell, Kathan Shukla, and Francis Huang. 2017. "Racial/Ethnic Differences in Perceptions of School Climate and Its Association with Student Engagement and Peer Aggression." *Journal of Youth and Adolescence* 46 (6): 1289–303.

Kornhauser, Ruth Rosner. 1978. *Social Sources of Delinquency: An Appraisal of Analytic Models.* Chicago: University of Chicago Press.

Kowalski, Robin, Gary Giumetti, Amber Schroeder, and Micah Lattanner. 2014. "Bullying in the Digital Age: A Critical Review and Meta-Analysis of Cyberbullying Research among Youth." *Psychological Bulletin* 140 (4): 1073.

Kowalski, Robin, and Susan Limber. 2013. "Psychological, Physical, and Academic Correlates of Cyberbullying and Traditional Bullying." *Journal of Adolescent Health* 53 (1): S13-S20.

Kramer, Alex. 2015. "One Strike and You're Out: The Application of Labeling Theory to the New Jersey Anti-Bullying Bill of Rights Act." *Seton Hall Law Review* 45 (1): 261–84.

Kreager, Derek. 2007. "Unnecessary Roughness? School Sports, Peer Networks, and Male Adolescent Violence." *American Sociological Review* 72 (5): 705–24.

Kuczynski, Leon, and Jan De Mol. 2015. "Dialectical Models of Socialization." In *Handbook of Child Psychology and Developmental Science*, 7th ed., edited by Richard M. Lerner, 1–46. Hoboken, NJ: Wiley.

Kulig, Teresa, Travis Pratt, Francis Cullen, Cecilia Chouhy, and James Unnever. 2017. "Explaining Bullying Victimization: Assessing the Generality of the Low Self-Control/Risky Lifestyle Model." *Victims & Offenders* 12 (6): 891–912.

Kupchik, Aaron, and Katie Farina. 2016. "Imitating Authority: Students' Perceptions of School Punishment and Security, and Bullying Victimization." *Youth Violence and Juvenile Justice* 14 (2): 147–63.

Kwak, Misung, and Insoo Oh. 2017. "Comparison of Psychological and Social Characteristics among Traditional, Cyber, Combined Bullies, and Noninvolved." *School Psychology International* 38 (6): 608–27.

Lacey, Anna, and Dewey Cornell. 2013. "The Impact of Teasing and Bullying on Schoolwide Academic Performance." *Journal of Applied School Psychology* 29 (3): 262–83.

Lacey, Anna, Dewey Cornell, and Timothy Konold. 2017. "The Relations between Teasing and Bullying and Middle School Standardized Exam Performance." *Journal of Early Adolescence* 37 (2): 192–221.

Ladd, Gary, Idean Ettekal, and Becky Kochenderfer-Ladd. 2017. "Peer Victimization Trajectories from Kindergarten through High School: Differential Pathways for Children's School Engagement and Achievement?" *Journal of Educational Psychology* 109 (6): 826–41.

Lafko, Nicole, Dianna Murray-Close, and Erin K. Shoulberg. 2015. "Negative Peer Status and Relational Victimization in Children and Adolescents: The Role of

Stress Physiology." *Journal of Clinical Child & Adolescent Psychology* 44 (3): 405–16.

Låftman, Sara, Susanne Alm, Julia Sandahl, and Bitte Modin. 2018. "Future Orientation among Students Exposed to School Bullying and Cyberbullying Victimization." *International Journal of Environmental Research and Public Health* 15 (4): 605.

Lai, Tianjian, and Grace Kao. 2018. "Hit, Robbed, and Put Down (but Not Bullied): Underreporting of Bullying by Minority and Male Students." *Journal of Youth and Adolescence* 47 (3): 619–35.

Lambe, Laura J., and Wendy M. Craig. 2020. "Peer Defending as a Multidimensional Behavior: Development and Validation of the Defending Behaviors Scale." *Journal of School Psychology* 78:38–53.

Lange, Benjamin P., Johannes Breuer, Benny Liebold, and Daniel Pietschmann. 2018. "Why an Evolutionary Psychological Approach to Digital Games?" In *Evolutionary Psychology and Digital Games*, edited by Johannes Breuer, Daniel Pietschmann, Benny Liebold, and Benjamin P. Lange, 1–13. New York: Routledge.

Langevin, Stephanie, Sara Mascheretti, Sylvana Côté, Frank Vitaro, Michel Boivin, Gustavo Turecki, Richard E. Tremblay, and Isabelle Ouellet-Morin. 2019. "Cumulative Risk and Protection Effect of Serotonergic Genes on Male Antisocial Behaviour: Results from a Prospective Cohort Assessed in Adolescence and Early Adulthood." *British Journal of Psychiatry* 214 (3): 137–45.

Langos, Colette. 2012. "Cyberbullying: The Challenge to Define." *Cyberpsychology, Behavior, and Social Networking* 15 (6): 285–89.

Latvala, Antti, Ralf Kuja-Halkola, Catarina Almqvist, Henrik Larsson, and Paul Lichtenstein. 2015. "A Longitudinal Study of Resting Heart Rate and Violent Criminality in More than 700 000 Men." *JAMA Psychiatry* 72 (10): 971–78.

Laub, John, & Robert Sampson. 2003. *Shared Beginnings, Divergent Lives: Delinquent Boys to Age 70*. Cambridge, MA: Harvard University Press.

Lauritsen, Janet, Robert Sampson, and John Laub. 1991. "The Link between Offending and Victimization among Adolescents." *Criminology* 29 (2): 265–92.

Lee, Byung. 2018. "Explaining Cyber Deviance among School-Aged Youth." *Child Indicators Research* 11 (2): 563–84.

Lee, Chang-Hun. 2010. "Personal and Interpersonal Correlates of Bullying Behaviors among Korean Middle School Students." *Journal of Interpersonal Violence* 25 (1): 152–76.

———. 2011. "An Ecological Systems Approach to Bullying Behaviors among Middle School Students in the United States." *Journal of Interpersonal Violence* 26 (8): 1664–93.

Lee, Chang-Hun, and Juyoung Song. 2012. "Functions of Parental Involvement and Effects of School Climate on Bullying Behaviors among South Korean Middle School Students." *Journal of Interpersonal Violence* 27 (12): 2437–64.

Lee, Joongyeup, and Philip Kavanaugh. 2015. "Discipline, Shaming and Antisocial Attitude in Philadelphia Middle Schools." *Sociological Spectrum* 35 (6): 504–17.

Lee, Sindy Sin-Ting, and Dennis Sing-Wing Wong. 2009. "School, Parents, and Peer Factors in Relation to Hong Kong Students' Bullying." *International Journal of Adolescence and Youth* 15 (3): 217–33.

Lee, Sunhee, Chun-Ja Kim, and Dong Hee Kim. 2015. "A Meta-analysis of the Effect of School-Based Anti-Bullying Programs." *Journal of Child Health Care* 19 (2): 136–53.

Lee, Talisha, and Dewey Cornell. 2009. "Concurrent Validity of the Olweus Bully/Victim Questionnaire." *Journal of School Violence* 9 (1): 56–73.

Lee, Yoona, Xiaodong Liu, and Malcolm Watson. 2016. "The Timing Effect of Bullying in Childhood and Adolescence on Developmental Trajectories of Externalizing Behaviors." *Journal of Interpersonal Violence* 31 (17): 2775–2800.

Lehman, Brett. 2017. "Supporting Gender Equality in Extracurricular Activities and the Impact on Female Bullying Victimization in School." *Social Psychology of Education: An International Journal* 20 (2): 445–70.

Lemert, Edwin. 1951. *Social Pathology: A Systematic Approach to the Theory of Sociopathic Behavior.* New York: McGraw-Hill.

Lenzi, Michela, Alessio Vieno, Gianluca Gini, Tiziana Pozzoli, Massimiliano Pastore, Massimo Santinello, and Frank J. Elgar. 2014. "Perceived Teacher Unfairness, Instrumental Goals, and Bullying Behavior in Early Adolescence." *Journal of Interpersonal Violence* 29 (10): 1834–49.

Lereya, Suzet Tanya, William Copeland, Stanley Zammit, and Dieter Wolke. 2015. "Bully/Victims: A Longitudinal, Population-Based Cohort Study of Their Mental Health." *European Child & Adolescent Psychiatry* 24 (12): 1461–71.

Lereya, Suzet Tanya, Muthanna Samara, and Dieter Wolke. 2013. "Parenting Behavior and the Risk of Becoming a Victim and a Bully/Victim: A Meta-analysis Study." *Child Abuse & Neglect* 37 (12): 1091–1108.

Lester, Leanne, Donna Cross, and Therese Shaw. 2012. "Problem Behaviours, Traditional Bullying and Cyberbullying among Adolescents: Longitudinal Analyses." *Emotional and Behavioural Difficulties* 17 (3–4): 435–47.

Letendre, Joan, Jason Ostrander, and Alison Mickens. 2016. "Teacher and Staff Voices: Implementation of a Positive Behavior Bullying Prevention Program in an Urban School." *Children & Schools* 38 (4): 235–43.

Lianos, Helen, and Andrew McGrath. 2018. "Can the General Theory of Crime and General Strain Theory Explain Cyberbullying Perpetration?" *Crime & Delinquency* 64 (5): 674–700.

Little, Todd D., Christopher C. Henrich, Stephanie M. Jones, and Patricia H. Hawley. 2003. "Disentangling the 'Whys' from the 'Whats' of Aggressive Behaviour." *International Journal of Behavioral Development* 27 (2): 122–33.

Liu, Jianghong. 2011. "Early Health Risk Factors for Violence: Conceptualization, Evidence, and Implications." *Aggression and Violent Behavior* 16 (1): 63–73.

Lopez, Rebecca A. 2003. "The Long Beach Unified School District Uniform Initiative: A Prevention-Intervention Strategy for Urban Schools." *Journal of Negro Education* 72 (4): 396–405.

Lu, Yu, Flor Avellaneda, Elizabeth D. Torres, and Jeff R. Temple. 2020. "Adolescent Bullying and Weapon Carrying: A Longitudinal Investigation." *Journal of Research on Adolescence* 30 (51): 61–65.

Lubke, Gitta, Daniel McArtor, Dorret Boomsma, and Meike Bartels. 2018. "Genetic and Environmental Contributions to the Development of Childhood Aggression." *Developmental Psychology* 54 (1): 39–50.

Lundwall, Rebecca, Jordan Sgro, and Tyson Wade. 2017. "SLC6A3 Is Associated with Relational Aggression in Children." *Journal of Individual Differences* 38:220–29.

Maiano, Christophe, Claude Normand, Marie-Claude Salvas, Gregory Moullec, and Annie Aimé. 2016. "Prevalence of School Bullying among Youth with Autism Spectrum Disorders: A Systematic Review and Meta-Analysis." *Autism Research* 9 (6): 601–15.

Mallinson, Daniel. 2016. "Schoolyard Politics: Measuring and Explaining Variation in State Antibullying Policy Comprehensiveness." *State and Local Government Review* 48 (2): 100–113.

Malouff, John, Sally Rooke, and Nicola Schutte. 2008. "The Heritability of Human Behavior: Results of Aggregating Meta-Analyses." *Current Psychology* 27 (3): 153–61.

Mann, Michael, Alfgeir Kristjansson, Inga Dora Sigfusdottir, and Megan Smith. 2015. "The Role of Community, Family, Peer, and School Factors in Group Bullying: Implications for School-Based Intervention." *Journal of School Health* 85 (7): 477–86.

Manuel, Natasha Rose. 2011. "Cyber-Bullying: Its Recent Emergence and Needed Legislation to Protect Adolescent Victims." *Loyola Journal of Public Interest Law* 13 (1): 219–52.

Marcus, Kenneth. 2011. "Bullying as a Civil Rights Violation: The US Department of Education's Approach to Harassment." *Engage* 12 (2): 54–58.

Marks, Stephen. 1974. "Durkheim's Theory of Anomie." *American Journal of Sociology* 80 (2): 329–63.

Martin, Randy, Robert Mutchnick, and W. Timothy Austin. 1990. *Criminological Thought: Pioneers Past and Present.* New York: Macmillan.

Martinez, Andrew. 2016. "State-Level Anti-Bullying Policy: Toward a System-Level Implementation Framework." PhD diss., DePaul University. https://via.library .depaul.edu/cgi/viewcontent.cgi?article=1152&context=csh_etd.

Marx, Robert, and Heather Hensman Kettrey. 2016. "Gay-Straight Alliances Are Associated with Lower Levels of School-Based Victimization of LGBTQ+ Youth: A Systematic Review and Meta-Analysis." *Journal of Youth and Adolescence* 45 (7): 1269–82.

Mason, Dehryl, and Paul Frick. 1994. "The Heritability of Antisocial Behavior: A Meta-Analysis of Twin and Adoption Studies." *Journal of Psychopathology and Behavioral Assessment* 16 (4): 301–23.

Matthews, Karen, J. Richard Jennings, Laisze Lee, and Dustin Pardini. 2017. "Bullying and Being Bullied in Childhood Are Associated with Different

Psychosocial Risk Factors for Poor Physical Health in Men." *Psychological Science* 28 (6): 808–21.

Matza, David. 1964. *Delinquency and Drift.* New York: Wiley.

Maunder, Rachel, and Sarah Crafter. 2018. "School Bullying from a Sociocultural Perspective." *Aggression and Violent Behavior* 38:13–20.

Mazur, Allan, and Alan Booth. 1998. "Testosterone and Dominance in Men." *Behavioral and Brain Sciences* 21 (3): 353–63.

Mazur, Joanna, Izabela Tabak, and Dorota Zawadzka. 2017. "Determinants of Bullying at School Depending on the Type of Community: Ecological Analysis of Secondary Schools in Poland." *School Mental Health* 9 (2): 132–42.

Mazzoli Smith, Laura, and Liz Todd. 2016. *Poverty Proofing the School Day: Evaluation and Development Report.* Newcastle, England: Research Center for Learning and Teaching, Newcastle University.

Mazzone, Angela, Marina Camodeca, Daniela Cardone, and Arcangelo Merla. 2017. "Bullying Perpetration and Victimization in Early Adolescence: Physiological Response to Social Exclusion." *International Journal of Developmental Science* 11 (3–4): 121–30.

Mazzone, Angela, Marina Camodeca, and Christina Salmivalli. 2018. "Stability and Change of Outsider Behavior in School Bullying: The Role of Shame and Guilt in a Longitudinal Perspective." *Journal of Early Adolescence* 38 (2): 164–77.

McDougall, Patricia, and Tracy Vaillancourt. 2015. "Long-Term Adult Outcomes of Peer Victimization in Childhood and Adolescence: Pathways to Adjustment and Maladjustment." *American Psychologist* 70 (4): 300–10.

McGuckin, Conor, and Stephen Minton. 2014. "From Theory to Practice: Two Ecosystemic Approaches and Their Applications to Understanding School Bullying." *Journal of Psychologists and Counsellors in Schools* 24 (1): 36–48.

McIver, Theresa, Rachael L. Bosma, Aislinn Sandre, Sarah Goegan, Janell A. Klassen, Julian Chiarella, Linda Booij, and Wendy Craig. 2018. "Peer Victimization Is Associated with Neural Response to Social Exclusion." *Merrill-Palmer Quarterly* 64 (1): 135–61.

Meier, Robert, and Terance Miethe. 1993. "Understanding Theories of Criminal Victimization." *Crime and Justice* 17:459–99.

Melnick, Shep. 2019. "The Strange Evolution of Title IX." *National Affairs*, no. 42. https://www.nationalaffairs.com/publications/detail/the-strange-evolution-of-title-ix.

Menard, Scott, and Jennifer Grotpeter. 2011. "Peer Influence, Social Bonding, Physical and Relational Aggression: Perpetration and Victimization in an Elementary School Sample." *Victims & Offenders* 6 (2): 181–206.

Menesini, Ersilia, and Christina Salmivalli. 2017. "Bullying in Schools: The State of Knowledge and Effective Interventions." *Psychology, Health & Medicine* 22 (sup 1): 240–53.

Menzer, Melissa, and Judith Torney-Purta. 2012. "Individualism and Socioeconomic Diversity at School as Related to Perceptions of the Frequency of Peer Aggression in Fifteen Countries." *Journal of Adolescence* 35 (5): 1285–94.

Meredith, Jessica. 2010. "Combating Cyberbullying: Emphasizing Education over Criminalization." *Federal Communication Law Journal* 63:311–40.

Merrell, Kenneth, Barbara Gueldner, Scott Ross, and Duane Isava. 2008. "How Effective Are School Bullying Intervention Programs? A Meta-Analysis of Intervention Research." *School Psychology Quarterly* 23 (1): 26–42.

Merrin, Gabriel, Kayla De La Haye, Dorothy Espelage, Brett Ewing, Joan Tucker, Matthew Hoover, and Harold D. Green Jr. 2018. "The Co-Evolution of Bullying Perpetration, Homophobic Teasing, and a School Friendship Network." *Journal of Youth and Adolescence* 47 (3): 601–18.

Merton, Robert. 1938. "Social Structure and Anomie." *American Sociological Review* 3 (5): 672–82.

Messner, Steven, and Richard Rosenfeld. 1994. *Crime and the American Dream.* 5th ed. Belmont, CA: Wadsworth.

Messner, Steven, Helmut Thome, and Richard Rosenfeld. 2008. "Institutions, Anomie, and Violent Crime: Clarifying and Elaborating Institutional-Anomie Theory." *International Journal of Conflict and Violence* 2 (2): 163–81.

Meyer, Ilan H., Feijun Luo, Bianca Wilson, and Deborah Stone. 2019. "Sexual Orientation Enumeration in State Antibullying Statutes in the United States: Associations with Bullying, Suicidal Ideation, and Suicide Attempts among Youth." *LGBT Health* 6 (1): 9–14.

Midgett, Aida, and Diana Doumas. 2019. "Witnessing Bullying at School: The Association between Being a Bystander and Anxiety and Depressive Symptoms." *School Mental Health* 11 (3): 454–63.

Midgett, Aida, Diana Doumas, and Rhiannon Trull. 2016. "Evaluation of a Brief, School-Based Bullying Bystander Intervention for Elementary School Students." *Professional School Counseling* 20 (1): 172–83.

Miethe, Terance. 1985. "The Myth or Reality of Victim Involvement in Crime: A Review and Comment on Victim-Precipitation Research." *Sociological Focus* 18:209–20.

Miethe, Terance, and Robert Meier. 1990. "Opportunity, Choice, and Criminal Victimization: A Test of a Theoretical Model." *Journal of Research in Crime and Delinquency* 27 (3): 243–66.

Miller, Walter. 1958. "Lower Class Culture as a Generating Milieu of Gang Delinquency." *Journal of Social Issues* 14 (3): 5–19.

Mishna, Faye, Charlene Cook, Michael Saini, Meng-Jia Wu, and Robert MacFadden. 2011. "Interventions to Prevent and Reduce Cyber Abuse of Youth: A Systematic Review." *Research on Social Work Practice* 21 (1): 5–14.

Mitsopoulou, Effrosyni, and Theodoros Giovazolias. 2013. "The Relationship between Perceived Parental Bonding and Bullying: The Mediating Role of Empathy." *European Journal of Counselling Psychology* 2 (1): 1–16.

———. 2015. "Personality Traits, Empathy and Bullying Behavior: A Meta-Analytic Approach." *Aggression and Violent Behavior* 21:61–72.

Modecki, Kathryn, Jeannie Minchin, Allen Harbaugh, Nancy Guerra, and Kevin Runions. 2014. "Bullying Prevalence across Contexts: A Meta-Analysis

Measuring Cyber and Traditional Bullying." *Journal of Adolescent Health* 55 (5): 602–11.

Modin, Bitte, Sara Låftman, and Viveca Östberg. 2017. "Teacher Rated School Ethos and Student Reported Bullying—A Multilevel Study of Upper Secondary Schools in Stockholm, Sweden." *International Journal of Environmental Research and Public Health* 14 (12): 1565.

Moffa, Giusi, Gennaro Catone, Jack Kuipers, Elizabeth Kuipers, Daniel Freeman, Steven Marwaha, Belinda R. Lennox, Matthew R. Broome, and Paul Bebbington. 2017. "Using Directed Acyclic Graphs in Epidemiological Research in Psychosis: An Analysis of the Role of Bullying in Psychosis." *Schizophrenia Bulletin* 43 (6): 1273–79.

Moffitt, Terrie. 2017. "Adolescence-Limited and Life-Course-Persistent Antisocial Behavior: A Developmental Taxonomy." In *Biosocial Theories of Crime*, edited by Kevin M. Beaver and Anthony Walsh, 69–96. London: Routledge.

Molcho, Michal, Wendy Craig, Pernille Due, William Pickett, Yossi Harel-Fisch, Mary Overpeck, and the HBSC Bullying Writing Group. 2009. "Cross-National Time Trends in Bullying Behaviour 1994–2006: Findings from Europe and North America." *International Journal of Public Health* 54 (2): 225–34.

Monk, Daniel. 2011. "Challenging Homophobic Bullying in Schools: The Politics of Progress." *International Journal of Law in Context* 7 (2): 181–207.

Montero-Carretero, Carlos, David Barbado, and Eduardo Cervelló. 2020. "Predicting Bullying through Motivation and Teaching Styles in Physical Education." *International Journal of Environmental Research and Public Health* 17 (1): 87.

Moon, Byongook, and Leanne Fiftal Alarid. 2015. "School Bullying, Low Self-Control, and Opportunity." *Journal of Interpersonal Violence* 30 (5): 839–56.

Moon, Byongook, Hye-Won Hwang, and John McCluskey. 2011. "Causes of School Bullying: Empirical Test of a General Theory of Crime, Differential Association Theory, and General Strain Theory." *Crime & Delinquency* 57 (6): 849–77.

Moon, Byongook, and Sung Joon Jang. 2014. "A General Strain Approach to Psychological and Physical Bullying: A Study of Interpersonal Aggression at School." *Journal of Interpersonal Violence* 29 (12): 2147–71.

Moore, Sophie, Rosana Norman, Shuichi Suetani, Hannah Thomas, Peter Sly, and James G. Scott. 2017. "Consequences of Bullying Victimization in Childhood and Adolescence: A Systematic Review and Meta-Analysis." *World Journal of Psychiatry* 7 (1): 60–76.

Moreno, Megan, Aubrey Gower, Heather Brittain, and Tracy Vaillancourt. 2019. "Applying Natural Language Processing to Evaluate News Media Coverage of Bullying and Cyberbullying." *Prevention Science* 20:1274–83.

Morrison, Brenda. 2002. "Bullying and Victimisation in Schools: A Restorative Justice Approach." *Trends and Issues in Crime and Criminal Justice*, no. 219, Canberra, Australian Institute of Criminology. https://www.aic.gov.au/publications/tandi/tandi219.

Motz, Ryan, Peter Tanksley, Hexuan Liu, Tesfaye Mersha, and J. C. Barnes. 2019. "Every Contact Leaves a Trace: Contact with the Criminal Justice System, Life

Outcomes, and the Intersection with Genetics." *Current Opinion in Psychology* 27:82–87.

Mulder, Rosa H., Esther Walton, Alexander Neumann, Lotte C. Houtepen, Janine F. Felix, Marian J. Bakermans-Kranenburg, Matthew Suderman et al. 2020. "Epigenomics of Being Bullied: Changes in DNA Methylation following Bullying Exposure." *Epigenetics.* Published ahead of print, January 28, 2020. https://doi.org/10.1080/15592294.2020.1719303.

Murray, Joseph, Pedro Hallal, Gregore Mielke, Adrian Raine, Fernando Wehrmeister, Luciana Anselmi, and Fernando C. Barros. 2016. "Low Resting Heart Rate Is Associated with Violence in Late Adolescence: A Prospective Birth Cohort Study in Brazil." *International Journal of Epidemiology* 45 (2): 491–500.

Musci, Rashelle, Amie Bettencourt, Danielle Sisto, Brion Maher, George Uhl, Nicholas Ialongo, and Catherine P. Bradshaw. 2018. "Evaluating the Genetic Susceptibility to Peer Reported Bullying Behaviors." *Psychiatry Research* 263:193–98.

Napoletano, Anthony, Frank Elgar, Grace Saul, Melanie Dirks, and Wendy Craig. 2016. "The View from the Bottom: Relative Deprivation and Bullying Victimization in Canadian Adolescents." *Journal of Interpersonal Violence* 31 (20): 3443–63.

National Center for Education Statistics. 2016. *The Condition of Education 2016.* Summary Report. http://nces.ed.gov/pubsearch/pubsinfo.asp?pubid=2016144.

Naylor, Paul, Helen Cowie, Fabienne Cossin, Rita de Bettencourt, and Francesca Lemme. 2006. "Teachers' and Pupils' Definitions of Bullying." *British Journal of Educational Psychology* 76 (3): 553–76.

Nelson, Helen, Sharyn Burns, Garth Kendall, and Kimberly Schonert-Reichl. 2019. "Preadolescent Children's Perception of Power Imbalance in Bullying: A Thematic Analysis." *PloS One* 14 (3): e0211124.

Nickerson, Amanda, Danielle Mele, and Dana Princiotta. 2008. "Attachment and Empathy as Predictors of Roles as Defenders or Outsiders in Bullying Interactions." *Journal of School Psychology* 46 (6): 687–703.

Nielsen, Morten Birkeland, Tone Tangen, Thormod Idsoe, Stig Berge Matthiesen, and Nils Magerøy. 2015. "Post-Traumatic Stress Disorder as a Consequence of Bullying at Work and at School: A Literature Review and Meta-Analysis." *Aggression and Violent Behavior* 21:17–24.

Nikiforou, Militsa, Stelios Georgiou, and Panayiotis Stavrinides. 2013. "Attachment to Parents and Peers as a Parameter of Bullying and Victimization." Special issue, *Journal of Criminology* 2013:1–9. http://doi.org/10.1155/2013/484871.

Nikolaou, Dimitrios. 2017. "Do Anti-Bullying Policies Deter In-School Bullying Victimization?" *International Review of Law and Economics* 50:1–6.

Nocentini, Annalaura, Ersilia Menesini, and Christina Salmivalli. 2013. "Level and Change of Bullying Behavior during High School: A Multilevel Growth Curve Analysis." *Journal of Adolescence* 36 (3): 495–505.

Nye, Francis Ivan. 1958. *Family Relationships and Delinquent Behavior.* New York: Wiley.

Obermann, Marie-Louise. 2013. "Temporal Aspects of Moral Disengagement in School Bullying: Crystallization or Escalation?" *Journal of School Violence* 12 (2): 193–210.

Odgers, Candace, and Nancy Adler. 2018. "Challenges for Low-Income Children in an Era of Increasing Income Inequality." *Child Development Perspectives* 12 (2): 128–33.

Olsson, Gabriella, Sara Brolin Låftman, and Bitte Modin. 2017. "School Collective Efficacy and Bullying Behaviour: A Multilevel Study." *International Journal of Environmental Research and Public Health* 14 (12): 1607.

Olweus, Dan. 1980. "The Consistency Issue in Personality Psychology Revisited—with Special Reference to Aggression." *British Journal of Social and Clinical Psychology* 19 (4): 377–90.

———. 1991. "Bully/Victim Problems among School Children: Basic Facts and Effects of a School-Based Intervention Program." In *The Development and Treatment of Childhood Aggression*, edited by Debra J. Pepler and Kenneth H. Rubin, 411–48. Hillsdale, NJ: Erlbaum.

———. 1993. *Bullying at School: What We Know and What We Can Do.* New York: WileyBlackwell.

———. 2013. "School Bullying: Development and Some Important Challenges." *Annual Review of Clinical Psychology* 9:751–80.

Olweus, Dan, Susan Limber, and Kyrre Breivik. 2019. "Addressing Specific Forms of Bullying: A Large-Scale Evaluation of the Olweus Bullying Prevention Program." *International Journal of Bullying Prevention* 1 (1): 70–84.

O'Malley Olsen, Emily, Laura Kann, Alana Vivolo-Kantor, Steve Kinchen, and Tim McManus. 2014. "School Violence and Bullying among Sexual Minority High School Students, 2009–2011." *Journal of Adolescent Health* 55 (3): 432–38.

O'Moore, Mona, and Colin Kirkham. 2001. "Self-Esteem and Its Relationship to Bullying Behaviour." *Aggressive Behavior* 27 (4): 269–83.

Ortiz, Jame, and Adrian Raine. 2004. "Heart Rate Level and Antisocial Behavior in Children and Adolescents: A Meta-Analysis." *Journal of the American Academy of Child & Adolescent Psychiatry* 43 (2): 154–62.

Orue, Izaskun, and Esther Calvete. 2018. "Homophobic Bullying in Schools: The Role of Homophobic Attitudes and Exposure to Homophobic Aggression." *School Psychology Review* 47 (1): 95–105.

———. 2019. "Psychopathic Traits and Moral Disengagement Interact to Predict Bullying and Cyberbullying among Adolescents." *Journal of Interpersonal Violence* 34 (11): 2313–32.

Osvaldsson, Karin. 2011. "Bullying in Context: Stories of Bullying on an Internet Discussion Board." *Children & Society* 25 (4): 317–27.

Ouellet-Morin, Isabelle, Andrea Danese, Lucy Bowes, Sania Shakoor, Antony Ambler, Carmine M. Pariante, Andrew S. Papadopoulos, Avshalom Caspi, Terrie E. Moffitt, and Louise Arseneault. 2011. "A Discordant Monozygotic Twin Design Shows Blunted Cortisol Reactivity among Bullied Children." *Journal of the American Academy of Child & Adolescent Psychiatry* 50 (6): 574–82.

Pabayo, Roman, Beth Molnar, and Ichiro Kawachi. 2014. "The Role of Neighborhood Income Inequality in Adolescent Aggression and Violence." *Journal of Adolescent Health* 55 (4): 571–79.

Papachristos, Andrew, Anthony Braga, Eric Piza, and Leigh Grossman. 2015. "The Company You Keep? The Spillover Effects of Gang Membership on Individual Gunshot Victimization in a Co-Offending Network." *Criminology* 53 (4): 624–49.

Papachristos, Andrew, and Christopher Wildeman. 2014. "Network Exposure and Homicide Victimization in an African American Community." *American Journal of Public Health* 104 (1): 143–50.

Pappa, Irene, Beate St. Pourcain, Kelly Benke, Alana Cavadino, Christian Hakulinen, Michel G. Nivard, Ilja M. Nolte et al. 2016. "A Genome-Wide Approach to Children's Aggressive Behavior: The EAGLE Consortium." *American Journal of Medical Genetics Part B: Neuropsychiatric Genetics* 171 (5): 562–72.

Pardini, Dustin, Adrian Raine, Kirk Erickson, and Rolf Loeber. 2014. "Lower Amygdala Volume in Men Is Associated with Childhood Aggression, Early Psychopathic Traits, and Future Violence." *Biological Psychiatry* 75 (1): 73–80.

Park, Sora, Eun-Yeong Na, and Eun-Mee Kim. 2014. "The Relationship between Online Activities, Netiquette and Cyberbullying." *Children and Youth Services Review* 42:74–81.

Park, Yeoju, and Christi Metcalfe. 2020. "Bullying Victimization as a Strain: Examining Changes in Bullying Victimization and Delinquency among Korean Students from a Developmental General Strain Theory Perspective." *Journal of Research in Crime and Delinquency* 57 (1): 31–65.

Pascoe, Cheri Joe. 2013. "Notes on a Sociology of Bullying: Young Men's Homophobia as Gender Socialization." *QED: A Journal in GLBTQ Worldmaking* 1:87–103. doi: 10.1353/qed.2013.0013.

Patchin, Justin, and Sameer Hinduja. 2011. "Traditional and Nontraditional Bullying among Youth: A Test of General Strain Theory." *Youth & Society* 43 (2): 727–51.

———. 2015. "Measuring Cyberbullying: Implications for Research." *Aggression and Violent Behavior* 23:69–74

———. 2018. "Deterring Teen Bullying: Assessing the Impact of Perceived Punishment from Police, Schools, and Parents." *Youth Violence and Juvenile Justice* 16 (2): 190–207.

Patton, Desmond Upton, Jun Sung Hong, Sadiq Patel, and Michael Kral. 2017. "A Systematic Review of Research Strategies Used in Qualitative Studies on School Bullying and Victimization." *Trauma, Violence, & Abuse* 18 (1): 3–16.

Paulhus, Delroy, and Kevin Williams. 2002. "The Dark Triad of Personality: Narcissism, Machiavellianism, and Psychopathy." *Journal of Research in Personality* 36 (6): 556–63.

Pauwels, Lieven, and Robert Svensson. 2015. "Schools and Child Antisocial Behavior: In Search for Mediator Effects of School-Level Disadvantage." *SAGE Open* 5, no. 2. https://doi.org/10.1177%2F2158244015592936.

Payne, Allison Ann, and Kelly Welch. 2010. "Modeling the Effects of Racial Threat on Punitive and Restorative School Discipline Practices." *Criminology* 48 (4): 1019–62.

Payne, Brian, Brittany Hawkins, and Chunsheng Xin. 2019. "Using Labeling Theory as a Guide to Examine the Patterns, Characteristics, and Sanctions Given to Cybercrimes." *American Journal of Criminal Justice* 44 (2): 230–47.

Payne, Elizabeth, and Melissa Smith. 2013. "LGBTQ Kids, School Safety, and Missing the Big Picture: How the Dominant Bullying Discourse Prevents School Professionals from Thinking about Systemic Marginalization or ... Why We Need to Rethink LGBTQ Bullying." *QED: A Journal in GLBTQ Worldmaking* (Fall): 1–36.

Pecjak, Sonja, and Tina Pirc. 2017. "Bullying and Perceived School Climate: Victims' and Bullies' Perspective." *Studia Psychologica: Journal for Basic Research in Psychological Sciences* 59 (1): 22–33.

Peguero, Anthony, Edwardo Portillos, Jun Hong, Juan Carlos González, Lindsay Kahle, and Zahra Shekarkhar. 2013. "Victimization, Urbanicity, and the Relevance of Context: School Routines, Race and Ethnicity, and Adolescent Violence." *Journal of Criminology* 2013:1–14, 240637. https://doi.org/10.1155/2013/240637.

Peguero, Anthony, and Zahra Shekarkhar. 2011. "Latino/a Student Misbehavior and School Punishment." *Hispanic Journal of Behavioral Sciences* 33 (1): 54–70.

Peguero, Anthony, and Lisa Williams. 2013. "Racial and Ethnic Stereotypes and Bullying Victimization." *Youth & Society* 45 (4): 545–64.

Pepler, Debra, Depeng Jiang, Wendy Craig, and Jennifer Connolly. 2008. "Developmental Trajectories of Bullying and Associated Factors." *Child Development* 79 (2): 325–38.

Perkins, H. Wesley, Jessica Perkins, and David Craig. 2014. "No Safe Haven: Locations of Harassment and Bullying Victimization in Middle Schools." *Journal of School Health* 84 (12): 810–18.

Phillips, Coretta. 2003. "Who's Who in the Pecking Order? Aggression and 'Normal Violence' in the Lives of Girls and Boys." *British Journal of Criminology* 43 (4): 710–28.

Piquero, Alex, Wesley Jennings, Brie Diamond, David Farrington, Richard Tremblay, Brandon C. Welsh, and Jennifer M. Reingle Gonzalez. 2016. "A Meta-analysis Update on the Effects of Early Family/Parent Training Programs on Antisocial Behavior and Delinquency." *Journal of Experimental Criminology* 12 (2): 229–48.

Piscitelli, Anthony, and Sean Doherty. 2018. "Connecting Social Disorganization to Broken Windows and Routine Activities." *Canadian Geographer/Le Géographe Canadien* 62 (4): 589–96.

Plexousakis, Stefanos Stylianos, Elias Kourkoutas, Theodoros Giovazolias, Kalliopi Chatira, and Dimitrios Nikolopoulos. 2019. "School Bullying and Post-Traumatic Stress Disorder Symptoms: The Role of Parental Bonding." *Frontiers in Public Health* 7 (75): 1–15.

Polanin, Joshua, Dorothy Espelage, and Therese Pigott. 2012. "A Meta-Analysis of School-Based Bullying Prevention Programs' Effects on Bystander Intervention Behavior." *School Psychology Review* 41 (1): 47–65.

Polanin, Megan, and Elizabeth Vera. 2013. "Bullying Prevention and Social Justice." *Theory into Practice* 52 (4): 303–10.

Pontzer, Daniel. 2010. "A Theoretical Test of Bullying Behavior: Parenting, Personality, and the Bully/Victim Relationship." *Journal of Family Violence* 25 (3): 259–73.

Popp, Ann Marie. 2012a. "The Difficulty in Measuring Suitable Targets When Modeling Victimization." *Violence & Victims* 27 (5): 689–709.

———. 2012b. "The Effects of Exposure, Proximity, and Capable Guardians on the Risk of Bullying Victimization." *Youth Violence and Juvenile Justice* 10 (4): 315–32.

Popp, Ann Marie, and Anthony Peguero. 2012. "Social Bonds and the Role of School-Based Victimization." *Journal of Interpersonal Violence* 27 (17): 3366–88.

Pornari, Chrisa, and Jane Wood. 2010. "Peer and Cyber Aggression in Secondary School Students: The Role of Moral Disengagement, Hostile Attribution Bias, and Outcome Expectancies." *Aggressive Behavior: Official Journal of the International Society for Research on Aggression* 36 (2): 81–94.

Powell, Melissa, and Linda Ladd. 2010. "Bullying: A Review of the Literature and Implications for Family Therapists." *American Journal of Family Therapy* 38 (3): 189–206.

Pranis, Kay. 2001. "Restorative Justice, Social Justice, and the Empowerment of Marginalized Populations." In *Restorative Community Justice: Repairing Harm and Transforming Communities*, edited by Gordon Bazemore and Mara Schiff, 287–306. Cincinnati: Anderson.

Prati, Gabriele. 2012. "A Social Cognitive Learning Theory of Homophobic Aggression among Adolescents." *School Psychology Review* 41 (4): 413–28.

Provenzano, Daniel, Andrew Dane, Ann Farrell, Zopito Marini, and Anthony Volk. 2018. "Do Bullies Have More Sex? The Role of Personality." *Evolutionary Psychological Science* 4 (3): 221–32.

Pyżalski, Jacek. 2012. "From Cyberbullying to Electronic Aggression: Typology of the Phenomenon." *Emotional and Behavioural Difficulties* 17 (3–4): 305–17.

Raine, Adrian. 2002. "Biosocial Studies of Antisocial and Violent Behavior in Children and Adults: A Review." *Journal of Abnormal Child Psychology* 30 (4): 311–26.

———. 2019. "A Neurodevelopmental Perspective on Male Violence." *Infant Mental Health Journal* 40 (1): 84–97.

Raine, Adrian, Rose Cheney, Ringo Ho, Jill Portnoy, Jianghong Liu, Liana Soyfer, Joseph Hibbeln, and Therese S. Richmond. 2016. "Nutritional Supplementation to Reduce Child Aggression: A Randomized, Stratified, Single-Blind, Factorial Trial." *Journal of Child Psychology and Psychiatry* 57 (9): 1038–46.

Randa, Ryan, Bradford Reyns, and Matt Nobles. 2019. "Measuring the Effects of Limited and Persistent School Bullying Victimization: Repeat Victimization, Fear, and Adaptive Behaviors." *Journal of Interpersonal Violence* 34 (2): 392–415.

Rawlings, Victoria. 2016. *Gender Regulation, Violence and Social Hierarchies in School: 'Sluts', 'Gays' and 'Scrubs.'* London: Palgrave Macmillan.

Reason, Lisa, Michael Boyd, and Casey Reason. 2016. "Cyberbullying in Rural Communities: Origin and Processing through the Lens of Older Adolescents." *Qualitative Report* 21 (12): 2331–48.

Reaves, Samantha, Susan McMahon, Sophia Duffy, and Linda Ruiz. 2018. "The Test of Time: A Meta-Analytic Review of the Relation between School Climate and Problem Behavior." *Aggression and Violent Behavior* 39:100–108.

Reid, Philippa, Jeremy Monsen, and Ian Rivers. 2004. "Psychology's Contribution to Understanding and Managing Bullying within Schools." *Educational Psychology in Practice* 20 (3): 241–58.

Reijntjes, Albert, Jan Kamphuis, Peter Prinzie, and Michael Telch. 2010. "Peer Victimization and Internalizing Problems in Children: A Meta-Analysis of Longitudinal Studies." *Child Abuse & Neglect* 34 (4): 244–52.

Reiss, Albert. 1951. "Delinquency as the Failure of Personal and Social Controls." *American Sociological Review* 16:196–207.

Reynolds, Arthur, Suh-Ruu Ou, Christina Mondi, and Alison Giovanelli. 2019. "Reducing Poverty and Inequality through Preschool-to-Third-Grade Prevention Services." *American Psychologist* 74 (6): 653–72.

Rhee, Soo Hyun, and Irwin Waldman. 2002. "Genetic and Environmental Influences on Antisocial Behavior: A Meta-Analysis of Twin and Adoption Studies." *Psychological Bulletin* 128 (3): 490–529.

Rigby, Ken. 2012. "Bullying in Schools: Addressing Desires, Not Only Behaviours." *Educational Psychology Review* 24 (2): 339–48.

———. 2018. "Exploring the Gaps between Teachers' Beliefs about Bullying and Research-Based Knowledge." *International Journal of School & Educational Psychology* 6 (3): 165–75.

Rigby, Ken, and Phillip Slee. 1993. "Dimensions of Interpersonal Relation among Australian Children and Implications for Psychological Well-Being." *Journal of Social Psychology* 133 (1): 33–42.

Rigby, Ken, and Peter Smith. 2011. "Is School Bullying Really on the Rise?" *Social Psychology of Education* 14 (4): 441–55.

Ringrose, Jessica, and Victoria Rawlings. 2015. "Posthuman Performativity, Gender and 'School Bullying': Exploring the Material-Discursive Intra-Actions of Skirts, Hair, Sluts, and Poofs." *Confero: Essays on Education, Philosophy and Politics* 3 (2): 1–37.

Rivers, Ian, V. Paul Poteat, Nathalie Noret, and Nigel Ashurst. 2009. "Observing Bullying at School: The Mental Health Implications of Witness Status." *School Psychology Quarterly* 24 (4): 211–23.

Roberts, Andrea, Margaret Rosario, Natalie Slopen, Jerel Calzo, and Bryn Austin. 2013. "Childhood Gender Nonconformity, Bullying Victimization, and Depressive Symptoms across Adolescence and Early Adulthood: An 11-Year Longitudinal Study." *Journal of the American Academy of Child & Adolescent Psychiatry* 52 (2): 143–52.

Rodkin, Philip, Dorothy Espelage, and Laura Hanish. 2015. "A Relational Framework for Understanding Bullying: Developmental Antecedents and Outcomes." *American Psychologist* 70 (4): 311–21.

Rodríguez-Hidalgo, Antonio, Juan Calmaestra, José Casas, and Rosario Ortega-Ruiz. 2019. "Ethnic-Cultural Bullying versus Personal Bullying: Specificity and Measurement of Discriminatory Aggression and Victimization among Adolescents." *Frontiers in Psychology* 10:46.

Romano, Isabella, Alexandra Butler, Karen Patte, Mark Ferro, and Scott Leatherdale. 2019. "High School Bullying and Mental Disorder: An Examination of the Association with Flourishing and Emotional Regulation." *International Journal of Bullying Prevention*. Published ahead of print, August 3, 2019. https://doi.org/10.1007/s42380-019-00035-5.

Rose, Chad, Amanda Nickerson, and Melissa Stormont. 2015. "Advancing Bullying Research from a Social-Ecological Lens: An Introduction to the Special Issue." *School Psychology Review* 44 (4): 339–52.

Rosen, Nicole, and Stacey Nofziger. 2018. "Boys, Bullying, and Gender Roles: How Hegemonic Masculinity Shapes Bullying Behavior." *Gender Issues* 36 (3): 295–318.

Rudo-Hutt, Anna, Yu Gao, Andrea Glenn, Melissa Peskin, and Yaling Yang. 2016. "Biosocial Interactions and Correlates of Crime." In *The Ashgate Research Companion to Biosocial Theories of Crime*, edited by Kevin M. Beaver and Anthony Walsh, 29–56. Oxon, England: Routledge.

Rudolph, Karen, Wendy Troop-Gordon, and Douglas Granger. 2010. "Peer Victimization and Aggression: Moderation by Individual Differences in Salivary Cortisol and Alpha-Amylase." *Journal of Abnormal Child Psychology* 38 (6): 843–56.

Runciman, William. 1966. *Relative Deprivation and Social Justice*. London: Routledge & Kegan Paul.

Rusby, Julie, Kathleen Forrester, Anthony Biglan, and Carol Metzler. 2005. "Relationships between Peer Harassment and Adolescent Problem Behaviors." *Journal of Early Adolescence* 25 (4): 453–77.

Russell, Katheryn. 1999. "Critical Race Theory and Social Justice." In *Social Justice/Criminal Justice: The Maturation of Critical Theory in Law, Crime, and Deviance*, edited by Bruce A. Arrigo, 178–88. Belmont, CA: Wadsworth.

Russell, Stephen, Katerina Sinclair, V. Paul Poteat, and Brian Koenig. 2012. "Adolescent Health and Harassment Based on Discriminatory Bias." *American Journal of Public Health* 102 (3): 493–95.

Rutten, Esther, Maja Deković, Geert Jan Stams, Carlo Schuengel, Jan Hoeksma, and Gert J.J. Biesta. 2008. "On- and Off-Field Antisocial and Prosocial Behavior in Adolescent Soccer Players: A Multilevel Study." *Journal of Adolescence* 31 (3): 371–87.

Rutten, Esther A., Carlo Schuengel, Evelien Dirks, Geert Jan J.M. Stams, Gert J.J. Biesta, and Jan B. Hoeksma. 2011. "Predictors of Antisocial and Prosocial Behavior in an Adolescent Sports Context." *Social Development* 20 (2): 294–315.

Ryoo, Ji Hoon, Cixin Wang, and Susan Swearer. 2015. "Examination of the Change in Latent Statuses in Bullying Behaviors across Time." *School Psychology Quarterly* 30 (1): 105–22.

Sabia, Joseph, and Brittany Bass. 2017. "Do Anti-Bullying Laws Work? New Evidence on School Safety and Youth Violence." *Journal of Population Economics* 30 (2): 473–502.

Sabic-El-Rayess, Amra, Naheed Natasha Mansur, Batjargal Batkhuyag, and Sarantsetseg Otgonlkhagva. 2019. "School Uniform Policy's Adverse Impact on Equity and Access to Schooling." *Compare: A Journal of Comparative and International Education.* https://doi.org/10.1080/03057925.2019.1579637.

Sacco, Dena, Katharine Baird Silbaugh, Felipe Corredor, June Casey, and Davis Doherty. 2012. *An Overview of State Anti-Bullying Legislation and Other Related Laws.* Research publication, Kinder & Braver World Project: Research Series, Born This Way Foundation & Berkman Center for Internet & Society, Harvard University. https://cyber.harvard.edu/sites/cyber.harvard.edu/files/State_Anti_bullying_Legislation_Overview_0.pdf.

Samek, Diana, Irene Elkins, Margaret Keyes, William Iacono, and Matt McGue. 2015. "High School Sports Involvement Diminishes the Association between Childhood Conduct Disorder and Adult Antisocial Behavior." *Journal of Adolescent Health* 57 (1): 107–12.

Sampson, Robert. 2018. "Organized for What? Recasting Theories of Social (Dis)organization." In *Crime and Social Organization*, edited by Elin Waring and David Weisburd, 113–28. Oxon, England: Routledge.

Sampson, Robert, and W. Byron Groves. 1989. "Community Structure and Crime: Testing Social-Disorganization Theory." *American Journal of Sociology* 94 (4): 774–802.

Sampson, Robert, and John Laub. 1993. *Crime in the Making: Pathways and Turning Points through Life.* Cambridge, MA: Harvard University Press.

———. 1997. "A Life-Course Theory of Cumulative Disadvantage and the Stability of Delinquency." In *Developmental Theories of Crime and Delinquency*, edited by Terence P. Thornberry, 133–55. New Brunswick, NJ: Transaction.

———. 2005. "A Life-Course View of the Development of Crime." *Annals of the American Academy of Political and Social Science* 602 (1): 12–45.

Sampson, Robert, and William Julius Wilson. 1995. "Toward a Theory of Race, Crime, and Urban Inequality." In *Race, Crime, and Justice: A Reader*, edited by John Hagan and Ruth D. Peterson, 37–54. Stanford, CA: Stanford University Press.

Sanchez, Jafeth E., Andrew Yoxsimer, and George C. Hill. 2012. "Uniforms in the Middle School: Student Opinions, Discipline Data, and School Police Data." *Journal of School Violence* 11 (4): 345–56.

Sánchez-Martín, J. R., Eduardo Fano, L. Ahedo, Jaione Cardas, Paul Brain, and Arantza Azpiroz. 2000. "Relating Testosterone Levels and Free Play Social Behavior in Male and Female Preschool Children." *Psychoneuroendocrinology* 25 (8): 773–83.

Sansone, Randy, Charlene Lam, and Michael Wiederman. 2010. "Being Bullied in Childhood: Correlations with Borderline Personality in Adulthood." *Comprehensive Psychiatry* 51 (5): 458–61.

Sawyer, Anne, Catherine Bradshaw, and Lindsey O'Brennan. 2008. "Examining Ethnic, Gender, and Developmental Differences in the Way Children Report Being a Victim of 'Bullying' on Self-Report Measures." *Journal of Adolescent Health* 43 (2): 106–14.

Schacter, Hannah, Samantha White, Vickie Chang, and Jaana Juvonen. 2015. "'Why Me?': Characterological Self-Blame and Continued Victimization in the First Year of Middle School." *Journal of Clinical Child & Adolescent Psychology* 44 (3): 446–55.

Scheider, Matthew. 2002. "Teaching Criminological Theory: Presentation According to the Dependent Variable." *Journal of Criminal Justice Education* 13 (2): 387–402.

Schiff, Mara. 2018. "Can Restorative Justice Disrupt the 'School-to-Prison Pipeline'?" *Contemporary Justice Review* 21 (2): 121–39.

Schoeler, Tabea, Shing Wan Choi, Frank Dudbridge, Jessie Baldwin, Lauren Duncan, Charlotte M. Cecil, Esther Walton, Essi Viding, Eamon McCrory, and Jean-Baptiste Pingault. 2019. "Multi–Polygenic Score Approach to Identifying Individual Vulnerabilities Associated with the Risk of Exposure to Bullying." *JAMA Psychiatry* 76 (7): 730–38.

Schoeler, Tabea, Lauren Duncan, Charlotte Cecil, George Ploubidis, and Jean-Baptiste Pingault. 2018. "Quasi-Experimental Evidence on Short- and Long-Term Consequences of Bullying Victimization: A Meta-analysis." *Psychological Bulletin* 144 (12): 1229–46.

Schumann, Lyndall, Wendy Craig, and Andrei Rosu. 2014. "Power Differentials in Bullying: Individuals in a Community Context." *Journal of Interpersonal Violence* 29 (5): 846–65.

Schwartz, David, Jennifer Lansford, Kenneth Dodge, Gregory Pettit, and John Bates. 2018. "Peer Victimization during Middle Childhood as a Marker of Attenuated Risk for Adult Arrest." *Journal of Abnormal Child Psychology* 46 (1): 57–65.

Schwartz, David, Laura Proctor, and Deborah Chien. 2001. "The Aggressive Victim of Bullying: Emotional and Behavioral Dysregulation as a Pathway to Victimization by Peers." In *School-Based Peer Harassment: The Plight of the Vulnerable and Victimized*, edited by Jaana Juvonen and Sandra Graham, 147–74. Boston: Guilford Press.

Schwartz, Joseph, Jukka Savolainen, Mikko Aaltonen, Marko Merikukka, Reija Paananen, and Mika Gissler. 2015. "Intelligence and Criminal Behavior in a Total Birth Cohort: An Examination of Functional Form, Dimensions of Intelligence, and the Nature of Offending." *Intelligence* 51:109–18.

Séguin, Jean Richard, and Philip David Zelazo. 2005. "Executive Function in Early Physical Aggression." In *Developmental Origins of Aggression*, edited by Richard E. Tremblay, William W. Hartup, and John Archer, 307–29. New York: Guilford Press.

Selkie, Ellen, Jessica Fales, and Megan Moreno. 2016. "Cyberbullying Prevalence among US Middle and High School–Aged Adolescents: A Systematic Review and Quality Assessment." *Journal of Adolescent Health* 58 (2): 125–33.

Serra-Negra, Júnia Maria, Isabela Almeida Pordeus, Patrícia Corrêa-Faria, Lívia Bonfim Fulgêncio, Saul Martins Paiva, and Daniele Manfredini. 2017. "Is There an Association between Verbal School Bullying and Possible Sleep Bruxism in Adolescents?" *Journal of Oral Rehabilitation* 44 (5): 347–53.

Sesar, Kristina, Nataša Simic, and Damir Sesar. 2013. "The Association between Bullying Behavior, Arousal Level, Coping Strategies and Psychological Adjustment." *Pedijatrija Danas/Pediatrics Today* 9 (1): 112–28.

Shaheen, Abeer, Sawsan Hammad, Eman Haourani, and Omayyah Nassar. 2018. "Factors Affecting Jordanian School Adolescents' Experience of Being Bullied." *Journal of Pediatric Nursing* 38:e66–e71.

Shapka, Jennifer, and Danielle Law. 2013. "Does One Size Fit All? Ethnic Differences in Parenting Behaviors and Motivations for Adolescent Engagement in Cyberbullying." *Journal of Youth and Adolescence* 42 (5): 723–38.

Shaw, Clifford Robe, and Henry Donald McKay. 1942. *Juvenile Delinquency and Urban Areas*. Chicago: University of Chicago Press.

Shaw, Therese, Donna Cross, and Stephen Zubrick. 2015. "Testing for Response Shift Bias in Evaluations of School Antibullying Programs." *Evaluation Review* 39 (6): 527–54.

Sherman, Lawrence, and Heather Strang. 2007. *Restorative Justice: The Evidence*. Research Report, The Smith Institute. http://www.iirp.edu/pdf/RJ_full_report.pdf.

Sherrill, Andrew, and Lauren Bradel. 2017. "Contact Sport Participation Predicts Instrumental Aggression, Not Hostile Aggression, within Competition: Quasi-experimental Evidence." *Journal of Aggression, Conflict and Peace Research* 9 (1): 50–57.

Sibold, Jeremy, Erika M. Edwards, Linnae O'Neil, Dianna Murray-Close, and James J. Hudziak. 2020. "Bullying Environment Moderates the Relationship between Exercise and Mental Health in Bullied US Children." *Journal of School Health* 90 (3): 194–99.

Side, Jeremy, and Kelley Johnson. 2014. "Bullying in Schools: Why It Happens, How It Makes Young People Feel and What We Can Do about It." *Educational Psychology in Practice* 30 (3): 217–31.

Silberg, Judy, William Copeland, Julie Linker, Ashlee Moore, Roxann Roberson-Nay, and Timothy P. York. 2016. "Psychiatric Outcomes of Bullying Victimization: A Study of Discordant Monozygotic Twins." *Psychological Medicine* 46 (9): 1875–83.

Simon, Joan, and Paul Nail. 2013. "Introduction to Special Issue on Bullying: A Social Influence Perspective." *Social Influence* 8 (2–3): 81–86.

Simon, Jonathan. 2007. *Governing through Crime: How the War on Crime Transformed American Democracy and Created a Culture of Fear*. New York: Oxford University Press.

Sims-Schouten, Wendy, and Simon Edwards. 2018. "'Man Up!' Bullying and Resilience within a Neoliberal Framework." *Journal of Youth Studies* 19 (10): 1382–1400.

Sittichai, Ruthaychonnee, and Peter Smith. 2015. "Bullying in South-East Asian Countries: A Review." *Aggression and Violent Behavior* 23:22–35.

Skiba, Russell, Mariella Arredondo, and Natasha Williams. 2014. "More than a Metaphor: The Contribution of Exclusionary Discipline to a School-to-Prison Pipeline." *Equity & Excellence in Education* 47 (4): 546–64.

Skrzypiec, Grace, Helen Askell-Williams, Phillip Slee, and Michael Lawson. 2018. "Involvement in Bullying during High School: A Survival Analysis Approach." *Violence and Victims* 33 (3): 563–82.

Smith, Peter, Helen Cowie, Ragnar Olafsson, and Andy Liefooghe. 2002. "Definitions of Bullying: A Comparison of Terms Used, and Age and Gender Differences, in a Fourteen-Country International Comparison." *Child Development* 73 (4): 1119–33.

Smith, Peter, Keumjoo Kwak, and Yuichi Toda. 2016. "Reflections on Bullying in Eastern and Western Perspectives." In *School Bullying in Different Cultures*, edited by Peter K. Smith, Keumjoo Kwak, and Yuichi Toda, 399–419. Cambridge: Cambridge University Press.

Smith, Peter, and Claire Monks. 2008. "Concepts of Bullying: Developmental and Cultural Aspects." *International Journal of Adolescent Medicine and Health* 20 (2): 101–12.

Smokowski, Paul, Caroline Evans, and Katie Cotter. 2014. "The Differential Impacts of Episodic, Chronic, and Cumulative Physical Bullying and Cyberbullying: The Effects of Victimization on the School Experiences, Social Support, and Mental Health of Rural Adolescents." *Violence and Victims* 29 (6): 1029–46.

Søndergaard, Dorte Marie. 2012. "Bullying and Social Exclusion Anxiety in Schools." *British Journal of Sociology of Education* 33 (3): 355–72.

Sønderlund, Anders, Kerry O'Brien, Peter Kremer, Bosco Rowland, Florentine De Groot, Petra Staiger, Lucy Zinkiewicz, and Peter G. Miller. 2014. "The Association between Sports Participation, Alcohol Use and Aggression and Violence: A Systematic Review." *Journal of Science and Medicine in Sport* 17 (1): 2–7.

Sourander, Andre, David Gyllenberg, Anat Brunstein Klomek, Lauri Sillanmäki, Anna-Marja Ilola, and Kirsti Kumpulaine. 2016. "Association of Bullying Behavior at 8 Years of Age and Use of Specialized Services for Psychiatric Disorders by 29 Years of Age." *JAMA Psychiatry* 73 (2): 159–65.

Spruit, Anouk, Eveline Van Vugt, Claudia van der Put, Trudy van der Stouwe, and Geert-Jan Stams. 2016. "Sports Participation and Juvenile Delinquency: A Meta-analytic Review." *Journal of Youth and Adolescence* 45 (4): 655–71.

Stark, Rodney. 1987. "Deviant Places: A Theory of the Ecology of Crime." *Criminology* 25 (4): 893–910.

Steffgen, Georges, Sophie Recchia, and Wolfgang Viechtbauer. 2013. "The Link between School Climate and Violence in School: A Meta-Analytic Review." *Aggression and Violent Behavior* 18 (2): 300–309.

Steiner, Riley, and Catherine Rasberry. 2015. "Brief Report: Associations between In-Person and Electronic Bullying Victimization and Missing School Because of Safety Concerns among U.S. High School Students." *Journal of Adolescence* 43:1–4.

Sternberg, Robert. 2018. "Theories of Intelligence." In *APA Handbooks in Psychology: APA Handbook of Giftedness and Talent*, edited by Steven I. Pfeiffer, Elizabeth Shaunessy-Dedrick, and Megan Foley-Nicpon, 145–61. Washington, DC: American Psychological Association.

Sterzing, Paul, Jeremy Gibbs, Rachel Gartner, and Jeremy Goldbach. 2018. "Bullying Victimization Trajectories for Sexual Minority Adolescents: Stable Victims, Desisters, and Late-Onset Victims." *Journal of Research on Adolescence* 28 (2): 368–78.

Sticca, Fabio, and Sonja Perren. 2015. "The Chicken and the Egg: Longitudinal Associations between Moral Deficiencies and Bullying: A Parallel Process Latent Growth Model." *Merrill-Palmer Quarterly* 61 (1): 85–100.

Strindberg, Joakim, Paul Horton, and Robert Thornberg. 2019. "Coolness and Social Vulnerability: Swedish Pupils' Reflections on Participant Roles in School Bullying." *Research Papers in Education*. Published ahead of print, May 13, 2019. https://doi.org/10.1080/02671522.2019.1615114.

Sulkowski, Michael, Sheri Bauman, Savannah Wright, Charisse Nixon, and Stan Davis. 2014. "Peer Victimization in Youth from Immigrant and Non-Immigrant US Families." *School Psychology International* 35 (6): 649–69.

Sung, Yu-Hsien, Li-Ming Chen, Cheng-Fang Yen, and Martin Valcke. 2018. "Double Trouble: The Developmental Process of School Bully-Victims." *Children and Youth Services Review* 91:279–88.

Sutherland, Edwin. 1947. *Principles of Criminology*. 4th ed. Chicago: J.B. Lippincott.

Sutin, Angelina, Eric Robinson, Michael Daly, and Antonio Terracciano. 2016. "Parent-Reported Bullying and Child Weight Gain Between Ages 6 and 15." *Childhood Obesity* 12 (6): 482–87.

Swearer, Susan, and Dorothy Espelage. 2004. "Introduction: A Social-Ecological Framework of Bullying among Youth." In *Bullying in American Schools: A Social-Ecological Perspective on Prevention and Intervention*, edited by Susan M. Swearer and Dorothy L. Espelage, 1–12. Nahwah, NJ: Lawrence Erlbaum Associates.

Swearer, Susan, and Shelley Hymel. 2015a. "Bullying and Discrimination in Schools: Exploring Variations across Student Subgroups." *School Psychology Review* 44 (4): 504–9.

———. 2015b. "Understanding the Psychology of Bullying: Moving toward a Social-Ecological Diathesis–Stress Model." *American Psychologist* 70 (4): 344–53.

Swearer, Susan, Meredith Martin, Marc Brackett, and Raul Palacios II. 2017. "Bullying Intervention in Adolescence: The Intersection of Legislation, Policies, and Behavioral Change." *Adolescent Research Review* 2:23–35.

Sweeting, Josiah A., Dana Rose Garfin, E. Alison Holman, and Roxane Cohen Silver. 2020. "Associations between Exposure to Childhood Bullying and Abuse and Adulthood Outcomes in a Representative National US Sample." *Child Abuse & Neglect* 101:104048. Published ahead of print, January 13, 2020. https://doi.org/10.1016/j.chiabu.2019.104048.

Sykes, Bryan, Alex Piquero, and Jason Gioviano. 2017. "Code of the Classroom? Social Disadvantage and Bullying among American Adolescents, US 2011–2012." *Crime & Delinquency* 63 (14): 1883–1922.

Sykes, Gresham, and David Matza. 1957. "Techniques of Neutralization: A Theory of Delinquency." *American Sociological Review* 22 (6): 664–70.

Tannenbaum, Frank. 1938. *Crime and the Community.* Boston: Ginn.

Tapper, Katy, and Michael Boulton. 2005. "Victim and Peer Group Responses to Different Forms of Aggression among Primary School Children." *Aggressive Behavior* 31 (3): 238–53.

Temko, Ezra. 2019. "Missing Structure: A Critical Content Analysis of the Olweus Bullying Prevention Program." *Children & Society* 33 (1): 1–12.

Teng, Zhaojun, George G. Bear, Chunyan Yang, Qian Nie, and Cheng Guo. 2020. "Moral Disengagement and Bullying Perpetration: A Longitudinal Study of the Moderating Effect of School Climate." *School Psychology* 35 (1): 99–109.

Terry, Amanda. 2018. "The Impact of State Legislation and Model Policies on Bullying in Schools." *Journal of School Health* 88 (4): 289–95.

Tholander, Michael. 2019. "The Making and Unmaking of a Bullying Victim." *Interchange* 50 (1): 1–23.

Tholander, Michael, Anna Lindberg, and Daniel Svensson. 2019. "'A Freak That No One Can Love': Difficult Knowledge in Testimonials on School Bullying." *Research Papers in Education:* 1–19. Published ahead of print, January 29, 2019. https://doi.org/10.1080/02671522.2019.1568534.

Thompson, Aisha, and Anne Gregory. 2011. "Examining the Influence of Perceived Discrimination during African American Adolescents' Early Years of High School." *Education and Urban Society* 43 (1): 3–25.

Thornberg, Robert. 2015a. "School Bullying as a Collective Action: Stigma Processes and Identity Struggling." *Children & Society* 29 (4): 310–20.

———. 2015b. "The Social Dynamics of School Bullying: The Necessary Dialogue between the Blind Men around the Elephant and the Possible Meeting Point at the Social Ecological Square." *Confero: Essays on Education, Philosophy and Politics* 3 (2): 161–203.

———. 2018. "School Bullying and Fitting into the Peer Landscape: A Grounded Theory Field Study." *British Journal of Sociology of Education* 39 (1): 144–58.

Thornberg, Robert, Lena Landgren, and Erika Wiman. 2018. "'It Depends': A Qualitative Study on How Adolescent Students Explain Bystander Intervention and Non-Intervention in Bullying Situations." *School Psychology International* 39 (4): 400–415.

Thornberg, Robert, Tiziana Pozzoli, Gianluca Gini, and Tomas Jungert. 2015. "Unique and Interactive Effects of Moral Emotions and Moral Disengagement on Bullying and Defending among School Children." *Elementary School Journal* 116 (2): 322–37.

Thorsborne, Margaret. 2013. "A Story of the Emergence of Restorative Practice in Schools in Australia and New Zealand: Reflect, Repair, Reconnect." In

Restorative Justice Today: Practical Applications, edited by Katherine S. van Wormer and Lorenn Walker, 43–52. Los Angeles: SAGE.

Tielbeek, Jorim, J. C. Barnes, Arne Popma, Tinca Polderman, James Lee, John R. B. Perry, Danielle Posthuma, and Brian D. Boutwell. 2018. "Exploring the Genetic Correlations of Antisocial Behaviour and Life History Traits." *BJPsych Open* 4 (6): 467–70.

Tielbeek, Jorim, Ada Johansson, Tinca Polderman, Marja-Riitta Rautiainen, Philip Jansen, Michelle Taylor, Xiaoran Tong et al. 2017. "Genome-Wide Association Studies of a Broad Spectrum of Antisocial Behavior." *JAMA Psychiatry* 74 (12): 1242–50.

Tielbeek, Jorim, Richard Karlsson Linnér, Koko Beers, Danielle Posthuma, Arne Popma, and Tinca J. C. Polderman. 2016. "Meta-Analysis of the Serotonin Transporter Promoter Variant (5-HTTLPR) in Relation to Adverse Environment and Antisocial Behavior." *American Journal of Medical Genetics Part B: Neuropsychiatric Genetics* 171 (5): 748–60.

Tippett, Neil, and Dieter Wolke. 2014. "Socioeconomic Status and Bullying: A Meta-Analysis." *American Journal of Public Health* 104 (6): e48–e59.

Toby, Jackson. 1957. "Social Disorganization and Stake in Conformity: Complementary Factors in the Predatory Behavior of Hoodlums." *Journal of Criminal Law, Criminology, and Police Science* 48 (1): 12–17.

Tokunaga, Robert. 2010. "Following You Home from School: A Critical Review and Synthesis of Research on Cyberbullying Victimization." *Computers in Human Behavior* 26 (3): 277–87.

Torres, Christopher E., Stewart J. D'Alessio, and Lisa Stolzenberg. 2020. "The Effect of Social, Verbal, Physical, and Cyberbullying Victimization on Academic Performance." *Victims & Offenders* 15 (1): 1–21.

Troop-Gordon, Wendy. 2017. "Peer Victimization in Adolescence: The Nature, Progression, and Consequences of Being Bullied within a Developmental Context." *Journal of Adolescence* 55:116–28.

Ttofi, Maria, and David Farrington. 2011. "Effectiveness of School-Based Programs to Reduce Bullying: A Systematic and Meta-Analytic Review." *Journal of Experimental Criminology* 7 (1): 27–56.

Ttofi, Maria, David Farrington, Friedrich Lösel, Rebecca Crago, and Nikolaos Theodorakis. 2016. "School Bullying and Drug Use Later in Life: A Meta-Analytic Investigation." *School Psychology Quarterly* 31 (1): 8–27.

Ttofi, Maria, David Farrington, Friedrich Lösel, and Rolf Loeber. 2011. "Do the Victims of School Bullies Tend to Become Depressed Later in Life? A Systematic Review and Meta-Analysis of Longitudinal Studies." *Journal of Aggression, Conflict and Peace Research* 3 (2): 63–73.

Ttofi, Maria, David Farrington, Alex Piquero, Friedrich Lösel, Matthew DeLisi, and Joseph Murray. 2016. "Intelligence as a Protective Factor against Offending: A Meta-Analytic Review of Prospective Longitudinal Studies." *Journal of Criminal Justice* 45:4–18.

Tucker, Corinna Jenkins, David Finkelhor, and Heather Turner. 2019. "Patterns of Sibling Victimization as Predictors of Peer Victimization in Childhood and Adolescence." *Journal of Family Violence* 34 (8): 745–55.

Turcotte Benedict, Frances, Patrick Vivier, and Annie Gjelsvik. 2015. "Mental Health and Bullying in the United States among Children Aged 6 to 17 Years." *Journal of Interpersonal Violence* 30 (5): 782–95.

Ullman, Jacqueline. 2018. "Breaking Out of the (Anti)bullying 'Box': NYC Educators Discuss Trans/Gender Diversity-Inclusive Policies and Curriculum." *Sex Education* 18 (5): 495–510.

Ünal, Halime, and Cem Çukur. 2011. "The Effects of School Bonds, Discipline Techniques in School and Victimization on Delinquency of High School Students." *Kuram Ve Uygulamada Egitim Bilimleri* [Educational Sciences: Theory & Practice] 11 (2): 560–70.

UNESCO (United Nations Educational, Scientific, and Cultural Organisation). 2018. *School Violence and Bullying: Global Status and Trends, Drivers, and Consequences.* Paris: UNESCO.

Ungvary, Stephen, Kristina McDonald, Carolyn Gibson, Andrea Glenn, and Albert Reijntjes. 2018. "Victimized by Peers and Aggressive: The Moderating Role of Physiological Arousal and Reactivity." *Merrill-Palmer Quarterly* 64 (1): 70–100.

United States Department of Education. 2011. *Analysis of State Bullying Laws and Policies.* Washington, DC: Office of Planning, Evaluation and Policy Development, Policy and Program Studies Service.

United States Department of Education. 2013. *Student Reports of Bullying and Cyber-Bullying: Results from the 2011 School Crime Supplement to the National Crime Victimization Survey.* Washington, DC: National Center for Education Statistics. https://nces.ed.gov/pubs2013/2013329.pdf.

United States Department of Education. 2016a. *Indicators of School Crime and Safety.* Washington, DC: National Center for Education Statistics and United States Department of Justice, Office of Justice Programs. https://nces.ed.gov/pubs2017/2017064.pdf.

———. 2016b. *Student Reports of Bullying: Results from the 2015 School Crime Supplement to the National Crime Victimization Survey.* Washington, DC: National Center for Education Statistics. https://nces.ed.gov/pubs2017/2017015.pdf.

———. 2016c. *2013–2014 Civil Rights Data Collection: A First Look.* Washington, DC: Office for Civil Rights. https://www2.ed.gov/about/offices/list/ocr/docs/2013–14-first-look.pdf.

Unnever, James, and Dewey Cornell. 2003. "Bullying, Self-Control, and ADHD." *Journal of Interpersonal Violence* 18 (2): 129–47.

Vaillancourt, Tracy, Heather Brittain, John Haltigan, Jamie Ostrov, and Cameron Muir. 2018. "Cortisol Moderates the Relation between Physical Peer Victimization and Physical Aggression in Preschoolers Attending High-Quality Child Care: Evidence of Differential Susceptibility across Informants." *Merrill-Palmer Quarterly* 64 (1): 101–34.

Vaillancourt, Tracy, Denys Decatanzaro, Eric Duku, and Cameron Muir. 2009. "Androgen Dynamics in the Context of Children's Peer Relations: An Examination of the Links between Testosterone and Peer Victimization." *Aggressive Behavior: Official Journal of the International Society for Research on Aggression* 35 (1): 103–13.

Vaillancourt, Tracy, Shelley Hymel, and Patricia McDougall. 2013. "The Biological Underpinnings of Peer Victimization: Understanding Why and How the Effects of Bullying Can Last a Lifetime." *Theory into Practice* 52 (4): 241–48.

Valdebenito, Sara, Maria Ttofi, and Manuel Eisner. 2015. "Prevalence Rates of Drug Use among School Bullies and Victims: A Systematic Review and Meta-Analysis of Cross-Sectional Studies." *Aggression and Violent Behavior* 23:137–46.

Van Bokhoven, Irene, Stephanie Van Goozen, Herman Van Engeland, Benoist Schaal, Louise Arseneault, Jean R. Séguin, Jean-Marc Assaad, Daniel S. Nagin, Frank Vitaro, and Richard E. Tremblay. 2006. "Salivary Testosterone and Aggression, Delinquency, and Social Dominance in a Population-Based Longitudinal Study of Adolescent Males." *Hormones and Behavior* 50 (1): 118–25.

van Dam, Daniella, Elsje van der Ven, Eva Velthorst, Jean-Paul Selten, Craig Morgan, and Lieuwe de Haan. 2012. "Childhood Bullying and the Association with Psychosis in Non-Clinical and Clinical Samples: A Review and Meta-Analysis." *Psychological Medicine* 42 (12): 2463–74.

Vandebosch, Heidi, and Katrien Van Cleemput. 2008. "Defining Cyberbullying: A Qualitative Research into the Perceptions of Youngsters." *CyberPsychology & Behavior* 11 (4): 499–503.

Van Donkelaar, Marjolein, Martine Hoogman, Irene Pappa, Henning Tiemeier, Jan Buitelaar, Barbara Franke, and Janita Bralten. 2018. "Pleiotropic Contribution of MECOM and AVPR1A to Aggression and Subcortical Brain Volumes." *Frontiers in Behavioral Neuroscience* 12:61.

van Geel, Mitch, Anouk Goemans, Fatih Toprak, and Paul Vedder. 2017. "Which Personality Traits Are Related to Traditional Bullying and Cyberbullying? A Study with the Big Five, Dark Triad and Sadism." *Personality and Individual Differences* 106:231–35.

van Geel, Mitch, Fatih Toprak, Anouk Goemans, Wendy Zwaanswijk, and Paul Vedder. 2017. "Are Youth Psychopathic Traits Related to Bullying? Meta-Analyses on Callous-Unemotional Traits, Narcissism, and Impulsivity." *Child Psychiatry & Human Development* 48 (5): 768–77.

van Hazebroek, Babette, Hilde Wermink, Lieke van Domburgh, Jan de Keijser, Machteld Hoeve, and Arne Popma. 2019. "Biosocial Studies of Antisocial Behavior: A Systematic Review of Interactions between Peri/Prenatal Complications, Psychophysiological Parameters, and Social Risk Factors." *Aggression and Violent Behavior* 47:169–88.

Van Ness, Daniel, and Karen Heetderks Strong. 2010. *Restoring Justice: An Introduction to Restorative Justice.* New Providence, NJ: LexisNexis Group.

Van Noorden, Tirza, Gerbert Haselager, Antonius Cillessen, and William Bukowski. 2015. "Empathy and Involvement in Bullying in Children and Adolescents: A Systematic Review." *Journal of Youth and Adolescence* 44 (3): 637–57.

van Reemst, Lisa, Tamar Fischer and Barbara Zwirs. 2016. "Social Information Processing Mechanisms and Victimization: A Literature Review." *Trauma, Violence, & Abuse* 17 (1): 3–25.

Varjas, Kris, Joel Meyers, Sarah Kiperman, and Alice Howard. 2013. "Technology Hurts? Lesbian, Gay, and Bisexual Youth Perspectives of Technology and Cyberbullying." *Journal of School Violence* 12 (1): 27–44.

Vaske, Jamie. 2017. "Policy Implications of Biosocial Criminology: An Introduction to the Special Issue." *Criminal Justice and Behavior* 44 (8): 989–92.

Vassos, Evangelos, David A. Collier, and Seena Fazel. 2014. "Systematic Meta-analyses and Field Synopsis of Genetic Association Studies of Violence and Aggression." *Molecular Psychiatry* 19 (4): 471–77.

Vaughn, Michael, Qiang Fu, Kimberly Bender, Matt DeLisi, Kevin M. Beaver, Brian E. Perron, and Matthew O. Howard. 2010. "Psychiatric Correlates of Bullying in the United States: Findings from a National Sample." *Psychiatric Quarterly* 81 (3): 183–95.

Veenstra, René, Jan Kornelis Dijkstra, Christian Steglich, and Maarten Van Zalk. 2013. "Network–Behavior Dynamics." *Journal of Research on Adolescence* 23 (3): 399–412.

Veldkamp, Sabine, Dorret Boomsma, Eveline de Zeeuw, Catharina van Beijsterveldt, Meike Bartels, Conor V. Dolan, and Elsje van Bergen. 2019. "Genetic and Environmental Influences on Different Forms of Bullying Perpetration, Bullying Victimization, and Their Co-Occurrence." *Behavior Genetics* 49 (5): 432–43.

Verlinden, Marina, René Veenstra, Ank Ringoot, Pauline Jansen, Hein Raat, Albert Hofman, Vincent W. V. Jaddoe, Frank C. Verhulst, and Henning Tiemeier. 2014. "Detecting Bullying in Early Elementary School with a Computerized Peer-Nomination Instrument." *Psychological Assessment* 26 (2): 628–41.

Vessey, Judith, Tania Strout, Rachel DiFazio, and Allison Walker. 2014. "Measuring the Youth Bullying Experience: A Systematic Review of the Psychometric Properties of Available Instruments." *Journal of School Health* 84 (12): 819–43.

Vitoroulis, Irene, and Katholiki Georgiades. 2017. "Bullying among Immigrant and Non-Immigrant Early Adolescents: School-and Student-Level Effects." *Journal of Adolescence* 61:141–51.

Vivolo-Kantor, Alana, Brandi Martell, Kristin Holland, and Ruth Westby. 2014. "A Systematic Review and Content Analysis of Bullying and Cyber-Bullying Measurement Strategies." *Aggression and Violent Behavior* 19 (4): 423–34.

Voisin, Dexter, and Jun Sung Hong. 2012. "A Meditational Model Linking Witnessing Intimate Partner Violence and Bullying Behaviors and Victimization among Youth." *Educational Psychology Review* 24 (4): 479–98.

Volk, Anthony, Joseph Camilleri, Andrew Dane, and Zopito Marini. 2012. "Is Adolescent Bullying an Evolutionary Adaptation?" *Aggressive Behavior* 38 (3): 222–38.

Volk, Anthony, Andrew Dane, and Zopito Marini. 2014. "What Is Bullying? A Theoretical Redefinition." *Developmental Review* 34 (4): 327–43.

Volk, Anthony, Andrew Dane, Zopito Marini, and Tracy Vaillancourt. 2015. "Adolescent Bullying, Dating, and Mating: Testing an Evolutionary Hypothesis." *Evolutionary Psychology* 13 (4): 1–11.

Volk, Anthony, and Larissa Lagzdins. 2009. "Bullying and Victimization among Adolescent Girl Athletes." *Athletic Insight* 11 (1): 12–25.

Volk, Anthony, Daniel Provenzano, Ann Farrell, Andrew Dane, and Elizabeth Shulman. 2019. "Personality and Bullying: Pathways to Adolescent Social Dominance." *Current Psychology*. https://doi.org/10.1007/s12144-019-00182-4.

Volk, Anthony, René Veenstra, and Dorothy Espelage. 2017. "So You Want to Study Bullying? Recommendations to Enhance the Validity, Transparency, and Compatibility of Bullying Research." *Aggression and Violent Behavior* 36:34–43.

Vreeman, Rachel, and Aaron Carroll. 2007. "A Systematic Review of School-Based Interventions to Prevent Bullying." *Archives of Pediatrics & Adolescent Medicine* 161 (1): 78–88.

Vveinhardt, Jolita, Diana Komskiene, and Zasha Romero. 2017. "Bullying and Harassment Prevention in Youth Basketball Teams." *Transformations in Business & Economics* 16 (1): 232–51.

Waasdorp, Tracy E., and Catherine Bradshaw. 2015. "The Overlap between Cyberbullying and Traditional Bullying." *Journal of Adolescent Health* 56 (5): 483–88.

Waasdorp, Tracy Evian, Elise Pas, Benjamin Zablotsky, and Catherine Bradshaw. 2017. "Ten-Year Trends in Bullying and Related Attitudes among 4th- to 12th-Graders." *Pediatrics* 139 (6): e20162615.

Wade, Kathleen Kiley, and Mary Stafford. 2003. "Public School Uniforms: Effect on Perceptions of Gang Presence, School Climate, and Student Self-Perceptions." *Education and Urban Society* 35 (4): 399–420.

Wade, Mark, Thomas Hoffmann, Ariel Knafo-Noam, Thomas O'Connor, and Jennifer Jenkins. 2016. "Oxytocin and Vasopressin Hormone Genes in Children's Externalizing Problems: A Cognitive Endophenotype Approach." *Hormones and Behavior* 82:78–86.

Waldmane, Ari Ezra. 2017. "Are Anti-Bullying Laws Effective?" *Cornell Law Review Online* 103:135–54.

Walsh, Anthony. 2012. *Criminology: The Essentials*. Los Angeles: SAGE.

Walsh, Anthony, and Craig Hemmens. 2011. *Introduction to Criminology: A Text/Reader*. 2nd ed. Los Angeles: SAGE.

Walters, Glenn. 2019. "Animal Cruelty and Bullying: Behavioral Markers of Delinquency Risk or Causal Antecedents of Delinquent Behavior?" *International Journal of Law and Psychiatry* 62:77–84.

Walters, Glenn, and Dorothy Espelage. 2019. "Latent Structure of Early Adolescent Bullying Perpetration: A Taxometric Analysis of Raw and Ranked Scores." *Educational and Psychological Measurement* 79 (4): 754–72. https://doi.org/10.1177%2F0013164418824142.

Walton, Gerald. 2005. "Bullying Widespread: A Critical Analysis of Research and Public Discourse on Bullying." *Journal of School Violence* 4 (1): 91–118.

———. 2011. "Spinning Our Wheels: Reconceptualizing Bullying beyond Behaviour-Focused Approaches." *Discourse: Studies in the Cultural Politics of Education* 32 (1): 131–44.

Wang, Cixin, Brandi Berry, and Susan Swearer. 2013. "The Critical Role of School Climate in Effective Bullying Prevention." *Theory into Practice* 52 (4): 296–302.

Wang, Cixin, Ji Hoon Ryoo, Susan Swearer, Rhonda Turner, and Taryn Goldberg. 2017. "Longitudinal Relationships between Bullying and Moral Disengagement among Adolescents." *Journal of Youth and Adolescence* 46 (6): 1304–17.

Wang, Cixin, Susan Swearer, Paige Lembeck, Adam Collins, and Brandi Berry. 2015. "Teachers Matter: An Examination of Student-Teacher Relationships, Attitudes toward Bullying, and Bullying Behavior." *Journal of Applied School Psychology* 31 (3): 219–38.

Ward, Michelle, Kylee Clayton, Jennifer Barnes, and Jennifer Theule. 2018. "The Association between Peer Victimization and Attachment Security: A Meta-analysis." *Canadian Journal of School Psychology* 33 (3): 193–211.

Weaver, Lori, James Brown, Daniel Weddle, and Matthew Aalsma. 2013. "A Content Analysis of Protective Factors within States' Antibullying Laws." *Journal of School Violence* 12 (2): 156–73.

Webber, Craig. 2007. "Reevaluating Relative Deprivation Theory." *Theoretical Criminology* 11 (1): 97–120.

Wertz, Jasmin, Avshalom Caspi, Daniel W. Belsky, Amber L. Beckley, Louise Arseneault, J. C. Barnes, David L. Corcoran et al. 2018. "Genetics and Crime: Integrating New Genomic Discoveries into Psychological Research about Antisocial Behavior." *Psychological Science* 29 (5): 791–803.

Williams, Frank, and Marilyn McShane. 2010. *Criminological Theory.* 5th ed. Columbus, OH: Prentice Hall.

Williams, Kirk, and Nancy Guerra. 2007. "Prevalence and Predictors of Internet Bullying." *Journal of Adolescent Health* 41 (6): S14–S21.

Williams, Susan, Anne Turner-Henson, Sara Davis, and Heather Soistmann. 2017. "Relationships among Perceived Stress, Bullying, Cortisol, and Depressive Symptoms in Ninth-Grade Adolescents: A Pilot Study." *Biological Research for Nursing* 19 (1): 65–70.

Williford, Anne, and Andrew Zinn. 2018. "Classroom-Level Differences in Child-Level Bullying Experiences: Implications for Prevention and Intervention in School Settings." *Journal of the Society for Social Work and Research* 9 (1): 23–48.

Winburn, Jonathan, Amanda Winburn, and Ryan Niemeyer. 2014. "Media Coverage and Issue Visibility: State Legislative Responses to School Bullying." *Social Science Journal* 51 (4): 514–22.

Winnaar, Lolita, Fabian Arends, and Unathi Beku. 2018. "Reducing Bullying in Schools by Focusing on School Climate and School Socio-Economic Status." *South African Journal of Education* 38 (1): 1–10.

Wolfgang, Martin. 1957. "Victim Precipitated Criminal Homicide." *Journal of Criminal Law and Criminology* 48 (1): 1–11.

Wolke, Dieter, William Copeland, Adrian Angold, and E. Jane Costello. 2013. "Impact of Bullying in Childhood on Adult Health, Wealth, Crime, and Social Outcomes." *Psychological Science* 24 (10): 1958–70.

Wolke, Dieter, Kirsty Lee, and Alexa Guy. 2017. "Cyberbullying: A Storm in a Tea-cup?" *European Child & Adolescent Psychiatry* 26 (8): 899–908.

Wong, Dennis, Christopher Cheng, Raymond Ngan, and Stephen Ma. 2011. "Pro-gram Effectiveness of a Restorative Whole-School Approach for Tackling School Bullying in Hong Kong." *International Journal of Offender Therapy and Comparative Criminology* 55 (6): 846–62.

Wong, Jennifer, Jessica Bouchard, Jason Gravel, Marin Bouchard, and Carlo Morselli. 2016. "Can At-Risk Youth Be Diverted from Crime? A Meta-Analysis of Restorative Diversion Programs." *Criminal Justice and Behavior* 43 (10): 1310–29.

Wong, Jennifer, and Matthias Schonlau. 2013. "Does Bully Victimization Predict Future Delinquency? A Propensity Score Matching Approach." *Criminal Justice and Behavior* 40 (11): 1184–1208.

Woods, Jordan. 2014. "Queer Contestations and the Future of a Critical 'Queer' Criminology." *Critical Criminology* 22 (1): 5–19.

Woods, Sarah, and Eleanor White. 2005. "The Association between Bullying Behaviour, Arousal Levels and Behaviour Problems." *Journal of Adolescence* 28 (3): 381–95.

Yang, An, and Christina Salmivalli. 2013. "Different Forms of Bullying and Victimization: Bully-Victims versus Bullies and Victims." *European Journal of Developmental Psychology* 10 (6): 723–38.

Yang, Fan, Debra Nelson-Gardell, and Yuqi Guo. 2018. "The Role of Strains in Negative Emotions and Bullying Behaviors of School-Aged Children." *Children and Youth Services Review* 94:290–97.

Yang, Y. Tony, and Erin Grinshteyn. 2016. "Safer Cyberspace through Legal Intervention: A Comparative Review of Cyberbullying Legislation." *World Medical & Health Policy* 8 (4): 458–77.

Ybarra, Michele, Dorothy Espelage, and Kimberly Mitchell. 2014. "Differentiating Youth Who Are Bullied from Other Victims of Peer-Aggression: The Importance of Differential Power and Repetition." *Journal of Adolescent Health* 55 (2): 293–300.

Yeung, Ryan. 2009. "Are School Uniforms a Good Fit? Results from the ECLS-K and the NELS." *Educational Policy* 23 (6): 847–74.

Zachry, Amber. 2018. "The Relationship between Virginia School Divisions' Anti-bullying Policy Scores and the Percentage of Student Offenses of Bullying." PhD diss., Liberty University. https://digitalcommons.liberty.edu/cgi/viewcontent.cgi?article=2952&context=doctoral.

Zara, Georgia, and David Farrington. 2016. "Chronic Offenders and the Syndrome of Antisociality: Offending Is Only a Minor Feature!" *Irish Probation Journal* 13:40–64.

Zehr, Howard. 1990. *Changing Lenses: A New Focus for Crime and Justice.* Scottsdale, AZ: Herald Press.

———. 2002. *The Little Book of Restorative Justice.* Intercourse, PA: Good Books.

Zeno v. Pine Plains Central School District, 702 F.3d 655 (2012).

Ziv, Yair, Inbal Leibovich, and Zipora Shechtman. 2013. "Bullying and Victimization in Early Adolescence: Relations to Social Information Processing Patterns." *Aggressive Behavior* 39 (6): 482–92.

Zuckerman, Marvin. 1990. "The Psychophysiology of Sensation Seeking." *Journal of Personality* 58 (1): 313–45.

Zuckerman, Marvin, and C. Robert Cloninger. 1996. "Relationships between Cloninger's, Zuckerman's, and Eysenck's Dimensions of Personality." *Personality and Individual Differences* 21 (2): 283–85.

Zych, Izabela, Anna Baldry, David Farrington, and Vicente Llorent. 2018. "Are Children Involved in Cyberbullying Low on Empathy? A Systematic Review and Meta-Analysis of Research on Empathy versus Different Cyberbullying Roles." *Aggression and Violent Behavior* 45:83–97.

Zych, Izabela, Maria Ttofi, and David Farrington. 2019. "Empathy and Callous–Unemotional Traits in Different Bullying Roles: A Systematic Review and Meta-analysis." *Trauma, Violence, & Abuse* 20 (1): 3–21.

Zych, Izabela, Maria Ttofi, Vicente Llorent, David Farrington, Denis Ribeaud, and Manuel Eisner. 2018. "A Longitudinal Study on Stability and Transitions among Bullying Roles." *Child Development* 91 (2): 527–45.

INDEX

Academic interest in school bullying, 1–4
age-graded theory, 145
Agnew, Robert, 81–82
Akers, Ronald, 95–96
anomie theory: Émile Durkheim and, 80; institutional anomie theory, 84–85; marketized mentality, 84–85; Robert K. Merton anomie theory, 80–81, 84
antisocial behavior: arousal and, 53–54; environmental risk factors and, 57–58; family risk and, 51–52; genetic influences of, 51–53; inequality and, 75; intelligence and, 63; interventions to reduce, 68–69, 93; sports participation and, 89
arousal, neurological, 53–54; reactivity, 54–55; resting heart rate and bullying, 54
attachment: age-grade theory and, 145; John Bolby and Mary Ainsworth theory of, 58; parental attachment and bullying involvement, 58–69; protective factor, as, 106, 107; school, attachment and bullying involvement, 82–83, 107, 108, 110, 141; social bond theory and, 104

Bandura, Albert, 64
Beccaria, Cesare, 29–31
Becker, Howard, 111–112
Bentham, Jeremy, 29–31
biological interventions and bullying, 70–71

biosocial theories, 50–58
bullycides: *see* suicidality and bullying
bully-victims: impairments of, 20; methodological considerations and, 18, 19; neurological arousal and, 54; prevalence of, 15; racialization of, 130
bystander(s), 49, 100, 119; and interventions, 101–102, 115–116

Chicago School, 77
classical school, 29–30
Clementi, Tyler, 25, 27
conceptualizing school bullying: *see* defining school bullying
control theories, 103–105; and victimization, 110
Cressey, Donald, 96
crime prevention through environmental design (CPTED), 45–47
criminalization: of bullying, 24–27, 28, 31–34; of schools, 47, 128–129, 133
critical criminology, 117–118
critical race theory, 126–129
cultural criminology, 118–119
cyberbullying: criminal offense, as, 32–34; defining, 9, 32; internalizing and externalizing symptoms, 19; lifestyle/routine activity theory and, 41; lower academic achievement and, 17; overlap with traditional bullying, 9, 15; peer influence, 97; power imbalance and, 9, 10; school risk factors for, 41–42; social bond theory and, 105; strain and, 83

defining school bullying: academic definitions, 8–9; criminal offense as, 32–33; cultural effects in, 10; cyberbullying, 10; importance of, 11–12; intra- and intergroup differences in, 10, 12; laypersons and, 10; legislative definitions, 11–12; media constructions, 10–11; overview, 7–12; Olweus definition, 8, 11, 13; neutralization theory and, 98–99; school resource officers and, 45; structural inequalities, considering when, 135

definitions: as component of social learning, 97–99

determinism, soft, 29. *See also* free-will, soft.

deterrence: and bullying, 31–35; general, 31; specific, 31; theory 30–31

developmental and life course theories, 144–151; adolescent-limited and life-course-persisting, 145–146, age-graded theory, 145–46; bullying perpetration and, 150–51; major questions, 146–147; social development model, 146; victimization and, 147–150

deviant places: theory of, 40

differential association: theory of, 95–96; as component of social learning, 96–97

differential involvement hypothesis, 130–131

differential reinforcement, 99–100

drift, 105

DNA: see genetic factors

Durkheim, Émile, 80, 103

empathy: *see* personality traits, empathy

endocrinology and bullying involvement: cortisol and alpha-amylase, 54–55; testosterone and androstenedione, 55–56

evolutionary theory: psychological, 67–68, 69–70

executive functioning, 63–64

exposure: and bullying victimization, 39–42

feminist theories, 119–121

free-will, soft, 29. *see also* determinism, soft

gender: bullying and construction of, 121–124; differences in bullying behaviors, 16, 119–120, 123;

genetic factors: and antisocial behavior generally, 51–52; and bullying, 52–53; methylation and bullying, 53; polygenic scores and bullying, 52–53; polymorphisms and bullying, 51–52

Goffman, Erving, 111

Glueck, Eleanor, 145

Glueck, Sheldon, 145

guardianship: bullying victimization and, 43–47; formal, 44–47; informal, 44

harms of school bullying: academic performance, 17; adult effects, 18; bystander harm, 20; causality of, 16–17, 18–19; externalizing behaviors, 18; healthy context paradox, and, 76; internalizing symptoms, and, 17–19; overview, 16–20; perpetrators, to, 19–20; physiological symptoms, 18; restorative justice and, 132; victims, to, 17–19

harassment, 11

hedonistic calculus, 29

heteromasculine norms, 82, 120, 127–128

Hirschi, Travis, 104–105; Gottfedson and, 104–105, 109–110

homophobia: *see* sexual minority youth

hormones: *see* endocrinology

imitation, as component of social learning, 100–103

intelligence: and bullying behaviors in children, 63; competing conceptualizations of, 63; criminal offending generally and, 62–63; moderating variable, as, 57; victimization risk factor, as, 53

integrationist theories, 138–144; fully integrated models, 139–143; end-to-end models, 143–44

Kohlberg, Lawrence: *see* moral development

labeling theories, 110–112; and bullying, 112–115

Laub, John H., 145

legislation: *see* prevention; legislation

Lemert, Edwin, 111

Founded in 1893,
UNIVERSITY OF CALIFORNIA PRESS
publishes bold, progressive books and journals
on topics in the arts, humanities, social sciences,
and natural sciences—with a focus on social
justice issues—that inspire thought and action
among readers worldwide.

The UC PRESS FOUNDATION
raises funds to uphold the press's vital role
as an independent, nonprofit publisher, and
receives philanthropic support from a wide
range of individuals and institutions—and from
committed readers like you. To learn more, visit
ucpress.edu/supportus.